The SAFE Mortgage Loan Originator National Exam Study Guide

Second Edition

PATRICIA O'CONNOR

About the Author

Pat O'Connor is a licensed Florida real estate broker and owner of The Veritas Real Estate Group, Inc. that she founded in 2004 in Fort Lauderdale. She was a licensed Florida mortgage broker for seven years.

The book has been updated and enhanced over the years and focuses on the information referenced in the NMLS content outline for the national exam. If you spot something that you believe needs changing, please contact me at poconnor@veritasrealestategroup.com. It is my goal to make this the best and most current resource on the market for prospective loan originators.

Table of Contents

Introduction

I wrote this guide to help prepare readers to take the SAFE Mortgage Loan Originator national exam. This is not an NMLS-approved course textbook; it is simply an exam prep. The material is continually updated as laws and guidelines change. There are summary highlights at the end of each chapter as well as practice questions with an answer key. The last section of this book contains two practice exams consisting of 100 multiple choice questions each. The student needs a 75% to pass. It's recommended that you not circle the answers in the book during the practice exams; instead, use an answer sheet numbered 1-100 so you can retake the tests multiple times.

When you take the exam read the entire question before choosing an answer and pay attention to the words NOT, ELSE and EXCEPT that may change the entire meaning of the question. Strategists will say that tests are designed so that answer A is frequently the wrong answer and will catch students who answer too quickly. Another strategy is to choose the longest answer if you can't narrow the choices down any other way. The longest answer is frequently the most complete answer and therefore, the correct answer.

The NMLS outline to exam topics and links to its source material is located at https://nationwidelicensingsystem.org/profreq/testing. In the right-hand column click on the National Test Outline link.

1

Federal Mortgage-Related Laws

Whenever there is money to be made, there are victims and profiteers. In most cases, the laws discussed in this chapter protect the individual from victimization. However, the intent of some legislation is to ensure the financial stability of the United States and prevent future financial meltdowns.

Changes to the first two laws discussed in this chapter (Real Estate Settlement Procedures Act (RESPA) and Truth-In-Lending Act (TILA) occurred when the TILA-RESPA Integrated Disclosure rule (TRID) went into effect on October 3, 2015. This rule modified disclosure requirements for most closed-end loans.

This new rule makes the presentation of the material a bit trickier. In a nutshell, reverse mortgages (an open-end loan) require four disclosures: an initial TILA Disclosure containing the annual percentage rate, a Good Faith Estimate of closing costs, the HUD-1 Settlement Statement, and a final TILA Disclosure.

Most closed end loans (including construction-only loans as well as loans for vacant land) are now required to use only two disclosures: a Loan Estimate form that contains the initial APR disclosure, and the Closing Disclosure form that contains the final APR disclosure. This eliminates the need for a separate TILA Disclosure for most closed-end loans.

To make things even more complicated, the following types of loans require a TILA Disclosure but not a Good Faith Estimate or Loan Estimate and not a HUD-1 Settlement Statement or Closing Disclosure: equity line of credit, a manufactured housing loan that is not secured by real estate, and some types of homebuyer assistance loans.

I.   Real Estate Settlement Procedures Act (Regulation X)

Congress passed the Real Estate Settlement Procedures Act (RESPA) in 1974 to provide consumer protection for loans on residential properties (1-4 units). This law is primarily involved with the disclosure of closing costs and the prevention of kickbacks that may raise the amount of closing costs to the consumer. The Department of Housing and Urban Development (HUD) was the original enforcer of the law, but enactment and enforcement responsibilities shifted to the Consumer Financial Protection Bureau (CFPB) in July 2011.

RESPA is implemented as Regulation X. (For test purposes, RESPA == RE**X**PA if that helps you remember that it is Reg. X.)

RESPA applies only to financed transactions and has no impact on cash purchases; it also applies to refinances, home improvement loans, assumptions, reverse mortgages and equity lines of credit. However, as noted earlier, the Good Faith Estimate and HUD-1 Closing Statement are only required for reverse mortgages. Borrowers receive a number of different RESPA disclosures prior to obtaining a mortgage loan, and students need to know the delivery timeframes for these disclosures.

Loan Application Disclosures

There are four disclosures that the lender or loan originator must give or mail the applicant within three business days of receiving the signed loan application. However, the requirements don't apply if the lender turns down the application during this three business day window. RESPA does not specify a penalty for noncompliance. The disclosures include:

- Special Information pamphlet that explains common mortgage terms and closing costs. This is only required for purchase mortgage loans.

- Good Faith Estimate (GFE) of the anticipated closing costs (reverse mortgages) or the Loan Estimate. (More details later in this chapter.)

- Mortgage Servicing Disclosure Statement that informs the applicant whether the lender intends to service the loan or transfer the servicing rights to another lender.

- List of 10 HUD-approved housing counseling agencies closest to the applicant's current address.

Pre-Settlement Disclosures

- **HUD-1 Settlement Statement (reverse mortgages) or Closing Disclosure**

  These forms show all credits and debits to the buyer and any disbursements to third parties. The HUD-1/Closing Disclosure is not required if the borrower has no closing costs. The borrower has the right to review the HUD-1 one business day before closing. The initial Closing Disclosure must be received at least three business days before closing.

- **Affiliated Business Arrangement**

  It's a fairly common occurrence for one parent company to own multiple service provider firms. The public likes the arrangement because it provides the opportunity for one-stop shopping. For example, one entity may own or have a partial controlling interest in real estate, mortgage and title companies. This type of situation is considered an affiliated business arrangement. RESPA requires that when one of these entities refers the applicant to another affiliated provider, the loan applicant receives an Affiliated Business Arrangement Disclosure at or prior to the time of referral. This disclosure states the relationship between the two companies and the charges for the second company.

Settlement Disclosures

- **Final HUD-1 Settlement Statement or Final Closing Disclosure.**

  The buyer signs the appropriate document at the time of the closing. (More Closing Disclosure details later in this chapter.)

- **Initial Escrow Statement**

  The borrower receives an Initial Escrow Statement at the closing or within 45 days after closing that estimates the first-year escrow payment for property taxes and homeowner's insurance.

Post-Settlement Disclosures

- **Servicing Transfer Statements**

  Servicing rights for loans may change hands frequently, and it's not unusual for homeowners to receive multiple notifications that instruct them to send the monthly mortgage payments to a different company and address. These Servicing Transfer Statements are required by RESPA, and the servicer must notify the borrower 15 days before the change goes into effect. The notice must contain the new servicer's name, address, toll-free phone number and effective date of the transfer.

Borrowers can't be penalized for non-payment if they continued to make payments to the prior servicer; this grace period expires after 60 days. By then, they should have received phone calls from the new servicer asking about the missing payments, and 60 days should be ample time to get the matter resolved.

- **Annual Escrow Analysis Statement**

   Lenders are required to conduct an annual analysis of all escrow accounts, inform the borrowers of the findings and refund any excess of $50 or more.

Good Faith Estimate/Loan Estimate Conditions

The Loan Estimate is very similar to the GFE except that, in addition to anticipated closing costs, it also includes the financing charges and terms, which eliminates the need for a separate TILA disclosure. The following conditions apply to both estimates:

- The GFE and Loan Estimate both have expiration dates for an interest rate lock.

- A charge for a credit report is the only fee that can be collected prior to the delivery of the Loan Estimate and the borrower's notification that he wishes to proceed with the loan. Checks or credit card information may not be collected for any other purpose until these conditions are satisfied. This applies even if cards are not charged or the checks cashed until after the conditions are met.

- Any estimate of costs provided to the borrower before the estimate must clearly state that the charges could change.

- The borrower cannot be required to submit any documents prior to the delivery of the estimate.

- The estimate may be provided by the lender or the loan originator.

- It must be delivered or mailed no later than three business days after a loan application is submitted. A business day for an estimate is defined as a day the office was open for business to the public.

- It must be delivered or mailed no later than seven business days prior to loan consummation. This can be waived if the borrower has an emergency, such as an impending foreclosure, that justifies an approved faster closing. The borrower must provide a written explanation of the emergency.

Good Faith Estimate/Loan Estimate Trigger

An estimate of closing costs is required when the creditor or loan originator receives an application that contains the following minimal amount of information:

- Consumer's name.

- Consumer's income.

- Consumer's social security number.

- Property address or zip code if address is unknown. If homeowner is investigating multiple properties, list multiple zip codes. This occurs with pre-approvals.

- Estimated property value.

- Requested amount of mortgage loan.

Good Faith Estimate/Loan Estimate Revisions

Creditors may not revise an estimate because of technical issues, incorrect calculations or low estimates. They can revise the estimate if changing circumstances:

- Increase the closing costs (interest rate increase on an unlocked loan).

- Affect the value of a property (storm damage or lien recorded).

- Negatively affects a borrower's ability to qualify for the loan (fired, documents prove less income).

- Consumer waits more than 10 business days to indicate an Intent to Proceed.

- Settlement is delayed more than 60 calendar days for a new construction loan if the original Loan Estimate includes the statement that the estimate can be revised for this reason.

Lenders must operate within the following timeframes when reissuing an estimate:

- Delivered or mailed within 3 business days after becoming aware of the new information that required the reissuance. In this case, a business day is a day the office is opened to the public.

- Delivery/mailing must precede the date the Closing Disclosure was delivered/mailed.

- Lender must ensure that the revised estimate is received at least 4 business days prior to loan consummation (mailed at least 7 business days prior). In this case, a business day is every day but Sunday and federal holidays. If the closing is scheduled before then, the changes may be reflected in the closing statement without reissuing the estimate.

Closing Costs Estimates Tolerance Levels

Fees are grouped into three categories with three different corresponding tolerance levels for variances between the closing costs estimate and the final closing statement. The TRID rule changed some of the variance levels.

GFE/HUD-1 tolerances (Reverse Mortgages) are as follows:

- Real estate transfer taxes, and creditor's or mortgage broker's charges for its own services (loan origination fees and interest rate) have zero variance. They must be identical on the GFE and HUD-1.

- Fees that the lender chooses or identifies (credit report, appraisal, government recording fees, and title insurance if selected or "recommended" by the lender) can't vary on the two documents by more than 10 percent.

- Fees for services that the owner chooses for themselves (hazard insurance or title insurance if the homeowner doesn't choose one of the lender-identified selections) and fees that are paid per diem (pre-paid mortgage interest) have no limit on the acceptable amount of variance between the estimates and the closing statement.

Lenders have **30 days** to refund any excessive variance between the GFE and the HUD-1.

Loan Estimate/Closing Disclosure tolerances are as follows:

- Real estate transfer taxes, creditor's or mortgage broker's charges for its own services (loan origination fees and interest rate), charges for services provided by an affiliate of the creditor or mortgage broker, and charges for services for which the creditor or mortgage broker does not permit the consumer to shop for (credit report, appraisal) have zero variance. They must be identical on the Loan Estimate and Closing Disclosure.

- Fees that the lender chooses or identifies (government recording fees, and title insurance if selected or "recommended" by the lender) can't vary on the two documents by more than 10 percent.

- Fees for services that the owner chooses for themselves (hazard insurance or title insurance if the homeowner doesn't choose one of the lender-identified selections) and fees that are paid per diem (pre-paid mortgage interest) have no limit on the acceptable amount of variance between the estimates and the closing statement.

Lenders have **60 days** to refund any excessive variance between the Loan Estimate and the Closing Disclosure.

Closing Disclosure

The borrower must receive the Closing Disclosure at least 3 business days before consummation. A business day for a Closing Disclosure is defined as every day except Sundays and federal holidays.

If the following items change, a new Closing Disclosure must be provided to the borrower and settlement is delayed for an additional 3 business days:

- APR.

- Loan product.

- Addition of a prepayment penalty.

If there are changes other than these three items, the borrower has the right to view the revised Closing Disclosure 1 business day before consummation.

One exception to this 3-business-day waiting period is for timeshares that are consummated within 3 business days of the application. In this case, borrowers are permitted to receive the disclosure at the time of loan consummation, and the requirement for a Loan Estimate is waived. A business day for a Closing Disclosure is defined as every day except Sundays and federal holidays.

Another exception is for emergencies when the wait would be a hardship. This might occur if the home was about to be sold at a foreclosure auction.

Lenders or closing agents prepare the Closing Disclosure. Sellers are permitted to receive a disclosure that only shows their costs and credits. They may receive the disclosure when the loan is consummated; there is no 3-business-day-receipt requirement for sellers.

In some cases, something may occur after loan consummation that results in changes to the Closing Disclosure. In this case, the lender has 30 calendar days after becoming aware of an event that changes the payment to a borrower or a seller, to deliver a revised Closing Disclosure.

Non-numeric clerical errors and tolerance violations trigger a new Closing Disclosure that must be delivered within 60 calendar days following loan consumption. Likewise, tolerance refunds must also be sent within 60 days.

Partial Payment Policy

There are times when a lender may allow a borrower to pay less than what's owed on the monthly statement. That situation may change when the loan is assigned to a new owner. That is the reason why mortgage transfer notices, for loans that fall under TRID compliance rules, must contain a partial payment disclosure. This notice informs the borrower whether or not the current owner (lender) accepts partial payments, how partial payments are handled, and a statement that the new owner may have a different policy.

Kickbacks, Referrals and Unearned Fees

Payment between service providers for illegal kickbacks, referrals and unearned fees is a violation of RESPA's Section 8. A kickback occurs when someone receives something of value in exchange for the referral of business. It becomes illegal when the participants are service providers. For example, a title company can't pay for a real estate agent's cruise, and loan originators can't distribute movie tickets to real estate agents who refer the most borrowers. The law allows referral fees between two real estate companies but that is the only exception.

In order for two loan originators to receive payment for one transaction, each originator must complete five distinct duties; HUD defines 14 separate tasks although others may be acceptable. Therefore, three loan originator disbursements on the same HUD-1 are a red flag for auditors since there are only 14 defined duties, and each originator must complete at least 5 unique tasks.

Violations may be treated as civil or criminal offenses. Civil penalties include reimbursement to the plaintiff in an amount equal to three times the actual cost of the service. Criminal penalties include a $10,000 fine and/or one year in jail per offense.

Title Insurance

Section 9 of RESPA prohibits the seller from picking the title company and requiring the buyer to purchase the services. In essence, whoever picks the title company pays for the services. This situation occurs in foreclosure sales in which the lender requires that the buyer close with the lender's choice of title company. In these cases, the buyer can't be charged for the title company's costs or the lender's title insurance policy.

Lender Escrow Accounts

RESPA doesn't require the lender to collect escrowed funds, but Section 10 regulates the accounts that do exist. Part of the monthly mortgage payment usually includes a partial payment for property taxes and hazard insurance, which the lender agrees to pay as the bills come due. RESPA limits the lender to collecting 1/12 of the annual property tax and 1/12 of the annual insurance premium each month. In addition, RESPA allows the lender to collect a maximum two months of property tax and two months of hazard insurance at closing as an escrow cushion in case the borrower misses some mortgage payments, or final charges are higher than estimated.

Escrow Closing Notice

When a consumer requests the cancellation of their escrow account, the lender must deliver an Escrow Closing Notice no later than 3 business days before closure. If the account is closed for some other reason (except for default or termination caused by refinancing, repayment or rescission), the notice must be sent 30 business days prior to closure. The notice must disclose:

- Account closing date.

- Account may also be called a trust or impound account.

- Reason for closure.

- Consumer must pay all taxes and insurance, which might require lump-sum payments.

- Cost to the consumer for closing the account.

- Consequences if consumer doesn't pay property tax and insurance costs.

- Contact number to discuss the status of the account and whether or not it can be kept open.

A business day for the Escrow Closing Notice is defined as every day except Sundays and federal holidays.

Servicer Complaints

Section 6 of RESPA requires that loan servicers adhere to the following rules:

- Loan servicers have 5 days to acknowledge a borrower's complaint, and 45 days to resolve or explain their position.

- Mortgage documents state that the borrower pays for hazard insurance. When the loan servicer believes that the policy has been canceled or not renewed, the servicer may choose an alternate insurance company and charge the borrower for the cost of continued coverage (force-placed insurance). Before a loan servicer chooses a replacement hazard insurance policy for a borrower, the servicer must notify the borrower 45 days before charging the borrower, and send a second notice 30 days after the initial notification. Furthermore, if the borrower escrows the insurance payments, the servicer is prohibited from choosing a force-placed insurance provider if the servicer can continue the payments; this applies even if the servicer must contribute funds to the borrower's escrow account.

- Servicers must attempt to speak to a delinquent borrower within 36 days after the missed mortgage payment and mail loss mitigation information within 45 days. Loss mitigation options include refinancing, loan modification, short sale and deed-in-lieu.

- Servicers must acknowledge the receipt of a loan mitigation application within five days and let the borrower know what additional information, if any, is needed to complete the application.

- If the servicer receives the mitigation application 37 days before a foreclosure sale, the borrower's situation must be evaluated for all applicable options within 30 days. The borrower may appeal a decision if the complete application package was submitted at least 90 days before a scheduled sale.

- A servicer can't file for foreclosure until the mortgage payment is 120 days late. If the borrower submits a complete application after 120 days but *before* the servicer files for foreclosure, the foreclosure process can't proceed until a number of conditions are satisfied. These conditions include the following: the servicer determines that the borrower is ineligible for mitigation and has no more possible appeals; the borrower declines any offers, or the borrower fails to honor the terms of an agreement.

Document Retention

Creditors have retention periods that differ from a loan originator's 3 year requirement. Creditors must retain the:

- Closing Disclosure and related documents for 5 years after consummation.

- Loan Estimate and related documents for 3 years after consummation.

- Escrow Cancellation Notice and Partial Payment Policy for 2 years after consummation.

II.   Truth-in-Lending Act (Regulation Z)

Congress passed the Truth-in-Lending Act (TILA) in 1968 as part of the Consumer Credit Protection Act. The law was implemented by the Federal Reserve Board as Regulation Z and was enacted to protect consumers during credit transactions. The Consumer Financial Protection Bureau administers TILA.

Regulation Z applies to residential mortgages (1-4 units) and doesn't include commercial or other nonresidential loans. The law covers three general areas:

- Disclosure of financing charges.

- Distribution of the Consumer Handbook on Adjustable-Rate Mortgages (CHARM) booklet to consumers who choose an adjustable-rate mortgage.

- Right of Rescission.

Truth-in-Lending Disclosure

The TILA-RESPA Integrated Disclosure (TRID) rule states that this separate TILA disclosure is only required for reverse mortgages, equity lines of credit, mortgages secured by a mobile home and dwellings not attached to land. It is not to be used in most closed-end transactions.

TILA requires that applicable consumers are informed of all extra credit charges so that they can compare offers based on total financing charges instead of simply looking at the interest rate. The disclosure includes:

- Annual Percentage Rate (APR).

- Finance charge.

- Amount financed.

- Total amount paid over the life of the loan.

The annual percentage rate (APR) reflects the total financing rate:

APR = interest rate + other loan financing costs

The APR represents the true yearly cost of borrowing. A finance charge is a fee the buyer would not pay if it were a cash deal. For example, wire transfers and mortgage interest payments contribute to the calculation of the APR; hazard insurance and home inspections don't. The law requires that a consumer receive this disclosure within three business days of signing a loan application and at least seven business days before closing. This form can be generated using whatever Loan Origination Software is standard for your office. If the APR is quoted incorrectly by more than 1/8 % for a fixed-rate loan or 1/4 % for an adjustable-rate loan, it must be re-disclosed before settlement. The APR must be finalized at least three days before closing.

Trigger Terms

TILA also addresses advertising practices and states that if any triggering term (interest rate, down payment, payment amount, number of payments, term of repayment or amount of any finance charge, etc.) is specified, then the APR and the amount and terms of repayment must also be disclosed. That is why in print ads, the banner may read "No Money Down!" and in tiny print at the bottom of the ad, the rest of the terms will be specified. The same thing happens with radio ads; one loan feature will be emphasized, and the rest of the terms will be specified so quickly that they are barely understandable. Phrases such as "easy loan payments" are non-specific and don't require further disclosure.

Consumer Handbook on Adjustable-Rate Mortgages (CHARM)

Adjustable-rate mortgages may be difficult for the consumer to understand. That's why Regulation Z requires creditors to give adjustable-rate applicants either the "Consumer Handbook on Adjustable-Rate Mortgages" pamphlet or something similar within three business days of receiving a signed loan application.

__Right of Rescission__

The Right of Rescission provides a three business day cooling-off period for consumers who use their primary residence as security for a refinance, home improvement or second mortgage loan. Upon applying for such a loan, the consumer is required to receive a Notice of Right to Rescind which states that the consumer must notify the lender in writing of their desire to cancel and ensure that it's delivered before midnight of the third business day after signing the loan contract. Saturday is considered a business day. The rescission period doesn't apply to a first mortgage on a purchase of a property or to any investment property. A business day is every day but Sunday and federal holidays for the Right of Rescission notice.

__High-Cost Home Loan__

The Home Ownership and Equity Protection Act of 1994 (HOEPA) amends the Truth-in-Lending Act and establishes requirements for certain loans on primary residences that have high rates and/or high fees. The rules for these loans are contained in Section 32 of Regulation Z, which implements the TILA, so the loans are called "Section 32 Mortgages." These loans are enforced by the Consumer Financial Protection Board.

Covered loans include:

- Purchase money mortgages.

- Home equity loans.

- Refinances.

Exempt loan types include:

- Reverse mortgages.

- FHA, VA and USDA loans.

- Investment properties.

- New construction loans.

The thresholds for determining if the loan is high-cost are as follows:

- First-lien transaction is more than 6.5 percent higher than the prime offer rate.

- Junior lien transactions are more than 8.5 percent higher than the prime offer rate.

- Total fees and points payable by the consumer at or before closing exceed five percent of the total loan amount.

Restrictions on high-cost loans include:

- No prepay penalties.

- Balloon mortgages are generally not allowed except short-term bridge loans (12 months or less) are allowed to finance the purchase of a new home for a consumer who is selling their home.

- No negatively amortizing loans.

- No refinancing any high-cost mortgage into another high-cost mortgage within 1 year after having extended credit, unless the refinancing is in the consumers' interest.

- No increase in interest rate upon default.

- Cannot accelerate the loan (call it due) after default.

- Borrowers must have a documented ability to repay the loan prior to funding.

- Borrowers must receive homeownership counseling from a HUD-approved counselor.

- No refinance into another high-cost mortgage, unless the refinancing is in the consumer's interest.

- Late fees may not exceed 4% of the past-due payment.

Higher-Priced Mortgage Loans

Higher-priced loans are ones in which the APR exceeds the Average Prime Offer Rate by at least 1.5% for first-lien loans or 2.5% for a jumbo loan or 3.5% for a subordinate lien.

- When the annual percentage rate (APR) for a mortgage loan on a primary residence exceeds a specified threshold, lenders must have an appraisal performed by a certified appraiser who enters the home and writes the report.

- The appraisal must be sent to the consumer promptly or at least three business days before closing.

- An additional appraisal is required if the purchase is a "flipped" home. Flips are defined as resells within 90 days with seller paying a minimum 10 percent price increase, or resells within the past 91-180 days with seller paying a minimum 20 percent price increase.

- These additional appraisals must be completed by a different appraiser and at no cost to the applicant.

- Refinancing a higher-priced mortgage may not result in a higher balance, balloon payments or negative amortization.

- Qualified mortgages, which are discussed later in this chapter, are exempt from this rule.

Higher-Priced Mortgage Loan Escrow Rules

- Lenders must require and maintain escrow accounts for property tax and hazard insurance on first-lien, closed-end, high-priced mortgage loans on principal residences for a minimum of five years, unless the debt is paid off earlier. The account may be eliminated upon request after five years if the loan-to-value is 80 percent or less (the borrower has 20 percent or more equity in the home based on the original purchase price), and the borrower is current on the mortgage payments.

- Hazard insurance escrows are not required for communities with a master insurance policy (condominiums).

- Small creditors in rural or under-served areas may be exempt from this rule.

Record Retention

Residential mortgage lenders must retain TILA disclosures for three years after loan consummation.

III.   Equal Credit Opportunity Act (Regulation B)

The Equal Credit Opportunity Act (ECOA) prohibits discrimination by lenders in any part of a credit transaction on the basis of:

- Race.

- Color.

- Religion.

- National origin.

- Sex.

- Marital status.

- Age (provided the applicant has attained the minimum legal age in the state).

- Receipt of income from a public assistance program.

- History of having exercised any rights under the Consumer Credit Protection Act.

The Consumer Financial Protection Bureau regulates and enforces ECOA.

Prohibited Factors

- Don't discuss applicant's spouse unless they are part of the transaction or it's a community property state or the applicant relies on alimony or child support as qualifying sources of income.

- No questions regarding birth control, current pregnancy or intent to have future children.

- Don't evaluate an elderly (age 62 or older) applicant differently from anyone else.

- Don't require a qualified applicant to provide a cosigner.

- Don't steer minority applicants into different types of loan products than other applicants.

- Don't treat men and women applicants differently.

- Don't require more documentation from a minority applicant.

Acceptable Factors

- Questions may be asked about applicant's immigration status and permanent residency, and the answers may affect the lending decision.

- An applicant's credit history may be taken into account.

- Part-time income, annuity, pension or other forms of retirement pay may be taken into account.

Property Appraisal

The borrower is entitled to a copy of the residential property appraisal report and any other property valuation as soon as it is completed or three business days before closing, whichever is earlier. The consumer can waive this timeframe (at least 3 business days prior to loan consummation) but must receive them at loan consummation. If the applicant submits a waiver and the transaction doesn't close, the applicant is entitled to a copy of the valuations no later than 30 days after the creditor determines that the transaction will not proceed.

Adverse Action Notice

An adverse action notice is sent to an applicant when a loan is denied. The notice must contain the following information:

- Action taken.

- Name and address of the creditor.

- A statement of the provisions of section 701(a) of the Equal Credit Opportunity Act.

- Name and address of the Federal agency that administers compliance with respect to the creditor.

- A statement of specific reasons for the action taken or a disclosure of the applicant's right to a statement of specific reasons within 30 days, if the statement is requested within 60 days of the creditor's notification. The disclosure shall include the name, address, and telephone number of the person or office from which the statement of reasons can be obtained.

If there are multiple applicants, the notice is only sent to the primary applicant, if that can be determined.

When an application is made by telephone and adverse action is taken, the creditor must request the applicant's name and address in order to provide written notification under this section. If the applicant declines to provide that information, then the creditor has no further notification responsibility.

A lender has 30 days after receipt of an application to notify the applicant of its action on the application. If the loan is not funded, the applicant is entitled to a written statement of reasons for the denial. If the lender did not provide this in the initial adverse action notice, then the applicant can request a statement of reasons within 60 days of receiving the original adverse action notice, and the lender has 30 days after the applicant's request to provide him with the information. If the applicant doesn't accept a counteroffer within 90 days, the lender notifies the applicant of an adverse action.

Incomplete Application

If some information on the loan application is missing, but there is enough to make a decision, the process can proceed. If critical information is missing, the creditor can deny the loan, orally notify the consumer of the need for additional information or send a Notice of Incompleteness, within 30 days to the applicant.

A Notice of Incompleteness must:

- Be in writing.

- Explain what additional information is required.

- Provide a reasonable deadline.

- State that the application process will terminate if the information is not received.

Marital Status

It is because of ECOA that loan originators can't ask an applicant if he's divorced. They can ask if the borrower is married, unmarried or separated **IF** a spouse is involved someway in the transaction. The term unmarried includes divorced, widowed and single.

Demographic Information

ECOA dictates the collection of demographic information in order to monitor the lenders compliance with the law. Specifically, on the bottom of the third page of the 1003 loan application are questions regarding an applicant's race, ethnicity and sex. If the applicant leaves these blank or declines to answer during an interview, the loan originator must guess based on visual observation or last name and make a notation on the application that the applicant declined to answer. The boxes MUST be checked.

Record Retention

The loan originator is required to retain the application for 25 months from the date a loan acceptance or denial notification is sent to the applicant.

Penalties

Failure to comply with the Equal Credit Opportunity Act's Regulation B can subject a financial institution to civil liability for actual and punitive damages in individual or class actions. Liability for punitive damages can be as much as $10,000 in individual actions and the lesser of $500,000 or 1 percent of the creditor's net worth in class actions.

IV.   Home Mortgage Disclosures Act (Regulation C)

Congress passed the Home Mortgage Disclosure Act (HMDA) in 1975. This law requires that mortgage lenders report a variety of demographic information about their borrowers. HMDA is implemented as Regulation C and provides industry watchdogs a tool for uncovering patterns of discrimination in local and regional lending. In addition, it allows for the identification of underfunded communities that might benefit from alternative types of lending.

Loan Application Register

Lending companies under HMDA jurisdiction must create a Loan Application Register (LAR) and enter the following information in the register for every application it receives and for every home purchase loan, home improvement loan and refinancing loans it originates or purchases:

- Loan amount.

- Purpose of the loan (home purchase, home improvement, refinancing).

- Loan type (conventional loan, FHA loan, VA loan or a loan guaranteed by the Farmers Home Administration).

- Location of the property.

- Race of the borrower.

- Age of the borrower.

- Ethnicity (Hispanic or non-Hispanic) of the borrower.

- Gender of the borrower.

- Whether or not the loan was granted.

- If the loan was denied, the reason why it was denied.

- If the loan was denied, whether the interest rate charged was over a certain threshold.

- The type of entity that purchased the loan if it was sold.

As previously noted, the monitoring information (race, ethnicity and gender) may be guesses on the part of the loan originator if the borrower refuses to provide the information.

Federal Financial Institutions Examination Council

The lending institutions submit their LARs to the Federal Financial Institutions Examination Council (FFIEC) every year. The FFIEC screens the collective data for errors, publishes it on the Internet and makes the information available on CDs. Individual institutions must make their LARs available to the public upon request.

HMDA does not prohibit any specific activity of lenders, and it does not establish a quota system of mortgage loans to be made in any geographic area. It does allow the public to monitor the lending history of institutions and uncover possible discrimination that might lead to further investigations for possible violations of the Equal Credit Opportunity Act.

V.   Fair Credit Reporting Act

Congress passed the Fair Credit Reporting Act (FCRA) in 1970 to protect an individual's privacy rights and to ensure accurate and fair credit reporting. It is enforced by the Federal Trade Commission.

Credit Reporting Agencies

Much of the law regulates the actions of the Credit Reporting Agencies (CRA) that compile databases of information received from creditors, and it explains the right of consumers to dispute incorrect information. The CRAs (Experian, TransUnion and Equifax) must take steps to verify information that is under dispute and can't retain negative information for an extended period of time. However, they can keep bankruptcies in the credit report for 10 years and tax liens for 7 years from the time they were paid.

Creditors

Other sections of the law regulate the actions of the creditors who report missed payments to the CRAs. These creditors are companies such as credit-card companies, auto financing companies and mortgage lenders. The creditors must provide complete and accurate information to the credit rating agencies.

Use of Credit Reports

The law also regulates who can use credit information: creditors, insurers, employers, and other businesses that use the information in the report to evaluate applications for credit, insurance, employment, or renting a home are among those that have a legal right to access the report. An employer can get a copy of the credit report only if the employee or job applicant agrees. A consumer reporting company may not provide information about employees to employers, or to prospective employers, without their written consent.

FCRA doesn't require any written authorization to pull credit; however, the loan application contains a clause that authorizes the loan originator to verify the borrower's credit history.

Adverse Action

Lenders must notify an applicant when a loan is denied (adverse action) because of the information contained in the credit report and provide the applicant with the contact information (name, address and phone number) of the CRA.

Borrowers are entitled to a free credit report if the lender takes adverse action against them, and they ask for their report within 60 days of receiving notice of the action. The notice will give them the name, address, and phone number of the consumer reporting company.

VI.   Fair and Accurate Credit Transaction Act

The Fair and Accurate Credit Transaction Act (FACT Act), which became law in 2003, is an extension of the 1970 Fair Credit Reporting Act.

Free Annual Credit Reports

The increase in identity theft was one of the driving forces behind the new regulation, and consequently, the FACT Act allows every individual to have a free copy of their credit report once a year from each of the three Credit Reporting Agencies (TransUnion, Experian and Equifax).

Fraud Alerts

The law also establishes a national fraud alert system. If someone feels that he has been the victim of an identity theft, he can call any one of the three credit reporting agencies, and an alert will be placed in all three CRA files. The alert requires lenders to take additional steps to verify the identity of the consumer before extending credit. The initial alert is in effect for 90 days and allows the consumer one free credit report during that time. If the consumers file an identity theft report with a law enforcement agency, they can then request an extended seven-year fraud alert that allows them to pull their credit two times during a twelve-month period from each of the CRAs.

Limited Disclosure

The FACT Act requires businesses that print debit and credit card receipts to use equipment that only prints the last five digits of the card number. Similarly, consumers can request the credit reporting agencies to print only the last four numbers of their social security number on their credit report.

Dispute Resolution

Prior to the passage of the FACT Act, the only recourse open to the public to dispute a credit report entry was to contact the credit reporting agency. Now, the consumer can contact the creditor that reported the negative information and request an investigation; no additional negative information on that matter can be reported until the issue is resolved.

Negative Information

If a consumer misses payments, or makes late or partial payments, the creditor must notify the individual within 30 days after reporting the information to a credit bureau. This notification may appear on the customer's monthly statement instead of being mailed as a separate notice.

Proper Disposal Methods

The FACT Act requires individuals and businesses that possess or maintain consumer report information for a business purpose to dispose of it properly. This means the business must take reasonable measures to protect against unauthorized access to the information. It does NOT require the business to dispose of credit reports; but, it has to take precautions if it does.

National Credit Score Disclosure Form

The National Credit Score Disclosure form is required of lenders by the FACT Act. The form states that consumers should contact their lender if they have questions about their application and that they should contact the Credit Reporting Agency if they have questions about their credit scores. The consumer is also told that the credit score is just one factor that the lender uses when evaluating a loan application. The range of possible credit scores is 300 to 850.

Red Flags Rule

This rule specifies five categories of potential identity theft indicators that financial institutions must take proactive measures to recognize. Measures include developing a written program to train employees in the recognition of these warning signs (red flags) and instructing them in the appropriate response to the threat. The program must be managed by the firm's Board of Directors or senior management and include methods for overseeing compliance by service providers. The law applies to companies that manage transactional accounts for credit cards, mortgage and car loans, checking and savings, cell phone and utilities, and margin accounts. The five red flag categories are:

- **Warnings From a Consumer Reporting Agency**

  Employees must pay attention to any consumer report warnings about the account including suspicious activity or address discrepancies.

- **Suspicious Documents**

  Employees need to stay on alert for documents that appear to be forged, and supporting material that doesn't match what is already on file for that account holder.

- **Suspicious Personal Identifying Information**

  Problems in this area involve social security numbers, addresses and phone numbers that don't match existing consumer report information or that have already been associated with suspicious activity.

- **Suspicious Use of Account**

  Changes in the pattern of use, customer failing to make initial payments, returned mail from an address of record and the reactivation of a dormant account are all possible indications of identity theft.

- **Reputable Source Notice of Possible Identity Theft Associated With Account**

  A customer or law enforcement officer notifies the business that an identity theft has occurred in an account.

VII.   Do Not Call / Do Not Fax

The Federal Communication Commission (FCC) and Federal Trade Commission (FTC) established a national Do-Not-Call Registry. The registry is nationwide in scope, applies to all telemarketers (with the exception of certain non-profit organizations), and covers both interstate and intrastate telemarketing calls. Registration is free, and an individual may enter a maximum of three personal phone numbers. Telemarketers may call registered numbers if they have obtained written permission from the individual. The 2022 penalty for violations is $43,792 per call.

Do Not Call Exemptions

Although there are six different types of exceptions, no telemarketer may ever call someone who has requested not to be contacted again including numbers that are not registered. Exempted telemarketers include:

- Political.

- Charitable.

- Telephone surveys.

- Established business relationship in which the business may continue to call for 18 months after the conclusion of business.

- Following customer inquiry in which the business may call for 3 months after receiving an inquiry or application.

- Obtained written permission to call from registered individual.

Registry Search

Telemarketers and sellers are required to search the do-not-call registry at least once every 31 days and drop from their call lists the phone numbers of registered consumers. In fact, all telemarketers are required to access the registry and pay any required fees; otherwise, they face the possibility of being fined for calling any numbers whether or not those numbers are registered.

Safe Harbor

Everybody makes mistakes, and companies won't be held liable if they have a written do-not-call policy, train employees, maintain an internal list of customers who requested not to be called and access the register every 31 days. They must be able to prove that the call was made in error.

Additional Telemarketing Violations

Commercial telemarketers may also be fined for the following offenses:

- Calling before 8 AM or after 9 PM.

- Leaving a message without including a phone number.

- Telemarketing company does not identify itself.

- Leaving a pre-recorded commercial message without having an established business relationship or permission to call.

- Offering debt-relief services without stating a timeframe for results; the amount of money needed to settle the debt with the creditor; the fact that missing monthly payments may have adverse consequences including lower credit score, law suit or submittal to a collection agency, and the fact that the customer has full rights to funds in any account opened in response to a request by the debt-relief service.

Do Not Fax

Advertisers may not send a message to anyone's fax number unless:

- They have an established business relationship.

- Fax number is public information.

- Recipient granted permission.

- Advertisement has clear opt-out instructions on the first page of the transmission for recipients who no longer wish to receive faxes from the sender.

VIII.   Homeowner's Protection Act

The Homeowners Protection Act (HPA) of 1998 is designed to protect people who buy primary residences using Private Mortgage Insurance (PMI). PMI is generally required for conventional loans that have less than a 20 percent down payment. The law does not apply to FHA loans and Mortgage Insurance Premiums (MIP).

The monthly PMI payments can be canceled under two circumstances:

- The lender MUST cancel the PMI when the loan-to-value ratio reaches 78%, based on the original value of the home, as long as the borrower is not in default.

- Borrowers may request cancellation when the loan-to-value ratio is 80% based on the original value of the home if they have a good payment history.

- Borrowers must be notified at closing if they are paying PMI and the procedure for canceling it. In addition, they must be sent an annual notice of their rights under the Homeowners Protection Act.

IX.   Dodd-Frank Wall Street Reform and Consumer Act

The Dodd-Frank Wall Street Reform and Consumer Act is a complex law passed in 2010 in response to the financial meltdown and recession. It's named after Senator Dodd and Representative Frank; the two Congressmen who were most instrumental in drafting the legislation. Because of the complexity of the law and opposition by financial firms, implementation of the rules and regulations was a slow process.

Some goals of the Dodd-Frank Act are to streamline federal regulatory agencies, provide better protection for consumers, increase the oversight of financial companies and establish liquidation procedures for failing financial institutions.

As part of the streamlining process, the Office of the Comptroller of the Currency absorbed the functions of the Office of Thrift Supervision, which was then eliminated. However, existing agencies couldn't support all the requirements of the new law, and several new ones now exist including the Consumer Financial Protection Bureau, the Financial Stability Oversight Council, the Orderly Liquidation Authority and the Federal Insurance Office.

The following three areas were affected by the Dodd-Frank Act and apply to residential (1-4 units) finance transactions:

- Refinancing

  - Refinancing a higher-priced mortgage may not result in a higher balance, balloon payments or negative amortization.

- Appraiser Independence Requirements (AIR)

  - Lenders may not accept an appraisal from anyone who has been selected, retained or compensated by a mortgage broker or real estate agent.

  - The appraiser's client is the lender.

  - Appraisers may not discuss valuations with loan staff. However, they may discuss it with real estate agents.

  - No one connected to the loan staff can order an appraisal.

  - No one must specify a desired or expected valuation although a sales purchase contract may be provided.

- A copy of the appraisal must be provided to the borrower at least three days prior to loan consummation, unless this timing requirement is waived by the borrower.

- Legal oversight over federal laws and regulations

  - The Consumer Financial Protection Bureau oversees federal finance regulation and enforcement. This includes RESPA, TILA and TRID among others.

Consumer Financial Protection Bureau (CFPB)

The role of CFPB is a multi-faceted one. It's the responsibility of this organization to:

- Simplify consumers' lending forms.

- Protect the public from predatory lending practices.

- Respond to consumer financial complaints.

- Educate the public and the employees of the financial institutions.

- Monitor and assess the risk level of current financial practices.

The Bureau is funded by the Federal Reserve, but its chairman is appointed by Congress. Congress can legislate changes in the Bureau or even abolish it.

Consumers can file complaints on the Bureau's website http://consumerfinance.gov

Financial Stability Oversight Council

The mission of the Financial Stability Oversight Council is to monitor the overall financial stability of the United States. In order to accomplish this, the group coordinates the development and sharing of policies among the member agencies, and it is empowered to request the Office of Financial Regulation to collect risk-assessment data from specific financial companies. The Oversight Council also plays a major role in recommending the breakup of companies such as large banks that may pose a threat to the financial stability of the United States.

Orderly Liquidation Authority

The Federal Deposit Insurance Company (FDIC) is tasked with the responsibility for becoming the receiver for some failing financial institutions. With its newly-granted Orderly Liquidation Authority, the FDIC has the power to replace the management of the failing companies and oversee the liquidation of assets, thereby avoiding the past issues associated with the bankruptcy (Lehman Brothers) and bailouts (Bank of America, Citicorp) of the "too big to fail" companies.

Federal Insurance Office

The AIG bailout is probably responsible for the increased scrutiny of insurance companies that is mandated by the Dodd-Frank Act. The Federal Insurance Office, which is housed within the U.S. Department of the Treasury Office, now monitors all non-health insurance providers and represents the U.S. on international insurance matters.

X.   Ability-to-Repay and Qualified Mortgage Rule

Prior to the financial meltdown of 2007, many borrowers were allowed to obtain mortgage loans without showing proof of income. These were known as no-doc or stated income loans; in essence, if an applicant had a decent credit score, he was approved for a loan without the need to provide much supporting documentation. In 2009, the rules changed and creditors started requiring proof of the borrower's ability to repay high-priced residential mortgages.

Ability-to-Repay

The Consumer Financial Protection Bureau changed the rules again on January 14, 2014, but the Ability-to-Repay law doesn't apply to home equity lines of credit, reverse mortgages, construction loans, vacant land or timeshare plans. They do apply to all other closed-end residential mortgage loans without regard to the loan amount and include investment property as well as primary residences. The rule is intended to protect the consumer from irresponsible lending and to assist in the stabilization of the mortgage market.

Although the ability-to-repay regulation doesn't instruct a creditor on specific underwriting guidelines, it does establish some relatively broad requirements. These include the following:

- Credit history.

- Current or reasonably expected income.

- Current employment status.

- Projected monthly mortgage payment for primary loan.

- Projected monthly mortgage payment for any simultaneous junior loan.

- Projected monthly payment for property tax, homeowner's insurance, mortgage insurance and any other mortgage-related monthly expenses.

- Current debt obligations including alimony and child support.

- Debt-to-income ratios or residual income (the amount of income remaining after all monthly debts, including mortgage, have been paid.)

- Debt that is stated by the borrower but doesn't appear on the credit report must be included in the calculation of debt-to-income ratios (see chapter 5.) However, the stated debt doesn't have to be verified. In addition, the creditor must consider any information the borrower volunteers regarding upcoming changes in employment such as retirement or a transition to part-time work.

Lenders must keep their files for three years, and borrowers may sue lenders within this time period if they are having difficulty making mortgage payments. If they win their claim that the lender didn't make a good-faith effort to determine the borrower's ability to pay, the lender may be required to reimburse the borrower for accumulated finance charges, fees and attorney costs. After three years, the lender's failure to properly qualify a borrower is only legally relevant during a foreclosure defense.

Qualified Mortgages

Qualified mortgages are a category of loans that are presumed to meet the ability-to-repay standards. While the ability-to-repay regulations address the borrower-qualification process, qualified mortgages deal with classifying those loan product types, features and fee limitations that should result in fewer borrower loan defaults and less lender liability.

With few exceptions, qualified mortgages have the following features:

- Positive amortization (the loan balance decreases over time rather than increasing).

- No balloon mortgages (a lump sum payoff is required before the loan is fully amortized).

- No interest-only periods.

- Maximum loan term of 30 years.

- Maximum debt-to-income ratio of 43 percent.

- Points and fees that don't exceed 3 percent of the loan amount (this threshold can be exceeded on loans less than $100,000 so that the loan originator may be adequately compensated.)

Additional issues concerning qualified mortgages include:

- **Lower APR Loans**

   The law allows a "safe harbor" for lower APR qualified mortgages; the lender is released from ability-to-repay liability for these loans.

- **Higher APR Loans**

   However, borrowers can still win ability-to-repay lawsuits against the lender for the higher-priced loans if they find themselves unable to make the mortgage payments. In order to prevail in the lawsuit, the consumer must prove that he didn't have sufficient funds to make the payments *at the time the loan closed.*

- **Small Creditor's Exceptions**

   The rule defines small creditors as businesses with less than $2 billion in assets and fewer than 500 closed-end, first-lien residential mortgages in the previous year. These lenders have special qualified mortgage guidelines in addition to positive amortization, no interest-only, and a cap on fees and loan term. These creditors are allowed to make qualified mortgages without meeting a specified debt-to-income threshold, and they can originate balloon mortgages in rural or under-served areas. The loans lose their qualified mortgage status if they are sold within three years.

- **Implementation Timeframes**

   These rules went into effect January 10, 2014. However, some loans that are bought by Fannie Mae and Freddie Mac and FHA, VA and USDA rural loans have a temporary maximum seven-year extension to allow their affiliated agencies time to implement the qualified mortgage standards. During this seven-year period, these loans will be underwritten according to the previously discussed criteria (positive amortization, maximum 30-year loan term, 3 percent cap on fees, no balloon or interest-only mortgages), but they don't have to meet the 43 percent maximum debt-to-income ratio requirement. This restriction may have been temporarily suspended because approximately 20 percent of these loans exceeded the 43 percent threshold in 2013 and to suddenly eliminate these prospective home buyers would cause a crushing slowdown in an already struggling housing market.

XI.   Mortgage Assistance Relief Services Rule

The Mortgage Assistance Relief Services (MARS) Rule helps to protect distressed homeowners from foreclosure-prevention scams. The law applies to everyone who offers to negotiate loan terms with a lender or loan servicer in order to prevent or delay foreclosure; this includes loan originators. The rule includes the following points:

- Fees may not be collected until a written agreement from the lender that the loan terms may be modified has been delivered and accepted by the customer. This law doesn't allow upfront payments.

- Borrowers can cancel their agreement with the loan negotiator at any time.

- The service agreement must state all costs; declare that the negotiator is not affiliated with the government or the lender and inform the borrower that the lender may not accept any change to the current loan or agree to a short sale.

- The negotiator can't advise borrowers to stop making mortgage payments unless the individuals are informed about the consequences of such an act, which include lower credit scores and the possibility of foreclosure.

- The negotiator can't interfere with the communication between the borrower and lender.

- The negotiator must present all lender offers and inform the borrowers that no fee is due until they accept an offer.

- The negotiator can't misrepresent his services or qualifications.

- Public advertising must include specific disclosures using the exact wording contained in the MARS rule. An additional negotiator disclosure must accompany all presented lender offers. See the following link for the exact wording required by law.

XII.   Bank Secrecy Act/Anti-Money Laundering

The Bank Secrecy Act and related Anti-Money Laundering (BSA/AML) laws protect the financial stability of the U.S. The Financial Crimes Enforcement Network (FinCEN), which is part of the U.S. Department of Treasury, analyzes submitted reports and uses the information to investigate possible criminal activity. The law requires reports in the following situations:

- Companies are required to develop policies, keep records and file a Currency Transaction Report with the IRS for cash purchases exceeding $10,000 in one day.

- Individuals transporting more than $10,000 in cash into or out of the country must file a Report of International Transportation of Currency or Monetary Instruments. Failure to comply is a federal offense subject to civil and criminal penalties.

- Any financial institution, which is subject to the Bank Secrecy Act, must electronically file a Suspicious Activity Report (SAR) if it detects suspicious or illegal behavior on the part of a customer or employee. This includes breaches of Internet firewalls (computer hacking).

- The SAR must be filed no later than 30 calendar days after the date of the initial detection by the reporting loan or finance company. If no suspect is identified on the date of such initial detection, a loan or finance company may delay filing a SAR for an additional 30 calendar days to identify a suspect. However, under no circumstances, can the reporting be delayed by more than 60 calendar days after the date of the initial detection.

- The contents or existence of a SAR is strictly confidential and cannot be disclosed even under subpoena.

- Individuals must submit an annual Report of Foreign Bank and Financial Accounts to the IRS naming any foreign bank account, brokerage account or mutual fund that they own.

XIII.   Gramm-Leach-Bliley Act

The Financial Modernization Act of 1999, also known as the "Gramm-Leach-Bliley Act" or GLB Act (named after the senators responsible for drafting the law), includes provisions to protect an individual's (not a business's) personal financial information held by financial institutions. The Federal Trade Commission (FTC) enforces the law for institutions and businesses that are not already regulated in these matters by federal or state agencies including private lenders, check cashing services, mortgage, title and tax-preparation firms. There are three principal parts to the privacy requirements: the Financial Privacy Rule, Pre-Texting and Safeguards Rules.

Financial Privacy Rule

The Financial Privacy Rule governs the collection and disclosure of personal financial information by financial institutions. It also applies to companies, whether or not they are financial institutions, who receive such information. The Privacy Rule distinguishes a consumer from a customer. A *consumer* is someone who obtains a specific product or service for personal use (check cashing service takes minutes), while a *customer* has an on-going significant relationship with the financial institution (obtaining a mortgage loan takes days or weeks). Consequently, the law provides a customer with more privacy protection.

For example, privacy notices provide an individual with the right to opt-out of sharing his financial information with a third party. A *consumer* is only entitled to a privacy notice if the business shares personal information with non-affiliated companies; a *customer* receives an annual privacy notice with the opportunity to opt-out of most information sharing. The notices can be delivered in writing or electronically.

Pre-Texting

The Pre-Texting provisions of the GLB Act protect consumers from individuals and companies that obtain their personal financial information under false pretenses.

Safeguards Rule

The Safeguards Rule requires all FTC-regulated financial institutions to take steps to protect their customer's private information. These steps include designing, implementing and maintaining customer safeguards. The Safeguards Rule applies to financial institutions that collect information from their own customers, as well as to financial institutions that receive customer information from other financial institutions. In addition to establishing and monitoring their own policy and procedures, the companies must also monitor the compliance efforts of their service providers.

XIV.   USA Patriot Act

After the 9/11 attacks, Congress rushed to pass legislation to help law enforcement officials monitor communications and control money laundering activity that might be funneling money to terrorists. A small piece of this applies to mortgage lenders and loan originators. It was the Patriot Act that required loan originators to acquire photo identification from loan applicants.

Loan originators and lenders must collect borrower's:

- Name.

- Address.

- Birth Date.

- Social security number or employee identification number.

- Government-issued photo identification.

All financial institutions must:

- Must establish a Customer Identification Program to verify the identity of all account holders.

- Maintain confidentiality of all documents.

- Establish an anti-money laundering policy.

- Report suspicious activity.

- Report any receipt of currency exceeding $10,000.

- Verify names of account holders against a federal database of known terrorists and fugitives.

- Train employees on policy compliance.

XV.   Mortgage Acts and Practices - Advertising (Regulation N)

It is illegal to misrepresent any loan terms in a commercial advertisement. This includes misrepresenting the:

- Interest rate.

- APR.

- Monthly payment.

- Fees.

- Property taxes and insurances.

- Ancillary products such as credit insurance or credit disability insurance.

- Prepayment penalties.

- Variability of terms.

- Number of payments.

- Actions that constitute a default.

- Effectiveness of debt consolidation.

- Government endorsement.

- Ability to obtain a mortgage or preapproval.

- Right of consumer to reside in property - particularly important for reverse mortgage.

- Availability of counseling services.

Retention of Records

Copies of all commercial communications and supporting documents must be kept for 2 years.

XVI.   The Electronic Signatures in Global and National Commerce Act

The Electronic Signatures in Global and National Commerce Act (E-Sign Act), which was enacted in 2000, allows electronic records and electronic signatures to be valid whenever a regulation requires a document to be in writing as long as the consumer has consented to its use. Financial institutions must provide the consumer with a statement explaining their rights to use and withdrawal of consent, and the hardware and software requirements for accessing and storing records. The consumer must be notified if their access to documents is affected by a change in the hardware or software and given new instructions for access or given the option to withhold consent for electronic storage.

Some of the ways a borrower's identity can be verified include the following:

- Email.

- Phone.

- Social network ID.

- Access codes.

- Knowledge based identity checks.

- Encryption keys.

XVII.   U.S. Department of Housing and Urban Development (HUD)

HUD is the primary federal agency tasked with creating and managing programs to provide quality affordable housing, prevent housing discrimination and help build sustainable communities.

Programs offered by HUD include:

- Section 8 housing for low income families.

- Rental assistance for the elderly.

- Housing for the disabled.

- Community Development Block Grants.

- Office of Fair Housing and Equal Opportunity.

- FHA loans.

- Government National Mortgage Association (Ginnie Mae).

HUD oversees the Federal Housing Administration (FHA).

A Housing Counseling Disclosure includes the names of 10 HUD-approved counseling agencies that are closest to the applicant's current zip code.

High cost home loans require the borrower to attend counseling by a HUD-approved counselor.

The Fair Housing Act is enforced by HUD and creates the following seven protected classes of individuals who cannot be legally discriminated against in residential housing transactions:

- Race.

- Color.

- Religion.

- Sex.

- National Origin.

- Disability (includes HIV/AIDS)

- Familial Status.

Important Points to Remember

1   The Real Estate Settlement Procedures Act (RESPA) provides consumer protection for loans on residential properties (1-4 units).

2   For test purposes, RESPA == REXPA if that helps you remember that it is Reg X.

3   RESPA (Regulation X) is primarily involved with the disclosure of closing costs and the prevention of kickbacks, which may raise the amount of closing costs to the consumer.

4   The Consumer Financial Protection Bureau enforces the RESPA regulations. HUD was the previous enforcer.

5   RESPA requires four pre-settlement disclosures: Special information booklet, Good Faith Estimate (GFE) of settlement costs for reverse mortgages or the Loan Estimate for most closed-end loans, Mortgage Servicing Disclosure Statement and list of housing counseling agencies. These must be sent to the borrower within three business days of receipt of the signed application.

6   RESPA states that a Servicing Transfer Statement is required if the loan servicer sells or assigns the servicing rights to a borrower's loan to another loan servicer.

7.   According to RESPA, the loan servicer must notify the borrower 15 days before the effective date of the loan transfer.

8.   As long the borrower makes a timely payment to the old servicer within 60 days of the loan transfer, the borrower cannot be penalized.

9.   Overages of $50 or more discovered in a borrower's escrow account during the annual audit analysis must be refunded to the borrower.

10.   RESPA requires two disclosures that must be given at settlement: the HUD-1 Settlement Statement (if the borrower has closing costs for reverse mortgages) or the Closing Disclosure, and the Initial Escrow Statement, which may be given shortly after closing.

11.   A referring party must give the Affiliated Business Arrangement Disclosure to the consumer at, or prior to, the time of referral.

12.   The HUD-1 Settlement Statement itemizes the costs and disbursements to the buyer and seller and must be made available, upon request by the borrower (for reverse mortgages), one business day prior to closing. The Closing Disclosure must be delivered three business days before closing.

13.   The HUD-1/Closing Disclosure is NOT required when there is no federally-related loan or no closing costs to the borrower or for most closed-end loans.

14.   The lender has 30 days after settlement to refund any portion of charges on the HUD-1 that exceeded acceptable variances. This refund timeframe is 60 days for the Closing Disclosure.

15.   An Annual Escrow Statement must be sent to the borrower yearly; it summarizes the activity in the escrow account.

16.   RESPA prohibits a person from giving or accepting anything of value for referrals of settlement service business related to a federally related mortgage loan.

17.   Illegal referral fees are known as kickbacks.

18.   RESPA prohibits a person from giving or accepting any part of a charge for services that are not performed.

19.   In order to protect itself from escrow shortages, the lender may require a cushion that doesn't exceed an amount equal to 1/6 of the total disbursements for the year.

20.   The Equal Credit Opportunity Act (ECOA) prohibits discrimination by lenders in any part of a credit transaction on the basis of: race, color, religion, national origin, sex, marital status, age (provided the applicant has attained the minimum legal age in the state), the receipt of income from a public assistance program or having exercised any rights under the Consumer Credit Protection Act.

21.   ECOA (Regulation B) also specifies that the borrower is entitled to a copy of the residential property appraisal report at least 3 business days before closing.

22.   It is because of ECOA that lenders cannot ask if a borrower is widowed or divorced. They can only ask if the person is married, unmarried or separated and these are the only choices on the loan application.

23.   ECOA dictates the collection of demographic information in order to monitor the lenders' compliance with the law. Specifically, on the bottom of the third page of the 1003 loan application the interviewer MUST specify the applicant's race, ethnicity and sex when the loan application is taken face-to-face.

24.   The Consumer Financial Protection Bureau enforces ECOA.

25.   A lender has 30 days after receipt of an application, to notify the applicant of its action on the application.

26.   An applicant can request a statement of reasons within 60 days of receiving the original adverse action notice

27.   A lender has 30 days after an applicant's request for an adverse action statement, to provide the information.

28.   The Truth-in-Lending Act (TILA) was passed by Congress in 1968 as part of the Consumer Credit Protection Act.

29.   TILA was implemented by the Federal Reserve Board as Regulation Z. It was enacted to protect consumers during credit transactions.

30.   TILA is administered by the Consumer Financial Protection Bureau.

31.   Regulation Z applies to residential mortgages (1-4 units) and does not include commercial or other nonresidential loans.

32.   Regulation Z covers three general areas: disclosure of financing charges (for reverse mortgages, equity lines of credit, mortgages secured by a mobile home and dwellings not attached to land), distribution of the Consumer Handbook on Adjustable-Rate Mortgages booklet and the right of rescission.

33.   APR disclosure must occur within 3 business days of receiving a signed loan application.

34.   If the APR is quoted incorrectly by more than 1/8 % for a fixed-rate loan, it must be re-disclosed before settlement.

35.   If the APR is quoted incorrectly by more than 1/4 % for an adjustable-rate loan, it must be re-disclosed before settlement.

36.   TILA states that if any triggering term is specified, then the APR and the amount and terms of repayment must also be disclosed.

37.   The Right of Rescission provides a 3 business day cooling-off period for a consumer who uses his primary residence as security for a refinance, home improvement or second mortgage loan.

38.   The rescission period does not apply to a first mortgage on a purchase of a property.

39.   The Truth-in-Lending Disclosure must be delivered at least 7 business days prior to funding for reverse mortgages, equity lines of credit, mortgages secured by a mobile home and dwellings not attached to land.

40.   The APR must be finalized at least three days before closing.

41. The Home Ownership and Equity Protection Act of 1994 (HOEPA) amends the Truth in Lending Act and establishes requirements for certain loans with high rates and/or high fees.

42. A high-cost home loan is one that charges the borrower more than 5% of the total loan amount for points and fees.

43. The Home Mortgage Disclosure Act (HMDA) is implemented by the Federal Reserve Board's Regulation C

44. HMDA requires lending institutions to report public loan data.

45. HMDA does NOT set lending quotas for protected classes of borrowers.

46. The Fair Credit Reporting Act (FCRA) was passed in 1970 to protect an individual's privacy rights and to ensure accurate and fair credit reporting.

47. The Fair Credit Reporting Act is enforced by the Federal Trade Commission. Much of the law regulates the actions of the Credit Reporting Agencies (CRA) that compile databases of information received from creditors, and the right of consumers to dispute incorrect information.

48. The three national credit reporting agencies are Experian, TransUnion and Equifax.

49. Lenders must notify an applicant when a loan is denied (adverse action) because of the information contained in the credit report and provide the applicant with the contact information (name, address and phone number) of the CRA.

50. Bankruptcies can be kept in the credit report for 10 years.

51. Tax liens can be kept in the credit report for 7 years from the time they were paid.

52. Examples of creditors who report missed payments are credit card companies, auto financing companies and mortgage lenders.

53. The Gramm-Leach-Bliley Act includes provisions to protect consumers personal financial information held by financial institutions.

54. The Gramm-Leach-Bliley Act requires companies to give consumers privacy notices that explain the institutions' information-sharing practices. In turn, consumers have the right to limit some sharing of their information.

55. The Gramm-Leach-Bliley Act requires all financial institutions to design, implement and maintain safeguards to protect customer information.

56. The Federal Communication Commission (FCC) and the Federal Trade Commission (FTC) established a national Do-Not-Call Registry.

57. Telemarketers and sellers are required to search the registry at least once every 31 days and drop from their call lists the phone numbers of consumers who have registered.

58. Violators of the telemarketing rules may be subject to fines of up to $43,792 per violation.

59. The National Do-Not-Call Registry does not limit calls by political organizations, charities, or telephone surveyors.

60. A company with which a consumer has an established business relationship may call for up to 18 months after the consumer's last purchase, last delivery, or last payment unless the consumer asks the company not to call again.

61. If a consumer makes an inquiry or submits an application to a company, the company can call for three months.

62. A company that is a seller or telemarketer could be liable for placing any telemarketing calls (even to numbers NOT on the registry) unless the seller has accessed the registry and paid the fee, if required.

63. Consumers should contact their lender if they have questions about their application, and they should contact the Credit Reporting Agency if they have questions about their credit scores.

64. The range of possible FICO credit scores is 300 to 850.

65. Borrowers are entitled to a free credit report if the lender takes adverse action against them, and they ask for their report within 60 days of receiving notice of the action.

66. The National Credit Score Disclosure will give the applicant the name, address, and phone number of the consumer reporting company.

67. The Fair and Accurate Credit Transaction Act (FACT Act) became law in 2003 and is an extension of the 1970 Fair Credit Reporting Act. The increase in identity theft was one of the driving forces behind the new regulation, and consequently, the FACT Act allows every individual to have a free copy of their credit report once a year from each of the three Credit Reporting Agencies.

68. The Red Flags Rule requires financial institutions and creditors to develop and implement written identity theft prevention programs.

69. The Red Flags Rule provides for the identification, detection, and response to patterns, practices, or specific activities – known as "red flags" – that could indicate identity theft.

70. Under the Red Flags Rule, financial institutions and creditors must develop a written program that identifies and detects the relevant warning signs – or "red flags" – of identity theft.

71. The Red Flags program must also describe appropriate responses that would prevent and mitigate the crime and detail a plan to update the program.

72. The Red Flags program must be managed by the Board of Directors or senior employees of the financial institution or creditor and include appropriate staff training and oversight of any service providers.

73. The Homeowner's Protection Act requires lenders to cancel the PMI when the LTV reaches 78% of the original purchase price. Borrowers can request a cancellation when it reaches 80%, which will usually be granted if they have a good payment history.

74. A finance charge is a fee the buyer would not pay if it were a cash deal. For example, wire transfers and mortgage interest payments contribute to the calculation of the APR while hazard insurance and home inspections do not.

75. According to the Truth-in-Lending Act, the term refinance applies to the satisfaction of an existing obligation and its replacement by a new obligation.

76. ECOA notification of adverse action must be in writing; a telephone call is not sufficient.

77. Loss mitigation options include refinancing, loan modification, short sale and deed-in-lieu.

78. If the servicer receives the mitigation application 37 days before a foreclosure sale, the borrower's situation must be evaluated for all applicable options within 30 days. The borrower may appeal a decision if the complete application package was submitted at least 90 days before a scheduled sale. A foreclosure sale is delayed until a loan modification is denied, appealed or canceled due to nonperformance.

79. High-cost home loans have the following restrictions: most balloon mortgages are prohibited; the borrower must prove an ability to repay the loan, and the borrower must speak to a HUD-approved housing counselor.

80. An additional appraisal may be required if a prospective purchase is a "flipped" home with a higher-priced mortgage loan. Flips are defined as resells within 90 days with seller paying a minimum 10 percent price increase, or resells within the past 91-180 days with seller paying a minimum 20 percent price increase.

81. Lenders must require a property tax and hazard insurance escrow account to be maintained for a minimum of five years if there is a first-lien high-priced home loan. The account can be canceled after five years if the LTV is 80 percent or less, and the borrower is current on the mortgage payments.

82. The 2010 Dodd-Frank Wall Street Reform and Consumer Act requires more regulation and oversight of lenders and non-health insurance companies. In order to implement the new legislation, the Consumer Financial Protection Bureau, the Financial Stability Oversight Council, the Orderly Liquidation Authority and the Federal Insurance Office were created.

83. Lenders must require proof of a borrower's ability to repay a mortgage loan.

84. A qualified mortgage is one that follows stated guidelines intended to reduce a lender's potential liability. These loans have no balloon or interest-only mortgages, positive amortization, maximum 30-year term, maximum 3 percent points and fees, and a maximum 43 percent debt-to-income ratio (FHA, VA and USDA loans don't have to conform to this ratio until 2021.)

85. The Mortgage Assistance Relief Services (MARS) Rule applies to negotiators assisting borrowers with mortgage loan modifications. They aren't allowed to collect upfront fees, and the borrower may cancel the agreement with the negotiator at any time without penalty.

86. The Bank Secrecy Act and Anti-Money Laundering laws require companies to file a Currency Transaction Report with the IRS for cash purchases exceeding $10,000 in one day. It also requires individuals transporting more than $10,000 in cash into or out of the country must file a report with the U.S. government.

87. Real estate transfer taxes, loan origination fees and interest rate have zero variance. They must be identical on the GFE and HUD-1 and between the Loan Estimate and the Closing Disclosure. The appraisal and credit report fees have zero variance between the Loan Estimate and the Closing Disclosure, but can have a 10 percent variance between the GFE and HUD-1.

88. Fees that the lender chooses or identifies (government recording fees, title insurance if selected or "recommended" by the lender) can't vary between the GFE and HUD-1 and between the Loan Estimate and the Closing Disclosure by more than 10 percent.

89. Fees for services that the owners choose for themselves (hazard insurance or title insurance if the homeowners don't choose one of the lender-identified selections) and fees that are paid per diem (pre-paid mortgage interest) have no limit on the acceptable amount of variance between the GFE and the HUD-1 Settlement Statement and between the Loan Estimate and the Closing Disclosure.

90. The lender has 30 business days after the closing for reverse mortgages to refund to the borrower any portion of the charges that exceeded the acceptable amount of variance. The refund deadline is 60 days for TRID-compliant loans.

91. Force-placed insurance occurs if the lender chooses the hazard insurance company when the borrower allows his policy to lapse.

92. Higher-priced loans are ones in which the APR exceeds the average prime rate by at least 1.5% for first-lien loans.

93.   TIL disclosure includes APR, finance charge, amount financed and total amount of payments.

94.   In October 2015, the TILA-RESPA Integrated Disclosure rule went into effect and modified disclosure requirements for most closed-end loans, but not for reverse mortgages.

95.   The TRID Loan Estimate combines the initial TILA disclosure and the GFE.

96.   The TRID Closing Disclosure combines the final TILA disclosure and the HUD-1.

97.   The Loan Estimate must be delivered or mailed no later than three business days after a loan application is submitted.

98.   The Loan Estimate must be delivered or mailed no later than seven business days prior to loan consummation. This can be waived if the borrower has an emergency such as an impending foreclosure auction.

99.   Creditors may not revise a Loan Estimate because of technical issues, incorrect calculations or low estimates.

100. Lender must ensure that the revised Loan Estimate is received at least 4 business days prior to loan consummation (mailed at least 7 business days prior).

101. The borrower must receive the Closing Disclosure at least 3 business days before consummation. THIS IS DIFFERENT FROM THE HUD-1 REQUIREMENT.

102. Changes in the APR, loan product or the addition of a prepayment penalty trigger a revised Closing Disclosure and an additional 3 business day waiting period.

103. Lenders or closing agents prepare the Closing Disclosure.

104. If changes to a seller or buyer payment occurs after closing, the lender has 30 calendar days to send a revised Closing Disclosure.

105. Non-numeric clerical errors and tolerance violations trigger a new Closing Disclosure that must be delivered within 60 calendar days following loan consumption. Likewise, Closing Disclosure tolerance refunds must also be sent within 60 days.

106. When a consumer requests the cancellation of their escrow account, the lender must deliver an Escrow Closing Notice no later than 3 business days before closure.

107. If the escrow account is closed for some other reason (except for default or termination caused by refinancing, repayment or rescission), the notice must be sent 30 business days prior to closure.

108. Lenders must retain the Closing Disclosure and related documents for 5 years, the Loan Estimate for 3 years and the Escrow Cancellation Notice and Partial Payment Policy for 2 years after loan consummation.

109. The USA Patriot Act requires mortgage applicants to provide their name, address, social security number or employee identification number and a government-issued photo ID.

110. The USA Patriot Act requires financial institutes to verify the identity of account holders, compare the account names to names in a federal database of fugitives and suspected terrorists, establish an anti-money laundering policy and train employees on the policy.

111. It is illegal to misrepresent any loan terms or conditions in an advertisement. Copies of commercial communications and supporting documents must be kept for 2 years.

112. The E-Sign Act allows electronic records and electronic signatures to be valid whenever a regulation requires a document to be in writing as long as the consumer has consented to its use.

113. The Fair Housing Act prohibits HIV/AIDS discrimination as part of the disability protected class.

114. High cost home loans require the borrower to obtain housing counseling.
115. HUD oversees the Federal Housing Administration (FHA) agency.
116. Loan originator should enter zip code(s) on the GFE/Loan Estimate if unknown property address, as may be the case when requesting lender's pre-approval.
117. If there are multiple co-signers, the ECOA Adverse Action Notice needs to be sent only to the primary borrower.
118. The loan originator must guess the ethnicity, race and sex of an applicant if they decline to provide that information. The monitoring section on the 1003 cannot be left blank.
119. ECOA requires an application must be retained for 25 months from the date a loan acceptance or denial notification is sent to the applicant.
120. A SARS report must be kept strictly confidential and existence or contents not disclosed even if subpoenaed.
121. Ten housing counseling agencies must be listed on the Housing Counseling Disclosures.
122. 12 months is the maximum term for a HOEPA balloon loan.
123. A borrower must indicate an Intent to Proceed within 10 business days after receiving the Loan Estimate.
124. In most cases, a TILA business day is a day the office is open for business to the public. However, a business day is defined as every calendar day except Sunday and federal holidays for delivery of the following three documents: Closing Disclosure, Escrow Closing Notice, and the Right of Rescission.
125. Servicers must attempt to speak to a delinquent borrower within 36 days after the missed mortgage payment, and mail loss mitigation information within 45 days.

Exam

1.   The Real Estate Settlement Procedures Act (RESPA) is implemented as:
   A.   Regulation B
   B.   Regulation X
   C.   Regulation A
   D.   Regulation Z

2.   Which government agency enforces the RESPA regulations?
   A.   CFPB
   B.   FCC
   C.   FHA
   D.   FTC

3.   RESPA is concerned with:
   A.   Kickbacks
   B.   Credit reports
   C.   Triggering terms in ads
   D.   U.S. security

4.   The Good Faith Estimate/Loan Estimate must be sent to the borrower within how many business days of receiving a loan application?
   A.   1
   B.   3
   C.   5
   D.   10

5.   The Special Information Booklet must be sent to the borrower within how many business days of receiving a loan application?
   A.   1
   B.   3
   C.   5
   D.   10

6.   The Mortgage Servicing Disclosure Statement must be sent to the borrower within how many business days of receiving a loan application?
   A.   1
   B.   3
   C.   5
   D.   10

7.   How often must a summary of escrow activity statement be sent to the borrower?
      A.   Once a month
      B.   Once every 3 months
      C.   Once every 6 months
      D.   Once a year

8.   RESPA requires which of the following to be given to the borrower when the loan servicer changes?
      A.   Servicing Transfer Statement
      B.   Good Faith Estimate
      C.   Truth In Lending Disclosure
      D.   Initial Escrow Statement

9.   When must a referring party give the Affiliated Business Arrangement Disclosure to the consumer?
      A.   Within 3 days of the loan application
      B.   Within 15 days of the loan application
      C.   At or prior to the time of referral
      D.   At closing

10.   A borrower is entitled to request and obtain a copy of the HUD-1 Settlement Statement how many days before closing?
      A.   1
      B.   3
      C.   5
      D.   7

11.   After an escrow account analysis, money must be refunded if the over-paid amount equals or exceeds:
      A. $50
      B. $100
      C. $250
      D. $500

12.   The servicer has how many days to notify the borrower if the servicing rights have been sold and are being transferred to another company?
      A.   3
      B.   5
      C.   10
      D.   15

13. A borrower who makes a timely payment to the old servicer after a loan transfer, can be penalized after how many days if he still is not sending the payment to the correct servicer?
    A. 30
    B. 60
    C. 90
    D. 120

14. What is the maximum criminal penalty for a kickback violation?
    A. $500 and 6 months in prison
    B. $1000 and 6 months in prison
    C. $10,000 and a year in prison
    D. $25,000 and a year in prison

15. The HUD-1 Settlement Statement is required for what type of transaction?
    A. Cash purchase of a condo
    B. Financed purchase of a warehouse
    C. Reverse Mortgage
    D. Cash purchase of a strip mall

16. The maximum escrow cushion that a lender can require is:
    A. 1/6 of total yearly disbursements
    B. 1/3 of total yearly disbursements
    C. 1/2 of total yearly disbursements
    D. 3/4 of total yearly disbursements

17. The lender has how many days after settlement to refund any portion of charges on the HUD-1 that exceeded the acceptable variance?
    A. 15
    B. 30
    C. 45
    D. 60

18. The Equal Credit Opportunity Act (ECOA) is implemented as:
    A. Regulation B
    B. Regulation X
    C. Regulation A
    D. Regulation Z

19. ECOA allows an applicant to have a copy of his:
    A. Credit score
    B. Credit report
    C. Property appraisal report
    D. Bank records

20.   What government agency enforces ECOA?
       A.   FCC
       B.   HUD
       C.   CFPB
       D.   FHA

21.   A lender can discriminate based on:
       A.   Age
       B.   Sex
       C.   Credit history
       D.   Race

22.   How many days does a lender have after receipt of an application to notify the applicant of its action on the application?
       A.   10
       B.   15
       C.   30
       D.   60

23.   How many days does an applicant have after receipt of an adverse action notice to request a statement of reasons from the lender?
       A.   10
       B.   15
       C.   30
       D.   60

24.   How many days does a lender have to send a statement of reasons for an adverse action after receiving a request from an applicant?
       A.   10
       B.   15
       C.   30
       D.   60

25.   The Truth-in-Lending Act (TILA) is implemented as:
       A.   Regulation B
       B.   Regulation X
       C.   Regulation D
       D.   Regulation Z

26.   The Truth-in-Lending Act (TILA) was implemented by the:
       A.   Federal Reserve Board
       B.   Fannie Mae
       C.   Federal Bureau of Investigation
       D.   Federal Express

27.   The Truth-in-Lending Act is administered by:
>   A.   DVA
>   B.   FCC
>   C.   FHA
>   D.   CFPB

28.   The TILA disclosure must be given to the applicant within how many days after receiving the signed loan application for a reverse mortgage?
>   A.   3 business days
>   B.   5 business days
>   C.   7 business days
>   D.   14 business days

29.   Which of the following is **NOT** a trigger term?
>   A.   5 % interest rate
>   B. $200 monthly payment
>   C.   Lowest rates in town
>   D.   48 easy payments

30.   The Right of Rescission does **NOT** apply to:
>   A.   Refinance loan
>   B.   Second mortgage
>   C.   Home improvement
>   D.   First mortgage on a purchase

31.   The TILA must be re-disclosed if the APR for a fixed-rate loan changes by more than:
>   A.   1/8 %
>   B.   1/2 %
>   C.   3/4 %
>   D.   1 %

32.   HOEPA considers a loan to be high cost if the total charges to the borrower exceed what percent of the loan amount?
>   A.   4 %
>   B.   5 %
>   C.   10 %
>   D.   12 %

33.   The Truth-in-Lending Disclosure must be delivered within how many business days prior to closing a reverse mortgage?
>   A.   3
>   B.   7
>   C.   10
>   D.   15

34.   The APR must be finalized at least how many days before closing?
    A.   1
    B.   3
    C.   5
    D.   7

35.   The Home Mortgage Disclosure Act (HMDA) was implemented by the:
    A.   Department of Housing and Urban Development
    B.   Department of Veterans Affairs
    C.   Federal Communication Commission
    D.   Federal Reserve Board

36.   HMDA is also known as:
    A.   Regulation B
    B.   Regulation C
    C.   Regulation X
    D.   Regulation Z

37.   HMDA does **NOT**:
    A.   Set lending quotas for protected classes
    B.   Require the loan amount to be reported
    C.   Require the location of the property to be reported
    D.   Require the race of the borrower to be reported

38.   Which of the following is **NOT** required HMDA borrower information?
    A.   Loan amount
    B.   Gender
    C.   Race
    D.   Income

39.   The Fair Credit Reporting Act is enforced by:
    A.   HUD
    B.   FCC
    C.   FHA
    D.   FTC

40.   Bankruptcies can be kept in the credit report for:
    A.   2 years
    B.   5 years
    C.   7 years
    D.   10 years

41.   Tax liens can be kept in the credit report for:
    A.   2 years
    B.   5 years
    C.   7 years
    D.   10 years

42.   Which of the following is **NOT** a credit repository?
    A.   FICO
    B.   TransUnion
    C.   Experian
    D.   Equifax

43.   Borrowers are entitled to a free credit report if the lender takes adverse action against them and they ask for their report within how many days of receiving notice of the action?
    A.   30
    B.   60
    C.   90
    D.   120

44.   Which Act includes provisions to protect consumers' personal financial information held by financial institutions?
    A.   Real Estate Settlement Procedures
    B.   Fair and Accurate Credit Transaction
    C.   Truth-in-Lending
    D.   Gramm-Leach-Bliley

45.   Which Act requires companies to give consumers privacy notices?
    A.   Real Estate Settlement Procedures
    B.   Fair and Accurate Credit Transaction
    C.   Truth-in-Lending
    D.   Gramm-Leach-Bliley

46.   What is the fine for Do Not Call violations?
    A. $3,000
    B. $9,000
    C. $43,792
    D. $60,000

47.   A company with which a consumer has an established business relationship may call for how many months after the consumer's last purchase?
    A.   6
    B.   13
    C.   18
    D.   24

48.   If a consumer makes an inquiry or submits an application to a company, the company can call for how many months?
    A.   3
    B.   6
    C.   9
    D.   12

49.   Which of the following is allowed to call numbers on the Do Not Call List?
  A.   Loan originators
  B.   Charities
  C.   Car dealerships
  D.   Dry cleaners

50.   The Fair and Accurate Credit Transaction Act:
  A.   Prohibits kickbacks to title companies
  B.   Provides that all the information in a credit report is verified
  C.   Allows consumers one free credit report per year from each repository
  D.   Changes credit scoring to a 1-5 ranking system

51.   Who does the consumer contact if he has questions about his credit score?
  A.   Credit Reporting Agency
  B.   Lender
  C.   Title company
  D.   Appraiser

52.   The range of possible credit scores is :
  A.   200 - 900
  B.   300 - 850
  C.   400 - 700
  D.   500 - 1000

53.   The Red Flags Rule is concerned with:
  A.   Identity theft
  B.   Kickbacks
  C.   Disclosure of the APR
  D.   Regulation of interest rates

54.   The Red Flags Rule is part of the:
  A.   Truth-in-Lending Act
  B.   Real Estate Settlement Procedures Act
  C.   SAFE Act
  D.   Fair and Accurate Credit Transactions Act

55.   Which of the following is a creditor as defined by the Red Flags Rule?
  A.   Mortgage Broker
  B.   Beauty shop
  C.   Grocery store
  D.   Appraiser

56.   Which of the following is **NOT** a requirement for a company's Red Flags program?
  A.   Be in writing
  B.   Identify and detect warning signs of identity theft
  C.   Detail appropriate responses to the warning signs
  D.   Managed by the Human Resources Department

57. If a Loan Estimate is mailed, It must be mailed how many days before loan consummation?
    A.   1
    B.   3
    C.   5
    D.   7

58. A lender has how many days to refund excessive variances on a Closing Disclosure?
    A.   10
    B.   30
    C.   60
    D.   90

59. A change to which of the following does NOT trigger a new 3-day waiting period?
    A.   Seller credits buyer money for landscaping
    B.   APR
    C.   Loan product
    D.   Addition of a prepayment penalty

60. How many business days before loan consummation is a borrower entitled to see a revised Closing Disclosure that did not trigger an additional 3-day waiting period?
    A.   1
    B.   2
    C.   3
    D.   4

61. How many days before loan consummation is a seller entitled to see the Closing Disclosure?
    A.   0 (closing day)
    B.   1
    C.   2
    D.   3

62. When a consumer requests the cancellation of their escrow account, the lender has how many business days prior to closing the account to deliver an Escrow Closing Notice?
    A.   1
    B.   3
    C.   10
    D.   30

63. When a lender cancels an escrow account for a reason other than default or termination caused by refinancing, repayment or rescission, they have how many business days prior to closing the account to deliver an Escrow Closing Notice?
    A.   1
    B.   3
    C.   10
    D.   30

64.   For how many years must a lender retain the Loan Estimate?
        A.   2
        B.   3
        C.   4
        D.   5

65.   For how many years must a lender retain the Closing Disclosure?
        A.   2
        B.   3
        C.   4
        D.   5

66.   For how many years must a lender retain the Escrow Cancellation Notice?
        A.   2
        B.   3
        C.   4
        D.   5

67.   For how many years must a lender retain the Partial Payment Policy?
        A.   2
        B.   3
        C.   4
        D.   5

68.   The borrower must receive the Closing Disclosure how many business days before
        consummation?
        A.   1
        B.   2
        C.   3
        D.   4

69.   Which of the following is NOT delivered to a reverse mortgage applicant?
        A.   TILA Disclosure
        B.   Loan Estimate
        C.   Good Faith Estimate
        D.   HUD-1

70.   Which of the following is NOT protected from discrimination by the Fair Housing Act?
        A.   HIV patients
        B.   Elderly
        C.   Pregnant women
        D.   Mexicans

71.   ECOA requires that a loan application is retained for how long after a denial?
        A.   6 months
        B.   25 months
        C.   36 months
        D.   60 months

72. What should a loan originator do if an applicant refuses to disclose their nationality?
    A.   Leave it blank on the application
    B.   Refuse the application
    C.   Select the box with their best guess
    D.   Pester the applicant until they answer

73. What should a loan originator do on a Loan Estimate address field when the borrower requests a pre-approval?
    A.   Leave it blank
    B.   Enter one or more zip codes of likely locations
    C.   Enter the applicant's personal address
    D.   Deny the loan application

74. How many housing counseling agencies must be listed on the Housing Counseling Disclosure?
    A.   1
    B.   3
    C.   5
    D.   10

75. What entity does HUD oversee?
    A.   Department of Health
    B.   Federal Housing Administration
    C.   Department of Veterans Affairs
    D.   Consumer Financial Protection Bureau

76. What is the maximum term for a HOEPA balloon bridge loan?
    A.   12 months
    B.   24 months
    C.   36 months
    D.   60 months

77. A borrower must indicate an Intent to Proceed within how many business days after receiving the Loan Estimate?
    A.   3
    B.   10
    C.   15
    D.   30

78. Which law enacted mandatory cancellation of PMI under certain circumstances?
    A.   Truth-in-Lending
    B.   RESPA
    C.   Homeowner's Protection Act
    D.   Equal Credit Opportunity Act

Answer Key

1.	B	26.	A	51.	A	76.	A
2.	A	27.	D	52.	B	77.	B
3.	A	28.	A	53.	A	78.	C
4.	B	29.	C	54.	D		
5.	B	30.	D	55.	A		
6.	B	31.	A	56.	D		
7.	D	32.	B	57.	D		
8.	A	33.	B	58.	C		
9.	C	34.	B	59.	A		
10.	A	35.	D	60.	A		
11.	A	36.	B	61.	A		
12.	D	37.	A	62.	B		
13.	B	38.	D	63.	D		
14.	C	39.	D	64.	B		
15.	C	40.	D	65.	D		
16.	A	41.	C	66.	A		
17.	B	42.	A	67.	A		
18.	A	43.	B	68.	C		
19.	C	44.	D	69.	B		
20.	C	45.	D	70.	B		
21.	C	46.	C	71.	B		
22.	C	47.	C	72.	C		
23.	D	48.	A	73.	B		
24.	C	49.	B	74.	D		
25.	D	50.	C	75.	B		

2

Uniform State Content

This chapter comprises approximately 20 percent of the national licensing exam, so pay close attention to the details.

I.   SAFE Act

The Secure and Fair Enforcement for Mortgage Licensing Act (SAFE Mortgage Licensing Act) was included as part of the Housing and Economic Recovery Act of 2008. The SAFE Act provides the framework for additional consumer protections, less regulatory burdens and a reduction in fraudulent activities by establishing minimum state licensing and renewal requirements for individuals and companies that provide residential mortgage loan services to the public. Although states can implement additional origination rules and regulations, the details of the SAFE ACT are part of the uniform state content that all loan originators need to know.

When the SAFE Act was first implemented, all states required a separate state exam in addition to a national exam. After a period of time, some states eliminated the state exam requirement. Consequently, the national exam was modified to include a larger percentage of questions that reference the material presented in this chapter.

Implementation

In order to implement the Safe Mortgage Licensing Act, the Conference of State Bank Supervisors (CSBS) and the American Association of Residential Mortgage Regulators (AARMR) created the Nationwide Mortgage Licensing System and Registry (NMLSR). The new policies streamlined the application and renewal policies. Previously, licensees who wished to operate in multiple states had to keep track of different regulatory websites, license expiration dates and continuing education (CE) requirements for each state. The new rules simplified the process; applicants may access each state's license application through the NMSLR website; NMSLR sets minimum CE requirements, and most states have an annual license renewal date of December 31 (although it's slightly earlier in a few states.)

Regulators and mortgage business owners now have a much easier method for tracking individuals who are licensed in multiple states; all the data is stored under the licensee's unique registration number. Interested parties can scan the account and immediately know where the licensee is authorized to do business. Expired licenses that weren't renewed are easily detected, which helps ensure that only licensed individuals are originating loans.

State Law and Regulation Definitions

The law requires that each licensee register with the NMLS. This is the first step in creating an entry in a searchable registry database that contains a loan originator's employment history, and disciplinary and criminal judgments that were uncovered during a background check. This information is intended to empower the consumer, and the database is available for public access on the Internet. Some states are going one step further than the national law by requiring national registration for non-mortgage state-licensed consumer finance companies, collection agencies and payday lenders. Information on these individuals and companies is included in the public database.

Definitions

CSBS/AARMR standardized the industry's terminology as part of the implementation of the SAFE Act. Specific definitions include the following:

- **Federal banking agencies** - Federal Reserve System Board of Governors, National Credit Union Administration, Comptroller of the Currency and the Federal Deposit Insurance Corporation.

- **Immediate family member** - spouse, parents, stepparents, child, stepchild, sibling, stepsibling, grandparent, grandchild and adopted members.

- **Individual** - a natural person.

- **Person** - natural person, limited liability corporation, association, company, corporation and partnership.

- **Loan originator** - individual who takes a residential loan application and explains the details of a loan and offers to negotiate the terms of a loan with a lender for compensation. This doesn't include real estate licensees, or individuals who only perform clerical and administrative duties or who only negotiate timeshare financing.

- **Clerical and administrative duties** - tasks that include the collection, analyzing and distribution of data needed for loan processing and underwriting. Communication with loan applicants is acceptable as long as the discussion doesn't include counseling or an offer to negotiate loan terms.

- **Underwriter and loan processor** - individual who performs clerical or support tasks under the direction of a state-licensed loan originator or registered loan originator.

- **Registered loan originator** - loan originator who is an employee of one of the following: a depository institution or a subsidiary owned and controlled by a depository institution that's regulated by a Federal banking agency, or an institution regulated by the Farm Credit Administration.

- **Residential real estate** - real property that is a dwelling or intended to be built as a dwelling.

- **Residential mortgage loan** - a loan for a personal, family or household dwelling that's secured by a mortgage or deed of trust. This includes vacant land intended for the construction of a home.

- **Unique identifier** - NMLSR applicant registration number.

- **Non-traditional mortgage product** - any offering that's not a 30-year fixed-rate loan.

State Authority

Although prospective loan originators access applications through the NMLSR, it's a state's responsibility to process and maintain the status of the application and license. This information is then communicated back to the NMLSR for inclusion in the national database. Specifically, a state is responsible for the following functions:

- Design the license application form.

- Assessing the fitness and character of applicant

- Collect transaction-processing fees.

- Establish minimum net worth or bonding requirements or establish a recovery fund which is funded by loan originators (fines, application and renewal fees)

- Conduct background checks.

- Issue licenses and write procedural regulations.

- Deny, suspend and revoke licenses.

- Audit loan origination records.

- Interpret, administer and enforce the SAFE Act within the state.

State Investigations

If a matter arises that warrants further investigation, each state has broad powers to gather information needed to establish the truth, including:

- Subpoena witnesses and documents.

- Documents must be produced on or before the date on the summons.

- Records may be requested from any licensee or person regulated by the SAFE Act.

- Any of the following individuals may be interviewed: officers, principals, mortgage loan originators, employees, independent contractors, agents, and customers of the licensee, individual or person subject to this Act concerning their business.

- No one involved in the investigation may withhold, destroy, alter or damage a record.

- Additional authority includes the right to issue cease and desist orders; enforce fines and penalties and order the termination of an employee or official who poses a threat to the public.

CSBS/AARMR Authority

The SAFE Act allows states to opt-out of managing the transition to the new system and overseeing future licensing and disciplinary activities. In these cases, CSBS/AARMR and the Consumer Financial Protection Bureau are empowered to implement its own systems and provide regulatory oversight in lieu of a state agency. Likewise, these national agencies may assume control of the licensing system if a state fails to maintain the required standards.

Additional oversight responsibilities include:

- Maintenance of the national registry.

- Approval of course material, schools and exams.

- Monitor the status of licensees.

- Request result of fingerprint background check from the FBI on behalf of the state.

- Assign unique identifier to MLO.

- Set penalty limits.

- Write Loan Originator Rule.

License Law and Regulation

The national law sets minimum standards for education and testing. Make sure you click on the link for individual state requirements before you register for a course. For example, if your state requires a separate state exam, try to enroll in a 20-hour course that includes the state law.

Exempted Licensing

The following individuals are exempt from MLO licensing:

- Exempt originators include: employees of a depository institution; a subsidiary that is owned and controlled by a depository institution, or an institution regulated by the Farm Credit Administration. This includes employees of a federally or state charted bank. These exempt employees are required to register with the NMLS and submit their fingerprints and personal biography of work experience. They aren't required to be licensed by the state or take pre-licensing and continuing education courses. These individuals are known as *registered* loan originators.

- Individuals who negotiate a mortgage loan for themselves or family members.

- Attorneys who negotiate loan terms as an ancillary service and who aren't compensated by a loan originator or lender.

- Commercial real estate loan originators.

- Employee of a non-profit housing organization when originating loans for that organization.

- An individual who does not act as a loan originator habitually or repeatedly, provided that the source of prospective financing does not provide mortgage financing or perform other loan origination activities habitually or repeatedly.

Loan Processors and Underwriters

The law states that loan processors and underwriters who function as *independent contractors* must be state-licensed loan originators and register with the NMLSR. *Supervised* loan processors and underwriters who don't represent to the public through any means, including business cards, that they can or will perform any of the activities of a loan originator aren't required to be a state-licensed loan originator. This is the minimal standard. Individual states may enforce stricter rules and require everyone, whether they are supervised or not, to be licensed.

Application Requirements

All candidates must submit fingerprints, personal history and experience, and sign an authorization that allows the NMLSR to access their credit report as well as information related to any administrative, civil or criminal findings by any governmental jurisdiction. Applicants must be licensed through a state.

The minimum standards for licensing and registration as a state-licensed loan originator include the following:

- Applicant has never had a loan originator license revoked in any governmental jurisdiction.

- Applicant has no felony conviction during the past seven years or no felony conviction ever if offense is related to fraud, dishonesty, money laundering or breach of trust.

- Applicant has demonstrated financial responsibility, character, and general fitness. The states determine if an individual applicant meets these requirements.

- Applicant has completed the pre-licensing education requirement.

- Applicant has passed a national exam and any additionally required state exam.

- Applicant has met either a net worth or surety bond requirement, or paid into a state fund, as required by the state.

Pre-Licensing Course Requirements

The requirements for pre-licensing courses are as follows:

- **National** - An applicant must complete at least 20 hours of NMLS-approved education in a pre-licensing course (called the core course) which includes at least:

  - 3 hours of Federal law and regulations.

  - 3 hours of ethics, which includes instruction on fraud, consumer protection, and fair lending issues.

  - 2 hours of training related to lending standards for the nontraditional mortgage product marketplace (any loan product that is not a 30-year fixed-rate loan).

  - The remaining 12 hours of content is left to the discretion of the course developer, and it may include state-specific information if the course is marketed in an individual state. All licensing courses must be approved by the NMLS.

- **State** - Individual states may require an additional state law component to be taken, but everyone needs to take the above 20 hours. Because this component is a national requirement, it will make it easier for individuals to be licensed in multiple states; they will only need to take the 20 hours one time, and it can be applied across the board to satisfy all the other states' core licensing requirements.

National Licensing Exam

An approved test provider administers the licensing test, which is developed by the NMLSR. The student must pass with a score of 75% or better. An individual may retake a test three consecutive times with each consecutive exam occurring at least 30 days after the preceding test. After failing three consecutive tests, an individual must wait a minimum six months before taking the test again. A state-licensed loan originator who fails to maintain a valid license for a period of five years or longer must retake the test.

State Licensing Exam

States have the option of designing their own state exams. Check the NMLS website to see which states (if any) still require state exams.

License Renewals and Continuing Education

Most licenses expire December 31 and all must be renewed annually. Background and credit checks are repeated each year following the renewal application.

Every state-licensed loan originator must complete a minimum of 8 hours of continuing education a year. CE must include at least:

- 3 hours of Federal law and regulations.

- 2 hours of ethics, which must include instruction on fraud, consumer protection and fair lending issues.

- 2 hours of training relating to lending standards for the nontraditional mortgage product marketplace.

- 1 hour of unspecified loan origination material.

Refer to the NMLS website for state-specific CE requirements, which may include one or more hours of state law.

Licensees can only receive credit for the year in which they complete the CE course. Courses for credit can't be taken more than once, and loan originators who are approved CE course instructors may receive two hours of CE credit for every hour taught.

Loan originators with expired licenses must complete the CE for the last year in which they were licensed in order to file for renewal or a new license.

Sponsorship

Loan originators who have met all the requirements for licensing are assigned a unique NMLS ID. However, before they can begin originating loans, they must be employed and sponsored by a qualified company. Sponsorship means the company agrees to oversee their work.

Change of Employer

The loan originator must notify current employer, update their NMLS employment history and grant the new employer access to their NMLS record so that they can be assigned to the new company.

Compliance

The model state law details violations that should be incorporated into state law and specifies that companies must report mortgage origination activity to the NMLSR.

Violations

The following 14 points are considered violations of the SAFE Act, which may result in a maximum civil penalty of $25,000 per offense; however, criminal charges may apply in some cases.

- Intentionally mislead or defraud anyone including borrowers and lenders.

- Engage in any unfair or deceptive practice.

- Obtain property by fraud or misrepresentation.

- Require borrowers to sign a contract in which they agree to pay a loan origination fee, even if they don't obtain a loan.

- Advertise or agree to loan terms that aren't available.

- Engage in regulated practices without a license.

- Fail to make required disclosures.

- Fail to comply with state or federal laws.

- Make false statements regarding available loan terms.

- Make false statements or negligent omissions in NMLSR reports or to investigating state or government officials.

- Make any payment, threat or promise in order to influence an appraiser or anyone else involved in the process of obtaining an approval for a mortgage loan.

- Attempt to collect a prohibited fee.

- Cause a borrower to obtain property insurance coverage in an amount that exceeds the replacement cost of the improvements as established by the property insurer.

- Fail to account for third-party funds.

Company Reports

Any mortgage company that is registered through the NMLSR must complete a Mortgage Call Report. This report consists of two parts: a quarterly report of residential loan origination activity and an annual report of the company's financial condition. Lenders and servicers must complete an Expanded Mortgage Call Report.

II.   Loan Originator Rule

The Loan Originator Rule is an amendment to the Truth-in-Lending Act and was written by the Consumer Finance Protection Board to address issues regarding loan originators' compensation and expand the SAFE Act and implement additional issues identified in the Dodd-Frank Act. Most portions of the rule are effective as of January 10, 2014.

The rules that concern compensation, qualifications, identifiers and written polices apply to all residential mortgage loans (1-4 units) except for vacant land, home equity lines of credit (HELOC) and timeshare plans.

The rules governing arbitration, waiver clauses, and certain credit insurance financing charges apply to all residential mortgage loans (1-4 units) except for vacant land and timeshare plans. They do apply to HELOCS on a primary residence.

Definitions

The rule expands the SAFE Act definition of a licensed loan originator to include the following duties:

- Take a loan application.

- Arrange a credit transaction.

- Assist a consumer in applying for credit.

- Offer or negotiate loan terms.

- Make an extension of credit.

- Refer a consumer to a creditor or loan originator for compensation.

- Advertise your loan origination services.

New terms include the following:

- **Individual loan originator** - a natural person.

- **Loan originator organization** - a sole proprietorship, trust, partnership, corporation, bank, credit union, finance company or thrift.

- **Loan originator** - can be either an individual loan originator or a loan originator organization.

The following loan origination services do NOT require a MLO license:

- Handling a loan application, without review, and forwarding it to loan approval personnel.

- Helping a borrower fill out a loan application without discussing particular loan products.

- Providing general explanations in response to consumer queries.

- Arranging the loan closing or other aspects of the loan process, without discussing any new loan terms with the borrower.

- Providing a borrower with information unrelated to loan terms.

- Describing the steps that a borrower or prospective borrower would need to take to obtain a loan offer without providing specific details related to a borrower's individual situation.

- Offering or negotiating loan terms solely through a third-party licensed loan originator.

- Volunteering without receiving or expecting to receive anything of value.

Compensation

Compensation includes commissions, bonuses, salaries, merchandise, trips and any other financial incentives. In the past, loan originators' compensation was partially based on the type and terms of the chosen loan product. While this was good for the originators, it was a disservice to the consumer since many were persuaded to select a more expensive product when another one would be more suitable. For the purpose of this discussion on compensation, creditors (including seller financiers) are considered as loan originators only when they use table-funding; otherwise, they are exempt from this portion of the rule. Table funding occurs when the lender uses borrowed money from an investor to fund the loan, and after closing, the mortgage and note are immediately assigned to that investor.

The Loan Originator Rule prohibits loan originators from receiving compensation from anyone, including employer, creditor or consumer, based on the terms of the loan or the terms for multiple loans. For example, they can't receive more money for steering a borrower into a loan with a higher interest rate or receiving additional compensation for generating more than 10 loans a month that have interest rates over 6 percent. The rule prohibits both the payment and receipt of this type of compensation.

Although loan originator organizations can receive compensation for selling additional products such as title insurance, individual loan originators may not.

Loan originators may lower their compensation if unforeseen circumstances increase the consumer's settlement charges after the Good Faith Estimate has been issued. For example, issues with title may cause the closing to be delayed, which leads to the interest rate lock expiring. In situations like this, loan originators can contribute part of their fees toward the purchase of another lock.

The rule identifies seven compensation methods that may be considered as safe harbors. This isn't an exhaustive list, but provides an employer with a good working template for compensation plans. The seven different methods are based on:

- Total volume of loans delivered to a lender based on loan amount or number of transactions.

- Long-term performance of the originator's loans. (Did they default?)

- Hourly pay rate for actual number of hours worked.

- Loans made to new customers as opposed to repeat customers.

- Predetermined commission structure for every originated loan.

- Percentage of originator's closed loans.

- Quality of the loan files with regards to accuracy and completeness that are submitted to the processor.

Loan originators may receive compensation as part of a company retirement or bonus plan that is based on mortgage-related business profits. However, the company must be careful how these plans are structured so that they comply with the rule's restrictions on receiving compensation that's based on the multiple closings of multiple originators.

In general, a loan originator is prohibited from receiving compensation from a consumer *and* another person, such as a creditor, for the same transaction. However, the rule does allow loan originator organizations that receive a fee directly from the consumer to split that money with their loan originators. At the same time, if the loan originator organization charges the consumer an *origination* fee that is directly paid by the consumer, there can be no additional compensation received from another person including a creditor.

Qualifications

Individual loan originators must adhere to the SAFE Act rules, and loan originator organizations must ensure that any of its loan originators are properly licensed or registered. It is the organization's responsibility to verify originators' credentials before they start originating loans.

The Loan Originator Rule specifies the responsibility of organizations that have employees who are required to register with the NMLS but don't need to be licensed (bank employees). These organizations must conduct background criminal checks, obtain a credit report and check civil and administrative penalties. If the organization is a depository institution, this information is accessible through the NMLSR for all registered employees. In addition, the organizations must provide training on federal and state laws and loan origination to employees who are registered, but not licensed, loan originators.

Record Keeping

Loan originator organizations must keep a record of payments from a creditor and payments to individual originators for three years. The files must also contain a copy of the compensation agreements that govern the payments.

Identification

If the unique identifiers have been issued, loan origination organizations must include its NMLSR unique identification number and the identification number of the loan originator on the loan application, the note or loan contract and the security instrument (mortgage or deed of trust).

Written Policies

Depository institutions, including credit unions, must have written policies detailing the steps taken to ensure and monitor compliance with the Loan Originator Rule by its employees, subsidiaries and their employees.

Contracts

Creditors may not include mandatory arbitration clauses or waivers of the consumer's right to file a lawsuit alleging federal violations in transactional agreements. This applies to home equity lines of credit (HELOCs) on a primary residence and all residential mortgage loans (1-4 units) except for vacant land and timeshare plans.

Credit Insurance Financing

Creditors are prohibited from financing any fee or premiums for credit insurance connected with HELOCs on a primary residence and all residential mortgage loans except for vacant land and timeshare plans.

Credit insurance is a policy that allows suspension or cancellation of mortgage payments under certain consumer finance-altering circumstances including diminished employment and health issues. The rule doesn't apply if the premiums are paid in full each month.

General Exceptions

Loan servicers or employees who assist in refinancing a loan or changing the debtors on an existing loan are considered loan originators. Assisting in a loan modification is not considered loan origination.

Similarly, HUD-approved counselors who receive or expect to receive compensation from creditors for recommending specific lenders or lender-specific products are considered loan originators. On the other hand, counselors who provide general explanations of loan types and terms and assist in mortgage applications are not loan originators. This holds true even if they receive a set fee (not a commission that is based on loan amount) from a creditor or loan originator (as long as that entity has an agreement with a government agency that allows such compensation.)

Seller Financier Exceptions

The loan origination rules regarding seller financing are a little more complicated than those for loan servicers and counselors. First of all, seller financiers are considered creditors if they:

- Extend more than 6 non-high-cost mortgages during the preceding year **or**

- Extend more than 1 high-cost mortgage in the past 12 months.

Secondly, if they do meet the qualifications of a creditor, they are exempt from being considered a loan originator for *compensation* purposes, unless they engage in table funding.

Seller financiers are also not considered loan originators for most of the other provisions in the Loan Originator Rule if they are a natural person, estate or trust that:

- Provided seller financing for only 1 property in a 12-month period.

- Owned the property being financed.

- Did not construct the property as a normal part of business.

- Provided a loan without negative amortization.

- Provided a fixed-rate loan or an adjustable-rate mortgage that has a minimal initial period of 5 years and reasonable rate increases. Reasonable is considered a maximum two percent periodic rate increase with a maximum six percent lifetime cap.

In addition, seller financiers are not considered loan originators if they:

- Provided seller financing for a maximum of 3 properties in a 12-month period.

- Owned the property being financed.

- Did not construct the property as a normal part of business.

- Provided loans that fully amortized (no balloon mortgages).

- Provided a fixed-rate loan or an adjustable-rate mortgage that had a minimal initial period of 5 years and reasonable rate increases.

- Determined that the borrower has the ability to repay the loan.

Temporary MLO

In 2018, the Temporary Authority to Operate provision was added to the Safe Act to streamline the application process for two categories of loan officers: federally registered MLOs employed by a depository institution who wish to transition to employment with a state-licensed mortgage company, and individuals seeking licensure in additional states.

Eligibility requirements include:

- Currently employed by a state-licensed mortgage company operating in the application state.

AND

- Continuously registered as an MLO in the NMLS for one year preceding the application.

OR

- Licensed as an MLO for 30 days preceding the application.

The temporary status lasts until:

- The application is withdrawn.

- The state denies the request.

- The state grants the license.

- 120 days after an incomplete application is submitted.

Important Points to Remember

1. SAFE is an acronym for **S**ecure **A**nd **F**air **E**nforcement.
2. The SAFE Act is part of the Housing and Economic Recovery Act of 2008.
3. The Conference of State Bank Supervisors, the American Association of Residential Mortgage Regulators and the Consumer Financial Protection Bureau oversee compliance with the SAFE Act.
4. Everyone's loan origination license expires annually. Most states have a December 31 renewal date.
5. Applicant information is stored in a national registry.
6. Consumers can search a separate database for non-confidential licensee information.
7. Federal banking agencies include Federal Reserve System Board of Governors, National Credit Union Administration, Comptroller of the Currency and the Federal Deposit Insurance Corporation.
8. Immediate family members include a spouse, parents, stepparents, child, stepchild, sibling, stepsibling, grandparent, grandchild and adopted members.
9. An individual is a natural person.
10. A person is a natural person, limited liability corporation, association, company, corporation and partnership.
11. A loan originator is an individual who takes a residential loan application, explains the details of a loan and offers to negotiate the terms of a loan with a lender for compensation.
12. Underwriters and loan processors are individuals who perform clerical or support tasks at the direction of a state-licensed loan originator or registered loan originator. They don't negotiate loan terms.
13. A registered loan originator may be an unlicensed bank employee who must be registered with the NMLS.
14. A nontraditional mortgage product is any offering that is not a 30-year fixed-rate loan.
15. States have the authority to design application forms; collect transaction fees; conduct background checks; issue licenses; write regulations; deny, suspend and revoke licenses; investigate complaints; subpoena witnesses and documents; assess penalties and order the termination of individuals who are regarded as threats to the public welfare.
16. Individual states interpret, administer and enforce the Safe Act within the state.
17. CSBS/AARMR maintains the registry, approves mortgage schools, courses, exams and oversees state compliance.
18. Individuals who negotiate a mortgage loan for themselves or family members are exempt from licensing.
19. Attorneys who negotiate loan terms as an ancillary service and who are not compensated by a loan originator or lender are exempt from licensing.
20. Loan processors and underwriters who function as independent contractors must be state-licensed loan originators and register with the NMLSR.
21. Supervised loan processors and underwriters who do not represent to the public that they can perform any of the activities of a loan originator are not required to be state-licensed loan originators.
22. All applicants need to provide their fingerprints, and credit report and criminal background check authorizations.

23. Applicants must never have had a loan originator license revoked in any governmental jurisdiction; had no felony conviction during the past seven years, or no felony conviction ever if offense is related to fraud, dishonesty, money laundering or breach of trust.

24. Applicant must meet either a net worth or surety bond requirement, or pay into a state fund.

25. A minimum of 20 hours of pre-licensing education is required for all loan originators.

26. Pre-licensing must include 3 hours of federal law, 3 hours of ethics, and 2 hours of training on nontraditional mortgage products.

27. A minimum of 8 hours of annual continuing education is required for all loan originators.

28. Continuing education must include 3 hours of federal law, 2 hours of ethics, and 2 hours of training on nontraditional mortgage products.

29. Licensees can only receive credit for the year in which they complete the CE course.

30. Continuing education courses for credit can't be taken more than once.

31. Loan originators who are approved CE course instructors may receive two hours of CE credit for every hour taught.

32. 75 % is the minimum passing score on the SAFE loan originator licensing exam.

33. The SAFE exam can be consecutively taken a maximum of 3 times.

34. The student must initially wait a minimum of 30 days to retake an exam but after 3 consecutive failures they must wait a minimum of 6 months before re-taking it again.

35. Loan originators may not advertise or commit to loan terms that aren't currently available.

36. Loan originators may not collect a commission if the loan doesn't close.

37. Loan originators may not attempt to illegally influence individuals responsible for loan approval including lenders, appraisers and underwriters.

38. Loan originators may not misrepresent a property.

39. Loan originators may not cause a borrower to obtain property insurance coverage in an amount that exceeds the replacement cost of the improvements as established by the property insurer.

40. Mortgage companies and lenders must submit Mortgage Call Reports to the NMLSR.

41. The Loan Originator Rule is an amendment to the Truth-in-Lending Act and was written by the Consumer Finance Protection Board to address issues regarding loan originators' compensation, expand the SAFE Act and implement additional issues identified in the Dodd-Frank Act.

42. Loan servicers or employees who assist in refinancing a loan or changing the debtors on an existing loan are considered loan originators. Assisting in a loan modification is not considered loan origination.

43. The rule prohibits loan originators from receiving compensation from anyone including employer, creditor or consumer on the basis of the terms of the loan or the terms for multiple loans.

44. Loan originator organizations can receive compensation for selling additional products such as title insurance, but individual loan originators may not.

45. Loan originator organizations must keep a record of payments from a creditor and payments to individual originators for three years. The files must also contain a copy of the compensation agreements that govern the payments.

46. Creditors may not include mandatory arbitration clauses or waivers of the consumer's right to file a lawsuit alleging federal violations in transactional agreements.

47. The maximum penalty for a SAFE Act violation is $25,000 per offense.
48. Subpoenaed books and records must be submitted on or before the date on the summons.
49. Exams must be repeated after 5 years of inactive status for returning MLOs.
50. A sponsor is a company that oversees the activities of an MLO.
51. An individual who originates loans for a non-profit housing organization is exempt from licensing.
52. A commercial real estate loan originator is exempt from licensing.
53. An individual who does not act as a loan originator habitually or repeatedly is exempt from licensing, provided that the source of prospective financing does not provide mortgage financing or perform other loan origination activities habitually or repeatedly.
54. The MLO NMLS ID number must appear in ads, on loan applications, on notes and on the security instrument (mortgage or deed of trust).
55. MLOs must keep compensation records for 3 years.
56. It is illegal to withhold, destroy or alter a record involved in an investigation.
57. A Temporary MLO is an MLO who is transitioning from a depository loan origination position to a state-licensed mortgage company, or a licensed MLO seeking to work in additional states. A temporary status allows the individual to work while the state is processing their application.
58. Applicants must be currently employed by a state-licensed mortgage company operating in the application state, and be continuously registered as an MLO in the NMLS for one year preceding the application or licensed as an MLO for 30 days preceding the application.
59. The temporary status terminates when: the application is withdrawn, the state denies the request, the state grants the request, or 120 days have lapsed since the application was marked incomplete.

Exam

1.   What is the minimum number of hours for loan originator pre-licensing education?
      A.   10
      B.   20
      C.   30
      D.   40

2.   What is the minimum number of hours for annual loan originator continuing education?
      A.   2
      B.   4
      C.   8
      D.   12

3.   Which of the following do **NOT** need to be licensed?
      A.   Independent contractors who are loan originators
      B.   Independent contractors who are underwriters
      C.   Independent contractors who are loan processors
      D.   Federally chartered bank employees

4.   Which of the following does **NOT** have to be submitted by a Loan Originator applicant?
      A.   Credit report authorization
      B.   Criminal background check authorization
      C.   References
      D.   Fingerprints

5.   Mortgage loan originator licenses renew:
      A.   Every 6 months
      B.   Every year
      C.   Every 2 years
      D.   Every 3 years

6.   The minimum passing score on the SAFE loan originator licensing exam is:
      A.   65 %
      B.   75 %
      C.   80 %
      D.   90 %

7.   What is the maximum number of times the SAFE exam can be consecutively taken?
      A.   2
      B.   3
      C.   4
      D.   5

8.   What is the minimum number of days a student must wait between his first two SAFE exam retakes?
    A.   10
    B.   15
    C.   30
    D.   60

9.   After three consecutive attempts to pass the SAFE exam, what is the minimum amount of time a student must wait before trying again?
    A.   1 month
    B.   3 months
    C.   6 months
    D.   9 months

10.   Which of the following is NOT an immediate family member?
    A.   Adopted brother
    B.   Aunt
    C.   Grandfather
    D.   Stepmother

11.   What may be true of registered loan originators?
    A.   They are independent contractors
    B.   They must take the national loan originator exam
    C.   They are bank employees
    D.   They are licensed loan originators

12.   Which of the following must be a licensed loan originator?
    A.   Commercial loan originator
    B.   Independent contractor who is an underwriter
    C.   Supervised loan processor employee
    D.   An individual who negotiates the terms of his own mortgage loan

13.   How often must a mortgage company submit a report on their financial condition?
    A.   Monthly
    B   Quarterly
    C.   Annually
    D.   Every 2 years

14.   What is the maximum fine for a SAFE Act violation?
    A. $1,000
    B. $5,000
    C. $15,000
    D. $25,000

15.   Returning MLOs must retake the national exam after how many years of inactivity?
       A.   1
       B.   3
       C.   5
       D.   7

Answer Key

1.   B
2.   C
3.   D
4.   C
5.   B
6.   B
7.   B
8.   C
9.   C
10.   B
11.   C
12.   B
13.   C
14.   D
15.   C

3

Introduction to Mortgage Lending

The lending environment changes with the times, but some aspects of mortgage loan origination remain fairly constant. People have been talking about notes, mortgages, liens and contracts for years and that's not likely to change. So, if you originated loans in the past, this is a refresher chapter. If you're new to the industry, it's an informative overview of standard documents and terminology.

I.   Summary of Basic Terms

There are a few terms that are used throughout this book that you need to become familiar with as soon as possible and there is a trick for some of these words to make it easier for you. There are GIVER and RECEIVER words; GIVER words end with the letters "or" and RECEIVER words end in the letters "ee".

GIVER WORDS	RECEIVER WORDS
Mortgag**or** (Promise to repay loan: borrower)	Mortgag**ee** (Receive promise to repay: lender)
Grant**or** (Holder of deed: homeowner)	Grant**ee** (Recipient of deed: new owner)
Assign**or** (Transfers contract rights)	Assign**ee** (Receives contract rights)

If the meaning of mortgagor and mortgagee confuses you, don't worry. Many people get confused. During normal conversation when we talk about a mortgage, we are talking about the loan amount. However, a mortgage is a document in which the borrower (mortgagor) pledges the property as collateral for the loan and gives certain promises to the lender.

The grantor is the current owner of the home who transfers title by signing the deed and giving it to the new owner of the property (grantee) who receives the deed.

The assignor is an individual who transfers contractual rights to a third party; the assignee is the individual who receives it.

II.   Promissory Note and Mortgage

There are two primary documents associated with the financing of a loan. These two documents are the promissory note and the mortgage.

The note is a legal document obligating a borrower to repay a loan at a stated interest rate during a specified period of time. The annual percentage rate (APR) is not on the note. The note is the legal evidence of the debt and is not recorded. It is the borrower's IOU. All borrowers and co-borrowers are required to sign the note, and all their credit scores may be affected if there are late mortgage payments.

The note is secured by a mortgage, which is a document in which the individuals who have an ownership interest in the real property (their names are on the deed) pledge their property as collateral for the loan (this is known as hypothecation). The borrower (mortgagor) also promises to repay the loan, keep the home in good repair, pay property taxes and pay hazard insurance.

A Purchase Money Mortgage (PMM) is a loan which is used for the purchase of a home and not a refinance, home improvement or equity line of credit loan. The deed is given to the borrower at closing, and the borrower makes mortgage payments to the seller.

III.   Liens

The United States is split about 50/50 between lien theory and title theory states. Florida is one example of a lien theory state because the borrower receives the deed at closing and obtains occupancy of the property. The mortgage secures the debt in lien theory states. The borrower holds full legal and equitable title to the property, and the lender has a recorded lien on the property as security for the loan.

Some other states, including Georgia, are known as title theory states in which the mortgagee (lender) or a third party keeps the deed until the loan is satisfied. The borrower has equitable title in which they are allowed to occupy, rent and sell the property, but the security instrument may be a deed of trust, instead of a mortgage. Once the loan is paid off, a Deed of Reconveyance is recorded which grants the homeowner full legal title. A few states, including California, have a mixture of equitable and legal types of home ownership. Both lien and title theory states require a note that is held by the lender.

Once the mortgage or deed of trust is recorded, a voluntary lien is placed on the property. A lien is a legal claim against property that is usually satisfied when the property is sold. When the borrower signs the mortgage document, they agree to allow the lender to have a lien on the property. In return, the borrower receives the loan money. The date and time of recording establish the position of the lien, *not* the date and time the document was signed. Lien position determines the order in which lien holders are paid when the property is sold.

Mortgage lien position also relates to interest rates. If the borrower receives a first and second mortgage at the same time, the interest rate on the second mortgage will be higher because it's a junior mortgage and has a lesser chance of being paid off if there is a foreclosure; the proceeds of the foreclosure sale may not be sufficient to pay off all the liens. It's a riskier loan for the lender because it has a lower lien position, and because it is riskier, the interest rate is higher. Typical lien priority and order of payoff are as follows:

1.   Government expenses of sale.

2.   Delinquent property taxes.

3.   Special assessment liens.

4.   Federal estate tax lien.

5.   1st mortgage   (Senior Mortgage).

6.   2nd mortgage   (Junior Mortgage).

7.   3rd mortgage   (Junior Mortgage).

    Unlimited possible number of additional junior mortgages, in order of recording time.

8.   IRS Tax Liens and other creditors.

Other types of liens are usually involuntary liens; the borrower did not agree to them. These are government liens that can result from failure to pay taxes; judgment liens that arise from a court order to place a lien on all real property owned by a convicted defendant, and mechanic's liens that can be filed by contractors if the homeowner does not pay for repairs or remodeling costs. All of these liens usually need to be paid by the property owner before a property is sold.

IV.   Default and Foreclosure

Within the mortgage document, borrowers promise to repay the loan, keep the home in good repair, pay property taxes and pay hazard insurance. If they fail to do any one of these things, they are in default of the loan, and the lender has certain rights, which could end in a public foreclosure auction with the homeowners losing their home to the highest bidder.

Foreclosure

A foreclosure is the enforcement of a lien. The lender can choose not to take legal action if the mortgagor is in default, and this is known as forbearance. Perhaps the mortgagor had been in an accident and was in traction and unable to work. If he called and explained the situation to the lender, the lender might work out a delayed payment plan for the mortgagor until he could get back on his feet.

In lien theory states, a lis pendens (Latin for litigation pending) is a notice which is filed when the lender files a foreclosure lawsuit; this is also known as a Notice of Default. This notice is recorded and becomes part of the county tax record where the property is located. In equitable theory states, foreclosures are quickly completed outside the court system (unless the homeowner objects and files a lawsuit) since the homeowner doesn't have full legal title.

Equitable Right of Redemption

Equitable right of redemption allows the mortgagor who is in default to pay the entire loan balance before the foreclosure auction, thereby keeping his property.

Deficiency Judgment

In some states, a deficiency judgment can occur when the proceeds of a foreclosure sale aren't sufficient to pay off the lender's loan balance. In these cases, the lender may request the court to allow it to file a lawsuit on the unpaid note and make a claim on the other assets of the borrower.

V.   Mortgage Clauses and Conditions

In the previous section, it was mentioned that the mortgagor promises to repay the loan; keep the home in good repair; pay property taxes and pay hazard insurance. Failure to do this means that he is in default of the terms of the mortgage, and the mortgagee has the legal right to take action. The rest of a mortgage document has a variety of clauses, some of which are beneficial to a lender and some to a borrower.

Clauses Beneficial to a Lender

- **Acceleration Clause** - gives the mortgage "teeth." It allows the mortgagee to call the entire loan balance due if the mortgagor is in default.

- **Escalation Clause** - allows the mortgagee to increase the interest rate under certain conditions. For example, a homeowner decides to move and rent out his primary residence. This home now becomes an investment property and is therefore, riskier to the lender, so it may increase the interest rate to reflect this. Why is it riskier? Well, imagine you have two homes; one you live in, and one you rent out. If you run into financial problems, which house are you most likely to stop making payments on? Most people would answer the rental house, and statistically, it has a greater chance of being foreclosed. Therefore, it's riskier for lenders, so they raise the interest rate to compensate for the increased risk. This usually applies only if the owner converts the owner-occupied property into an investment property during the first 12 months of the loan.

- **Due-on-Sale Clause** - stipulates that the mortgagee may require that the loan balance be paid off when the property is sold or transferred. In other words, the loan is *not* assumable by the new owner. This is also known as the alienation clause.

- **Prepayment Penalty Clause** - states that a mortgagor is required to pay a fee if he makes a larger than required monthly payment, or if he pays off the loan before the due date.

Clauses Beneficial to a Borrower

- **Defeasance Clause** - prevents the lender from foreclosing unless the borrower is in default. In addition, the clause requires the lender to provide a recordable Satisfaction of Mortgage notice to the mortgagor within sixty days of closing.

- **Exculpatory Clause** - prevents the lender from requesting a deficiency judgment against the borrower when the foreclosure proceeds are not sufficient to pay off the loan balance. The borrower has no personal liability to repay the note (non-recourse loan). This is more common in commercial lending than in residential financing.

- **Prepayment Privilege Clause** - allows the mortgagor to pay all or part of the loan before it is due without penalty.

- **Open-End Clause** - permits future additional advances from the same lender without rewriting the mortgage. This applies to a home equity line of credit loan.

Clauses Beneficial to a Developer

- **Subordination Clause** - allows subsequent mortgages on the same property to have a more superior lien position than the earlier-recorded mortgage. For example, if a developer bought a large tract of land from the seller and the seller provided financing, this loan would have the senior position since it is the first mortgage recorded. Six months later the developer is ready to go to a commercial lender for a construction loan. This lender, however, requires its loan to have a senior position. In order for this to be accomplished, the original mortgage for the land must have a subordination clause in it. Owners of large tracts of land realize this and usually agree to the clause because they may not be able to sell the land otherwise.

- **Blanket Mortgage** - a loan to developers who purchase one or more tracts of land that will be developed into smaller parcels of land. The mortgage encompasses ("blankets") the land and structures.

- **Partial Release Clause** - clause in a blanket mortgage that allows the lien to be removed from each parcel as it is sold, thus allowing the purchaser to have clear title to the parcel unencumbered by the developer's lien. The developer will pay the lender a specified sum of money to release the lien each time a parcel is sold.

VI.   Contracts

A contract is a binding agreement between two or more individuals. A valid contract has four essentials:

- **Competent Parties** - signers must be mentally sound and of legal age.

- **Mutual Agreement** - both parties agree on all the terms of the contract.

- **Legal Object** - seller must have the legal right to transfer ownership of the property.

- **Consideration** - money, valuables or good intentions to proceed with the deal.

A bilateral contract (purchase agreement) is signed by both parties and is binding on both parties. A unilateral contract (purchase option) is signed by two parties but is only binding on the party offering the option.

Attorney-in-Fact

An attorney-in-fact is a person named in a written power-of-attorney document to act on behalf of the person who signs the contract if one of the parties is not able or competent to sign.

Assignment

Contracts can be assigned to another individual, and this often happens with pre-construction contracts when the asking price for a unit is much lower before the developers break ground. As the building process continues and the initial Phase One units have sold, the asking price for similar subsequent units will increase as demand increases. Parties holding contracts for the earlier units may assign these for a nice price to another party if they have not yet closed on the deal. Maybe Phase Four units are selling for $80,000 more than Phase One; the Phase One contract holder could make a relatively quick $50,000 or more by assigning his contract to another individual. The assignor is the party transferring the contractual rights to another, and the assignee is the individual who receives it. The assignment of the mortgage and note will be covered in a later chapter.

VII.   Deeds

A deed is a written instrument used to convey title or the transfer of ownership from the original owner (grantor) to the new owner (grantee). In order for a deed to be valid, it must:

- Identify the seller and buyer.

- Include the legal description of the property.

- Be in writing.

- Signed by a competent grantor and two witnesses. The grantee does not sign the deed. The deed is recorded to give constructive notice of the change in ownership.

Deed restrictions may be placed in the deed and control the use of an individual property. They cannot be discriminatory and are said to "run with the land," which means they continue indefinitely. A restrictive covenant is a deed restriction that affects the entire subdivision.

A Deed in Lieu of Foreclosure occurs when the borrower voluntarily conveys the deed to the lender in exchange for the satisfaction of the debt. Junior mortgage liens remain the responsibility of the mortgagor.

VIII.   Forms of Real Estate Ownership

When individuals purchase real estate, they are purchasing the land, the structures on the land, and air and mineral rights. They also gain a bundle of rights (real property) associated with ownership. These rights include right of disposition, right of use (control), right of possession and right of exclusion (quiet enjoyment).

Freehold estates can be held indefinitely by the owner. There are two kinds of freehold estates:

- **Fee Simple** - the most desirable form of property ownership

- **Life Estate** - owned during a lifetime, but title reverts to the grantor or a predetermined party (remainderman) upon the death of the estate holder.

Fee Simple ownership represents absolute ownership of real property (as compared to leasehold estates, which involve a tenancy). However, even though the property is owned outright, the owner must abide by state and federal regulations including zoning, condemnation, health and building codes and taxation.

A property owner can deed a property to an individual for the remainder of his lifetime. This is usually done within families for financial planning purposes and is known as a Life Estate. A Life Estate lasts only for the owner's lifetime and then reverts back to the grantor or to named third parties (remaindermen).

When more than one individual's name is on the title, there exists some form of concurrent ownership. This can be in the form of one of three types of estates: Tenancy in Common, Joint Tenancy or Tenancy by the Entirety.

FORMS OF CONCURRENT OWNERSHIP

	Tenancy In Common	Joint Tenancy	Tenancy by the Entirety
Eligibility	2 or more persons	2 or more persons	Married couple
% of Ownership	Same or different %	Same %	Each 100 %
Time of title	Same or different	Same for all	Same
Inheritable ?	Yes	No, right of survivorship	No, right of survivorship

Tenancy in Common is a statutory form of ownership that exists when there is more than one owner. The owners can purchase equal or unequal "undivided interest" in the property, buy at the same or different times and will or sell their share to anyone else.

Joint Tenancy is another statutory form of ownership that exists when there is more than one owner. The owners purchase an equal "undivided interest" in the property, buy at the same time and can sell their share to anyone else; but, the share cannot be willed. If one owner dies, the Right of Survivorship requires the remaining owners to divide his share equally among themselves.

Tenancy by the Entirety is similar to Joint Tenancy With Right of Survivorship for married couples with both names on title; it's available in some states. However, the couple owns *in severalty*, which means 'as one entity'. They each own 100% of the property.

IX.   Transfer of Real Estate Ownership

A new owner can buy a property in a number of ways. He can pay cash for the property, which means that the previous owner must pay off their existing mortgage, if there is one, at closing.

Assumption

The purchaser may take over the mortgagor's monthly mortgage payments with the knowledge, but without the qualification, of the lender. This is known as an assumption; the purchaser and previous owner share liability, and the buyer makes the monthly payments with the same terms. Shared liability was common a few years ago when buyers could assume a government loan without being qualified by the lender. The lenders allowed it under the condition that the sellers shared liability.

Assumption With Novation

More commonly, however, the loan is assumed with novation in which the original borrower is released from all liability for the note. This is what is usually meant when someone states he is assuming a loan.

Subject to the Mortgage

The situation can also arise in which the buyer is not qualified by the lender. There is no new note, and the original buyer retains all liability. This is known as transferring title subject to the mortgage.

Satisfaction of Mortgage

When a mortgage is paid off, the lender has 60 days to send the borrower a recordable Satisfaction of Mortgage letter, which states that the loan has been paid in full. This payoff letter should be recorded in the county records. Lenders usually take care of the recording but aren't legally required to do so. This can cause title issues when the property is being sold; closing may be delayed because the mortgage lien is still on the property.

Important Points to Remember

1. The two types of documents associated with a loan are the mortgage and the note.
2. The note is the legal evidence of the debt and is not recorded.
3. The date and time of recording establish lien position of the mortgage.
4. The borrower is the mortgagor.
5. The lender is the mortgagee.
6. The APR is not included in the note.
7. Mortgagors promise to repay the loan; pay property tax; pay hazard insurance and keep the property in good repair. They are in default if they fail to do any one of these.
8. A Purchase Money Mortgage is for the purchase a home.
9. A mortgage is a voluntary lien; special assessments and mechanic's liens are involuntary liens.
10. The first mortgage recorded is referred to as the senior mortgage. Subsequent mortgages are known as junior mortgages.
11. There is an unlimited possible number of junior mortgages and no restrictions on terms.
12. Florida is a Lien Theory state since the borrower obtains the deed to the property at closing and agrees to allow the lender to place a lien on the property in exchange for the loan. The mortgage is the security instrument.
13. States, like Georgia, where the borrower does not receive the deed at closing are known as Title Theory states. The deed of trust may be the security instrument.
14. A foreclosure is the enforcement of a lien.
15. Forbearance is the choice by the lender not to take action even though the borrower is in default of the loan.
16. A lis pendens is a notice filed by the lender when it initiates a foreclosure lawsuit.
17. The equitable right of redemption allows the mortgagor in default to pay the entire balance due and keep the property from being foreclosed.
18. A deficiency judgment allows the lender to claim other assets from the borrower when the proceeds of the foreclosure sale are insufficient to satisfy the mortgage lien.
19. The mortgage acceleration clause allows the lender to call the entire loan balance due if the borrower is in default.
20. The mortgage escalation clause allows the lender to increase the interest rate of the loan under certain conditions.
21. The mortgage due-on-sale clause requires that the loan balance is paid off when the title is transferred.
22. The mortgage prepayment penalty clause requires the borrower to pay a fee if the loan is paid off early.
23. The mortgage defeasance clause prevents the lender from foreclosing unless the borrower is in default. It also requires the lender to send a Satisfaction of Mortgage notice to the borrower within sixty days of paying off the loan.
24. The mortgage exculpatory clause prevents the lender from requesting a deficiency judgment against the borrower when the proceeds of the foreclosure are insufficient to pay off the mortgage lien.
25. The mortgage prepayment privilege clause allows the borrower to pay all or part of the loan before it is due without penalty.
26. The mortgage open-end clause permits future additional advances from the same loan.

27. A blanket mortgage covers multiple tracts of land.
28. A mortgage subordination clause permits a senior mortgage to assume a junior lien position.
29. A partial release clause in a blanket mortgage allows the developer's lien to be released as the parcel is sold.
30. A valid contract has four elements: competent parties, mutual agreement, legal object and consideration.
31. An attorney-in-fact is an individual with power of attorney who is able to sign the contract if one of the parties is not able or competent to sign.
32. The assignor is the party transferring contractual rights to another.
33. The assignee is the party receiving the contractual rights.
34. The grantor is the owner of a property.
35. The grantee is the party receiving the title transfer.
36. A deed is a written instrument used to convey title or transfer ownership.
37. Deed restrictions may be placed in the deed and control the use of the property.
38. Deed restrictions "run with the land" and cannot be discriminatory.
39. A Deed in Lieu of Foreclosure occurs when the mortgagor voluntarily conveys the deed to the lender in exchange for satisfaction of the debt.
40. Real estate is the land, structures on the land, air rights and mineral rights.
41. Real property is the associated bundle of rights with real estate.
42. Fee simple is the highest type of personal property interest in the law. A buyer owns the land as well as the improvements on the land.
43. There are three types of concurrent real estate ownership: tenancy in common, joint tenancy and tenancy by the entirety.
44. Tenants in common are two or more parties buying the same or unequal percentage of the property, buying at the same or different times and the individual's share can be sold or willed.
45. Joint tenants are two or more parties buying at the same time, buying equal shares and the shares can't be willed. The right of survivorship dictates that the remaining co-owners receive the deceased's interest in the property.
46. A mortgage assumption implies a shared liability between the original mortgagor and the new mortgagor.
47. Novation is an assumption in which the original borrower is released from all liability.
48. Subject to the mortgage is a transfer of title in which there is no new note and the original buyer retains all the liability.
49. Freehold estates can be held indefinitely by the owner.
50. There are two types of freehold estates: fee simple and life estate.
51. A life estate title reverts to the original grantor or a remainderman upon the death of the life estate holder.
52. IRS tax liens have a lower lien position (recorded later) than property taxes, senior mortgages and junior mortgages because no lender would loan money to someone with an outstanding IRS lien.

Exam

1. The mortgagor is the:
    A. Lender
    B. Borrower
    C. Mortgage broker
    D. Real estate agent

2. The mortgagee is the:
    A. Lender
    B. Borrower
    C. Mortgage broker
    D. Real estate agent

3. Mortgages are a(n):
    A. Involuntary lien
    B. Voluntary lien
    C. Special assessment
    D. Mechanics lien

4. What establishes the lien position?
    A. Date and time of signing
    B. Date and time the loan was approved
    C. Date and time of recording
    D. Date and time of the title search

5. Junior mortgages are:
    A. Involuntary liens
    B. Limited to 30 year terms
    C. Limited to a total of 2
    D. Voluntary lien

6. Which is **NOT** a promise by the mortgagor:
    A. Keep the home in good repair
    B. Obey all state and county laws
    C. Pay the hazard insurance
    D. Pay the mortgage payment

7. What is the enforcement of a lien?
    A. Arrest
    B. Bankruptcy
    C. Foreclosure
    D. Mediation

8. A lender may choose **NOT** to take legal action upon default and this is known as:
    A. Forbearance
    B. Exculpation
    C. Fortitude
    D. Deficiency

9. Which clause allows the lender to increase the interest rate?
    A. Acceleration clause
    B. Escalation clause
    C. Deficiency judgment
    D. Exculpatory clause

10. Which of the following is **NOT** beneficial to a developer?
    A. Blanket mortgage
    B. Subordination clause
    C. Development clause
    D. Partial release clause

11. Which is **NOT** essential for a valid contract:
    A. $2,000 in reserves
    B. Competent parties
    C. Consideration
    D. Mutual agreement

12. Tenancy in Common does **NOT** have:
    A. Equal or unequal ownership
    B. Buy at same or different times
    C. Multiple owners
    D. Right of survivorship

13. Joint Tenancy does **NOT** have:
    A. Equal ownership
    B. Right of survivorship
    C. Only one individual's name on title
    D. Buy at same time

14. How many days after settlement does the lender have to send the Satisfaction of Mortgage letter?
    A. 10 days
    B. 15 days
    C. 30 days
    D. 60 days

15.   When there is no new note and the original buyer retains all the liability, this is known as transferring title by:
    A.   Creative financing
    B.   Assumption
    C.   Novation
    D.   Subject to the mortgage

16.   When there is a new note and the original borrower is released from all liability, this is known as transferring title by:
    A.   Creative financing
    B.   Assumption
    C.   Novation
    D.   Subject to the mortgage

17.   The assignor:
    A.   Transfers contract rights
    B.   Receives contract rights
    C.   Must be a United States citizen
    D.   Must be an attorney

18.   Which of the following is **NOT** an involuntary lien?
    A.   Judgment lien
    B.   Mortgage lien
    C.   Mechanic's lien
    D.   IRS tax lien

19.   The pledging of property as collateral for a loan:
    A.   Defeasance
    B.   Hypothecation
    C.   Exculpation
    D.   Intermediation

20.   The conveyor of the deed is the:
    A.   Grantor
    B.   Lender
    C.   Grantee
    D.   Mortgagor

21.   The receiver of the deed is the:
    A.   Grantee
    B.   Grantor
    C.   Mortgagee
    D.   Assignee

22.   Which document is **NOT** recorded?
    A.   Note
    B.   Satisfaction of Mortgage
    C.   Mortgage
    D.   Deed

23.   The borrower's IOU is the:
    A.   Mortgage
    B.   Note
    C.   Loan-to-Value Ratio
    D.   Equity

24.   A clause in some mortgages which allows subsequent mortgages on the same property to have a higher claim than the current mortgage is a:
    A.   Subordination clause
    B.   Penalty clause
    C.   Privilege clause
    D.   Inferior clause

25.   Which of the following does include the Right of Survivorship?
    A.   Good Faith Estimate
    B.   Tenants in Common
    C.   Joint Tenancy
    D.   Truth-in-Lending disclosure

26.   The document conveying title from one party to another and guaranteeing that the title is good is known as a:
    A.   Good Faith
    B.   Warranty Deed
    C.   Usury limit
    D.   Red Flags document

27.   A mortgage lien on an entire tract of land is known as a:
    A.   Buy-down mortgage
    B.   Chattel mortgage
    C.   Blanket mortgage
    D.   Pillow mortgage

28.   Liens which are subsequent to the first recorded mortgage lien are known as:
    A.   Junior liens
    B.   Unavailable liens
    C.   Estoppel liens
    D.   Homestead liens

Answer Key

1. B
2. A
3. B
4. C
5. D
6. B
7. C
8. A
9. B
10. C
11. A
12. D
13. C
14. D
15. D
16. C
17. A
18. B
19. B
20. A
21. A
22. A
23. B
24. A
25. C
26. B
27. C
28. A

4

General Mortgage Knowledge

This chapter discusses various mortgage types and products. Definitions of common lending terms are also included.

I.   Down Payment Funds

Meeting the requirement for a down payment can be challenging for many prospective homebuyers. Fortunately, underwriting policies allow gifts from approved donors to help borrowers meet this obligation.

Gift Funds

Both government and conventional loans allow cash gifts from approved classes of donors to be used to pay the down payment. This gift must be accompanied by a letter that includes:

- Dollar amount of the gift and the date the funds were transferred.

- Donor's statement that no repayment is expected.

- Donor's name, address, telephone number, and relationship to the borrower.

Approved cash gift donors include:

- Relative of the borrower.

- Domestic partner.

- Fiancee or fiance.

- Employer.

- Charitable organization.

- Government or public entity providing homebuyer assistance.

Down payment donors may NOT include parties that have an interest in the purchase transaction including:

- Seller.

- Builder.

- Real estate agent.

- Loan originator.

Note: builders, real estate agents and loan originators may be allowed, with lender approval, to credit part of their transaction earnings toward payment of **other types of borrower closing costs** (appraisal fee, loan origination fee, discount points, etc.). Sellers are always allowed to contribute toward such costs.

Borrower Funds

Lenders want to see a paper trail for the funds the borrower uses for the down payment and closing costs. If the source of the cash-on-hand is undocumented it may not be acceptable. Acceptable sources include:

- Bank and brokerage accounts.

- IRA, 401k and other retirement funds.

- Documented sale of assets.

- Net proceeds from a loan against the cash value (or surrender) of a life insurance policy.

II.   Mortgage Types

There are three loan types (FHA, VA, USDA) that are either government insured for the entire loan amount or partially guaranteed by the government for part of the loan amount. Insured and guaranteed refer to the amount of funding lenders receive if they suffer a loss on the loan. Conventional loans have no government reimbursement policies.

FHA Mortgages

The Federal Housing Administration (FHA) is a government organization within the Department of Housing and Urban Development (HUD). The FHA does not lend the money to build homes; instead, it guarantees that approved lenders are reimbursed for losses suffered if there is a foreclosure or short sale in which the property sells for less than the mortgage balance. Under the FHA Direct Endorsement (DE) program, the mortgagee can underwrite and close FHA loans without HUD review or approval.

So where is HUD getting the money to insure the loan? Primarily, from two sources: the first is a one-time closing cost (Up Front Mortgage Insurance Premium or UFMIP) that is a small percentage of the total loan amount, and the second source of funds is the monthly Mortgage Insurance Premium (MIP) that is paid by the borrower every month. This fee is paid on all FHA loans with terms greater than 15 years, regardless of the amount of down payment.

Borrowers may finance the up-front MIP cost as part of the loan amount and pay the MIP premiums along with the monthly PITI payment. The MIP continues for the life of the loan.

FHA loans are for primary residences only and require a minimum 3.5% down payment. The entire down payment can be a gift.

The maximum FHA seller concession is 6% which cannot be used to pay the down payment.

Because the FHA guarantee allows financing that is less risky for the lender, interest rates may be quite competitive. The lenders set the interest rates, not the FHA or HUD. So why doesn't everybody get one? Low credit scores, an unacceptable amount of debt, inadequate employment history and insufficient income level may keep individuals from qualifying.

FHA loans have maximum loan amounts depending on the borrower's county, and the maximum is based on the loan amount not including the UFMIP. The FHA maximum loan limits differ between counties. There is no due-on-sale clause in FHA mortgages, so these loans are assumable by qualified borrowers. They have no prepayment penalties.

FHA requires appraisers to perform a limited home inspection with the appraisal.

The maximum term for an FHA loan is 30 years. Borrowers must have a Social Security Number, and the late fee is 4% of the monthly P&I.

An FHA early payment default is a mortgage loan that is 60 days past due within the first six months.

VA Mortgages

The Department of Veteran's Affairs (DVA) partially guarantees VA loans, which are made to qualified U.S. active duty servicemen and veterans. While the DVA may fund some loans, this is generally done by authorized lenders. There is no maximum VA loan although the DVA does control the amount of the guaranty that reimburses lenders if they suffer a loss due to a foreclosure or short sale. To do this, the DVA sets maximum loan limits (for reimbursement calculations) based on the county. The 2022 amount is $647,200 for most counties. The DVA guarantees lenders 25 percent of this limit as reimbursement for losses.

Lenders will generally lend up to four times the amount of a veteran's entitlement without requiring a down payment. This means that VA loans can have 100% financing on first mortgages for primary residences only.

The entitlement amount is shown on the veteran's Certificate of Eligibility. Interest rates on these loans may be quite competitive, since they are partially guaranteed. If for some reason, the veterans can't use the online Automated Certificate of Eligibility request process, they will have to fill out a Request for Certificate of Eligibility and send in a photocopy of their DD-214 (proof of discharge) to prove the status of their discharge. If they were discharged with a status less than honorable, they may have trouble qualifying for a VA loan.

The one-time funding fee that's paid by the borrower at closing creates a pool of money that makes the partial guarantee possible. The funding fee is paid by the veteran and may be added to the loan balance and amortized over the life of the loan. The lender sets the interest rate on VA loans, not the VA. These loans are assumable (no due-on-sale clause) and have no prepayment penalty. There is no monthly insurance premium. A VA appraisal is known as a Certificate of Reasonable Value (CRV) and is performed by a VA approved appraiser who operates on a rotation system.

The maximum term for a VA loan is 30 years, and the late fee is 4% of the monthly P&I.

The vast majority of VA loans are for 100% financing. However, down payment gifts are allowed if needed.

Sellers may contribute up to 4% of the sale price, plus reasonable and customary loan costs. The payments that fall under the 4% maximum include:

- Property taxes and insurance

- Discount points above 2% of the loan amount

- Borrower's judgments and debts.

- VA funding fee

Other standard closing costs (appraisals, origination and lender fees, etc.) can also be paid by the seller in addition to the just-mentioned 4%.

USDA Mortgages

USDA home loans are also known as farm loans or rural development loans. They are similar to the VA loans in that they are partially guaranteed by the US government, allow for 100% financing, have a one-time funding fee (guaranty fee) paid at closing and require monthly mortgage insurance. To qualify, the property must be located in a rural area as defined by the Department of Agriculture. These loans are all lower-income, owner-occupied, 30-year fixed-rate loans. Gifts are allowed, and repair costs can be included in the loan amount. There is no prepay penalty, and an FHA appraiser is usually used. The late fee is 4 % of the monthly P&I.

Seller may contribute up to 6% of the sales price toward the buyer's reasonable closing costs and down payment gifts are allowed.

Conventional Mortgages

A conventional loan is a loan that is not FHA insured or VA guaranteed and is below a set maximum value that is established each year. The 2022 maximum loan limit is $647,200 for a first mortgage on a single-family house. Any single-family loans above that amount are called nonconforming or jumbo loans and are not bought by Fannie Mae or Freddie Mac.

Lenders may allow a minimum 3% down payment on a first mortgage Fannie Mae loan if the borrower purchases Private Mortgage Insurance (PMI). PMI is required on all loans where the borrower puts down less than 20 % of the loan amount at closing. This monthly mortgage insurance payment creates a pool of money, which will help compensate the lender if it takes a loss on a foreclosure sale. The less money down, the riskier the loan is for the lender and the higher the PMI payment. However, the use of PMI allows the borrower to use leverage and buy a more expensive property than he might if he had to make a larger down payment. The PMI insures the top 20% of the loan and once it is paid down or canceled when the loan balance reaches 78%, there is no insurance coverage for the lender on the remaining loan balance. The borrower's monthly payment is less without any included PMI.

The conventional mortgage may have a due-on-sale clause, and there may or may not be a prepayment penalty. Conventional mortgages are issued for investment properties, primary residences and second homes.

The late fee is 5% of the monthly P&I.

Down payment gifts are allowed.

The amount of a conventional mortgage seller concession depends on the LTV:

- 75% LTV or less = 9% seller concessions.

- 75% - 90% LTV = 6% seller concessions.

- 90% or more = 3% seller concessions.

Note: Investment properties have a maximum 2% seller concession.

Because non-owner occupied rental properties are considered riskier than owner-occupied ones, lenders will usually charge a higher interest rate and a larger down payment (usually a minimum of 20%.)

Nonconforming Mortgages

A nonconforming loan is one that doesn't meet the Fannie Mae or Freddie Mac underwriting guidelines. This could occur for a number of reasons: the loan amount is too high; the borrower's credit score is too low; the borrower doesn't have enough assets, or the borrower has too much debt. If any of these are true, Fannie and Freddie will not buy the mortgage and note in the secondary mortgage market, and the lender will have to find alternative investors. The interest rate will be higher on these loans.

A jumbo loan exceeds the Fannie/Freddie allowable loan limits.

An Alt-A mortgage is a type of U.S. mortgage that's considered riskier than A-paper (prime) and less risky than subprime. Alt-A interest rates, which are determined by credit risk, tend to be between those of prime and subprime home loans. Typically, Alt-A mortgages are characterized by borrowers with less than full documentation, higher loan-to-value ratios, or higher debt-to-income ratios (see Chapter 5.)

	FHA	VA	USDA	CONVENTIONAL
Government Involvement	100 % Insured	Partially Guaranteed	Partially Guaranteed	None
Minimum Down Payment	3.5 %	0 %	0 %	3 %
Special Closing Fee	Up-front mortgage insurance premium	Funding Fee	Guaranty Fee	None
Monthly Mortgage Insurance	Mortgage Insurance Premium (MIP)	None	Mortgage Insurance premium (MIP)	Private Mortgage Insurance (PMI) if less than 20% down
Due-on-Sale	No (assumable)	No (assumable)	No (assumable)	Yes (usually)
Investment Properties	No	No	No	Yes
Appraisal	FHA approved appraiser	Certificate of Reasonable Value (CRV) - VA appraiser	FHA approved appraiser	Standard
Late Fees	4 %	4 %	4 %	5 %

III.   Nontraditional Mortgages

If you were in the business in 2005 or bought a home during that time, you know that lenders had very liberal lending criteria; if you were breathing, you got a loan. Supposedly, the reason for this liberal underwriting policy was the fact that property values were appreciating; so, even if the property went into foreclosure, the lender could turn around and sell it for more than the loan balance.

During 2006 - 2007, the housing bubble burst, home values started to go down and more existing mortgages were found to be fraudulent, which forced the lenders to buy them back. Lenders started going out of business because of the defaulting loans; commercial banks tightened up the warehouse credit lines, and the regulatory agencies saw the writing on the wall and began issuing guidelines for the riskiest type of products and borrowers.

In September 2006, five federal financial regulatory agencies (IRREA) jointly issued "Interagency Guidance on Nontraditional Mortgage Product Risks" to address risks posed by different types of adjustable-rate mortgages, including "interest-only" mortgages and "payment option" adjustable-rate mortgages that could result in negative amortization. These types of loans are called nontraditional or exotic. Guidelines were first issued to the banks and savings associations. The Conference of State Bank Supervisors (CSBS) and the American Association of Residential Mortgage Regulators (AARMR) then issued parallel guidelines for the rest of the lenders. Some primary areas of concern involve:

- Qualifying a borrower based on a low introductory interest rate rather than the final fully indexed rate.

- Allowing adjustable-rate mortgages to be combined with interest-only, reduced documentation or second mortgage loans. The process of combining multiple risky loan features into one package is called risk layering.

- Lenders need to implement strict controls and monitoring practices if a high percentage of their business involves risky loans. In addition, they need to monitor the practices of third party loan originators.

- The products and the risks must be fully explained to consumers.

- Lenders must ensure that the borrowers receive all the required state and federal disclosures.

IV.   Subprime Lending

In June 2007, the same financial regulatory agencies that had addressed the dangers of specific nontraditional loan products in 2006, issued the "Statement on Subprime Mortgage Lending," which addresses risks relating to certain subprime mortgages and the qualifications of the borrower. Generally, subprime borrowers will display a range of credit risk characteristics that may include one or more of the following:

- Two or more 30-day delinquencies in the last 12 months or one or more 60-day delinquencies in the last 24 months.

- Judgment, foreclosure, repossession, or charge-off in the prior 24 months.

- Bankruptcy in the last 5 years.

- Relatively high default probability as evidenced by, for example, a credit score of 660 or below.

- Debt-to-income ratio of 50% or higher.

Products that the agencies were particularly concerned about include:

- Low initial payments based on a fixed introductory rate that expires after a short period and then adjusts to a variable index rate plus a margin for the remaining term of the loan.

- Very high or no limits on how much the payment amount or the interest rate may increase ("payment or rate caps") on reset dates.

- Limited or no documentation of borrowers' income.

- Product features likely to result in frequent refinancing to maintain an affordable monthly payment.

- Substantial prepayment penalties and/or prepayment penalties that extend beyond the initial fixed interest rate period.

Predatory Lending

Subprime lending is not synonymous with predatory lending, and loans with features described above are not necessarily predatory in nature. Typically, predatory lending involves at least one of the following elements:

- Making loans based predominantly on the foreclosure or liquidation value of a borrower's collateral rather than on the borrower's ability to repay the mortgage according to its terms.

- Inducing a borrower to repeatedly refinance a loan in order to charge high points and fees each time the loan is refinanced ("loan flipping").

- Engaging in fraud or deception to conceal the true nature of the mortgage loan obligation, or ancillary products, from an unsuspecting or unsophisticated borrower.

- Loans to borrowers who don't demonstrate the capacity to repay the loan may lack sufficient consumer protection safeguards and are generally considered unsafe and unsound.

Providers offering mortgage loans such as these face an elevated risk that their conduct will violate Section 5 of the Federal Trade Commission Act (FTC Act) or other state laws, which prohibit unfair or deceptive acts or practices.

Consumer Protection Principles

The lender needs to inform the subprime borrower about:

- Potential payment increases, including how the new payment will be calculated when the introductory fixed rate expires.

- The existence of any prepayment penalty, how it will be calculated, and when it may be imposed.

- The existence of any balloon payment.

- Whether there is a pricing premium attached to a reduced documentation or stated income loan program.

- The requirement to pay possibly substantial real estate taxes and insurance in addition to the loan payments.

V.   Definitions

Amortization - process of fully paying off a loan in regular payments over a specified period of time. The portion of each monthly payment that goes to reduce the outstanding principal balance gradually increases with each payment throughout the life of the loan, and the portion used to pay interest gradually decreases each month.

Positive Amortization - occurs when the monthly mortgage payment decreases the loan balance. This occurs in a fixed-rate mortgage, as one example.

Negative Amortization - occurs in a mortgage repayment plan in which the borrower makes payments that amount to less than the interest due. The unpaid interest is added to the outstanding loan balance, causing the outstanding loan balance to increase instead of decrease.

Escrow Impounds - usually collected by the lender as part of the monthly mortgage payment. They include the monthly amount for property taxes, hazard insurance and flood insurance, if required.

PITI - Principal, Interest, Taxes and Insurance (Hazard, Flood and Mortgage). It's also called the monthly housing expense. PITI also includes any monthly homeowner's association fees.

P&I (Debt Service) - monthly principal and interest payment. Late fees are either 4% or 5% of the debt service, not the PITI.

Senior Mortgage - has the superior lien position.

Junior Mortgage - has a lower, or more subordinate, lien position than the Senior Mortgage.

Payment-Option ARM - nontraditional adjustable-rate mortgage that allows borrowers to pick their type of payment each month. Possible options may include a minimal payment based on a starter interest rate, an interest-only payment or a fully amortized payment. If the minimum payment option is less than the interest accruing on the loan, the difference is added to the loan balance, which results in negative amortization. The interest-only option avoids negative amortization but doesn't provide for principal amortization. If the borrower continually chooses the interest-only option, the required monthly payment amount eventually will be recast so that the outstanding balance fully amortizes over the remaining loan term.

Reduced Documentation - loan feature that is commonly referred to as "low doc/no doc," "no income/no asset," "stated income" or "stated assets." For mortgage loans with this feature, a lender sets minimal documentation standards.

Simultaneous Second-Lien Loan - lending arrangement where either a closed-end second-lien or a home equity line of credit (HELOC) is originated simultaneously with the first lien mortgage loan, typically in lieu of a higher down payment.

VI.   Mortgage Subcategories

Fixed-Rate Mortgage - one example of a fully amortized loan. Loan terms are generally 15 or 30 years. During the first few years of the loan, most of the monthly P & I is going toward paying the interest. Payments during the last few years are almost entirely principal repayment. A 15-year loan has a lower interest rate, but the shorter timeframe makes the monthly payments higher than with a 30-year loan. The borrower needs to decide if he wants to build up equity faster with a 15-year loan or minimize monthly payments with a 30-year loan.

Balloon Mortgage - partially amortized loan. Monthly payments are usually calculated as if it had a 30-year term, but the balance of the loan will come due before that time and has to be paid in one lump sum; 5, 7 and 10-year terms are popular. Interest rates are typically lower than on a fixed-rate mortgage. A 360/180 loan is a balloon amortized over 30 years with a lump-sum payment due after 15 years. Balloon mortgages are accepted as Qualified Mortgages in a very few circumstances including loans made by small lenders or a short term (12 months or less) bridge loan to provide closing funds while the buyer is in the process of selling another house. In all cases of Qualified Mortgages, the borrower must show a documented ability to re-pay the loan.

Adjustable-Rate Mortgage (ARM) - consists of two parts: an index that fluctuates and a margin that's fixed.

Index + Margin = Fully Indexed Rate

Interest rates are usually lower for ARMS than for fixed-rate mortgages. Some mortgages may allow an ARM to be converted to a fixed-rate loan during designated times. This may involve the payment of a fee. Some of the major features of an ARM include the following:

- The index is a known, reliable, fluctuating financial indicator expressed as a percent. Two common indices are the U.S. Treasury Securities rate and the London Inter-Bank Offered Rate (LIBOR). The index used must be beyond the control of the lender and verifiable by the borrower. If the index has increased at the start of the adjustment period, the mortgagor will have a higher monthly mortgage payment. If the index has decreased, the monthly mortgage payment will be less.

- The margin is a fixed percentage rate (typically 2% to 3%) that is added to the specified index at each adjustment period to determine the fully indexed rate. It reflects the lender's profit and overhead. The margin is expressed in basis points where 100 basis points = 1%.

- The adjustment period specifies the initial term before the first interest rate adjustment. After this first period, the loan typically adjusts every year. Common terms are one year, three year and five-year ARMs. A five-year ARM will have a fixed interest rate for the first five years and adjust annually after that. This is referred to as a 5/1 ARM.

- Rate caps limit how much the interest rate can change at each adjustment and over the life of the mortgage. Rate caps typically are 1% to 3% per adjustment period, and 5% to 6% over the life of the loan. A 2/3/6 cap allows the loan to adjust a maximum of 2% the first adjustment period, 3 % for subsequent adjustment periods and a lifetime cap of 6%.

- Borrowers must be notified of a rate change six months before the initial reset.

- Payment caps limit the amount the monthly payment may increase at the time of each adjustment. Any interest that is not paid because of the cap is added to the balance of the loan. A payment cap can limit the amount of the monthly payment increases, but it can also add to the loan balance. If that occurs, it results in negative amortization.

Bi-Weekly Mortgage - borrower must make a mortgage payment every two weeks. This allows the borrower to build up equity faster and pay less interest over the life of the loan.

Term Mortgage - non-amortizing interest-only loan. The balance is due at the end of the term in a balloon payment.

Reverse Mortgage/ Home Equity Conversion Mortgage (HECM) - negatively amortizing loan that allows elderly homeowners to convert the equity in their primary residence into a monthly cash flow or a line of credit. HECM loans have no maximum payout.

The requirements are:

- Youngest borrower is at least age 62.

- Home is a 1-unit primary residence, including condominiums.

- No existing mortgage on the property or one that can be satisfied with the first reverse mortgage payment.

- Borrower must receive counseling from a HUD-approved home counseling agency.

- Borrower must maintain hazard insurance, pay property taxes, pay monthly mortgage insurance premiums (MIP, added to loan balance), and possibly pay monthly servicing fees, which would also be added to the loan balance.

- Payments can continue for as long as the borrower lives, or the property is vacant for more than 12 consecutive months for health reasons or the borrower violates the terms of the mortgage (hazard insurance, property tax, etc.).

- New FHA appraisal.

Reverse mortgage interest can be fixed or an ARM that adjusts annually with a 2% annual cap and a 5% lifetime cap. Lenders may also offer an ARM that adjusts monthly with only a lifetime cap. The type of interest cannot be changed after closing,

The choice of payout plans (that can be changed by borrower during the course of the mortgage) include:

- **Tenure.** Payments continue for the life of the borrower as long as it remains the principal residence.

- **Term**. Borrowers select the desired number of monthly payments.

- **Line of Credit.** Borrowers withdraw money as needed.

- **Modified Tenure.** Tenure combined with a line of credit.

- **Modified Term.** Term combined with a line of credit.

Disclosures include:

- Notice of the Right of Rescission.

- ARM disclosure (if borrower selected an adjustable rate mortgage).

- Initial payment plan details.

- HUD-1 closing statement.

- HUD-1 certification statement.

Closing costs may include fees for:

- Appraisal.

- Credit report.

- Deposit Verification.

- Document preparation.

- Property survey.

- Title examination and title policy (equal to the full value of the house at the time of closing).

- Attorney.

- Settlement.

- Mortgage broker (if retained independently by the borrower).

- Recording fees and taxes.

- Property tests or treatments.

- Courier services.

Reverse mortgage advertisements must NOT:

- Misrepresent a government affiliation.

- Provide inaccurate information about interest rates.

- Provide misleading statements concerning the costs of reverse mortgages.

- Misrepresent the amount of cash or credit available to a consumer:

Lenders calculate how much a borrower is authorized to borrow overall, based on age, the interest rate, and the value of the home. This number is known as the initial principal limit, and it increases every year of the loan. Limits on first year withdrawals are:

- 60% of the initial principal limit.

- Enough to pay off an existing mortgage (if it's more than the allowable 60%) plus 10% of the principal limit.

This loan doesn't have to be repaid until the last borrower dies or the home is vacant for more than a year. The owner retains the deed and possession. These are non-recourse loans since the heirs are not personally liable for the note; if the lien is greater than the market value of the home, the lender must accept the sold price and cannot file for a deficiency judgment against the heirs. The HECM loan is the FHA's reverse mortgage loan.

Buy-Down Mortgage - begins at a rate below the existing market rate and then rises, usually every year, at a predetermined amount. A developer may work with a lender and in return for a certain volume of business, a lender may offer lower interest rates for two or three years if a borrower uses the developer's financing. This is good for the borrower and good for the developer because the financing terms are likely to attract more buyers to the properties.

Package Mortgage - can be either amortizing or non-amortizing, and the lien includes personal property as well as real property. This is more common in commercial lending than residential; for example, a mortgage on a restaurant may include the ovens and other restaurant equipment.

Graduated Payment Mortgage (GPM) - payment starts low and increases over time. The initial payment is used for qualifying purposes so this might be a good product for individuals who expect their income to increase over time.

Wraparound Mortgage - usually a type of seller financing in which the seller finances enough money to cover the existing loan balance as well as any additional funds needed by the borrower. The original loan can't have a due-on-sale clause, since the seller will continue to make these payments after title is transferred to the new purchaser. This only makes sense if the interest rate on the wraparound mortgage is higher than the rate on the existing lien, because that is how the seller/lender is making a profit.

Growing Equity Mortgage (GEM) - fixed interest rate and increasing payments so that the loan balance is paid off more quickly.

Home Equity Line of Credit (HELOC) - form of revolving credit in which the home serves as collateral. The amount of the available credit line usually depends on the borrower's equity in the home (appraised value – loan balance = borrower's equity). Funds can be withdrawn for a stated period of time, such as 10 years, after which the repayment period starts (also a stated number of years). Interest rates tend to be varied, so the repayment amount may vary from month to month. Lenders can cancel the credit line at any time.

Bridge Loan (swing loan) - "bridges" the gap between the purchase of a new home and the sale of the borrower's current home. The borrower's current home is used as collateral, and the loan is used to close on the new home before the current home is sold. The borrower usually needs to have a signed contract to sell his current house.

Construction Loan - usually a short-term temporary loan in which money is advanced in stages as the construction progresses, and the borrower pays the interest on each draw. Because there's usually no structure yet to act as collateral, interest rates, down payments and borrower credit score requirements tend to be higher than residential purchase mortgages.

Construction-to-Permanent Loan - lenders sometimes allow a borrower to apply for two types of loans with one application. Payments on the permanent loan begin after the final inspection or issuance of the Certificate of Occupancy. Creditors are allowed to treat multiple advance loans to finance construction of a dwelling that may be permanently financed by the same creditor either as a single transaction or as more than one transaction.

Interest-Only Mortgage - borrowers pay only the monthly interest due during the specified term of the loan. When the term is about to expire, borrowers may be given several options:

- Make a lump sum loan payoff.

- Refinance into an amortizing fixed rate or adjustable mortgage.

- Start paying off the balance at a higher interest rate.

Interest-only mortgages are not considered to be Quality Mortgages, so it might be difficult finding a lender willing to assume the risk.

Jumbo Mortgage - loans that exceed the Fannie Mae lending limits. Interest rates may be higher on these loans than for conforming mortgages.

Important Points to Remember

1. The Federal Housing Administration (FHA) is a government agency within the Department of Housing and Urban Development (HUD).
2. The FHA provides 100 % insurance to its approved lenders. The lenders recover any losses experienced during a foreclosure or short sale because the FHA makes up the difference to the lenders.
3. FHA loans have a required Up Front Mortgage Insurance Premium (UFMIP) and a Monthly Insurance Premium (MIP) regardless of the down payment amount.
4. The lenders set the interest rate, not FHA or HUD.
5. FHA loans are assumable; there is no due-on-sale clause.
6. FHA loans have a 4% late fee.
7. FHA loans have a minimum down payment of 3.5%. This can be a gift from a relative.
8. FHA loans require the use of an FHA-approved appraiser.
9. FHA loans have a maximum loan amount in each county, which does not include the Up Front Mortgage Insurance Premium.
10. A 5/1 ARM has a fixed interest rate for 5 years and adjusts annually after that.
11. A 2/3/6 rate cap indicates that there is an initial 2% adjustment, then 3 % every adjustment period after that with a lifetime cap of 6%.
12. The Department of Veteran's Affairs (DVA) partially guarantees VA loans.
13. VA loans are made to qualified military servicemen and women.
14. VA loans require no down payment (100% financing).
15. VA loans require no monthly insurance premium.
16. VA loans do require a one-time funding fee at closing.
17. VA loans require a veteran to produce a Certificate of Eligibility, which shows the amount of his entitlement.
18. The lenders set the interest rate, not the VA.
19. A VA appraisal is known as a Certificate of Reasonable Value (CRV).
20. A VA loan is assumable; it does not have a due-on-sale clause.
21. VA loans have a 4% late fee.
22. USDA loans are partially guaranteed by the US government, allow for 100% financing, have a one time funding fee that is paid at closing and have required monthly mortgage insurance.
23. The USDA loans are lower-income, owner-occupied, 30 year fixed-rate loans.
24. To qualify for a USDA loan, the property must be located in a rural area as defined by the Department of Agriculture.
25. A conventional mortgage is not insured or guaranteed by the government.
26. A conventional mortgage requires a minimum 3% down payment.
27. A conventional mortgage requires Private Mortgage Insurance on loans with less than a 20% down payment.
28. Most conventional mortgages are not assumable; they do have a due-on-sale clause.
29. A conventional mortgage has a 5% late fee.
30. A nonconforming loan is one that does not meet Fannie's or Freddie's underwriting guidelines.
31. A jumbo loan exceeds Fannie/Freddie maximum loan amount.
32. Alt-A loans are characterized by reduced documentation, high ratios or limited assets.

33.   Subprime loans are the riskiest and are associated with poor credit scores.

34.   Amortization is the process of fully paying off a loan in regular payments over a specified period of time. The portion of each monthly payment that goes to reduce the outstanding principal balance gradually increases with each payment throughout the life of the loan, and the portion used to pay interest gradually decreases each month.

35.   Positive amortization occurs when the monthly mortgage payment decreases the loan balance.

36.   Negative amortization occurs in a mortgage repayment plan in which the borrower makes payments that amount to less than the interest due. Unpaid interest is added to the outstanding loan balance, causing the outstanding loan balance to increase instead of decrease.

37.   P&I (Debt Service) is the monthly principal and interest payment.

38.   Late fees are either 4% or 5% of the debt service, not the PITI.

39.   Escrow impounds are usually collected by the lender as part of the monthly mortgage payment. They include the monthly amount for property taxes, hazard insurance and flood insurance, if required.

40.   PITI is Principal, Interest, Taxes and Hazard, Flood and Mortgage Insurance. It is also called the monthly housing expense.

41.   A senior mortgage has the superior lien position.

42.   A junior mortgage has a lower or more subordinate lien position than the senior mortgage.

43.   A Fixed-Rate Mortgage is one example of a fully amortized loan. During the first few years of the loan, most of the monthly P & I is going toward paying the interest. Payments during the last few years are almost entirely principal repayment.

44.   A Balloon Mortgage is partially amortized. Monthly payments are usually calculated as if it was a 30-year term but the balance of the loan will come due before that time and has to be paid in one lump sum; 5, 7 and 10-year terms are popular.

45.   A 360/180 loan is a balloon amortized over 30 years with a lump sum payment due after 15 years.

46.   An Adjustable-Rate Mortgage (ARM) consists of two parts: an index which fluctuates and a margin which is fixed. Index + Margin = Fully Indexed Rate.

47.   The index is a known, fluctuating, published economic indicator outside of the control of the lender.

48.   U.S. Treasury Securities rate and the London Inter-Bank Offered Rate (LIBOR) are two common indices.

49.   The margin is a fixed percentage rate (typically 2% to 3%) that is added to the specified index at each adjustment period to determine the fully indexed rate. It reflects the lender's profit and overhead.

50.   The margin is expressed in basis points where 100 points = 1%.

51.   The adjustment period specifies the initial term before the first interest rate adjustment. After this first period, the loan typically adjusts every year.

52.   Rate caps limit how much the interest rate can change at each adjustment and over the life of the mortgage. A 2/3/6 has a max first adjustment of 2%, subsequent max adjustments of 3% and a lifetime max adjustment of 6%.

53.   A Bi-Weekly Mortgage is one in which the borrower must make a mortgage payment every two weeks. This allows the borrower to build up equity faster and pay less interest over the life of the loan.

54. A Term Mortgage is a non-amortizing interest-only loan. The balance is due at the end of the term in a balloon payment.

55. A Reverse Mortgage is a negatively amortizing loan for homeowners of primary residences who are 62 years or older and have a large percentage of their current mortgage paid off. They are non-recourse loans, and the lenders cannot file a deficiency judgment against the heirs. The heirs are not personally liable for the note.

56. A Buy-Down Mortgage is a loan that begins at a rate below the existing market rate and then rises, usually every year, at a predetermined amount.

57. A Package Mortgage can be either amortizing or non-amortizing, and the lien includes personal property as well as real property.

58. A Graduated Payment Mortgage (GPM) is a mortgage in which the payment starts low and increases over time.

59. A Wraparound Mortgage is usually a type of seller financing in which the seller finances enough money to cover the existing loan balance as well as any additional funds needed by the borrower. The original loan cannot have a due-on-sale clause since the seller will continue to make these payments after title is transferred to the new purchaser.

60. A Growing Equity Mortgage (GEM) has a fixed interest rate and increasing payments so that the loan balance is paid off more quickly.

61. A Home Equity Line of Credit is a form of revolving credit in which the home serves as collateral. The amount of the available credit line usually depends on the borrower's equity in the home (appraised value – loan balance = borrower's equity).

62. The HECM loan is the FHA's reverse mortgage loan.

63. The borrower generally must use his or her own funds to make the required minimum cash down payment, although that down payment may be supplemented with a gift from a relative, domestic partner, fiancé, or fiancée.

64. A gift must be accompanied by a gift letter that specifies the dollar amount of the gift, and the date the funds were transferred. The letter must also contain the donor's statement that no repayment is expected and include the donor's name, address, phone number and relationship to the borrower.

65. The maximum FHA seller concession is 6%.

66. The maximum VA seller concession is 4% + other standard closing costs.

67. The maximum USDA seller concession is 6%.

68. Conventional seller concessions are: 75% LTV or less = 9%, 75% - 90% LTV = 6%, 90% or more = 3%.

69. Seller concessions may NOT be applied to the down payment.

70. Because non-owner occupied rental properties are considered riskier than owner-occupied ones, lenders will usually charge a higher interest rate and a larger down payment (usually a minimum of 20%).

71. The monthly mortgage payment on a conventional loan is reduced when the borrower pays down the loan to the point where he has 22% equity (78% LTV), and the PMI is automatically canceled. He can request a cancelation with 20% equity.

72. Borrowers must be notified of an ARM rate change six months before the initial reset.

73. Reverse mortgage interest can be fixed or an ARM that adjusts annually with a 2% annual cap and a 5% lifetime cap. Lenders may also offer an ARM that adjusts monthly with only a lifetime cap.

74. Reverse mortgage title insurance must equal the full value of the house at the time of closing.

75.   Creditors are allowed to treat multiple advance loans to finance construction of a dwelling that may be permanently financed by the same creditor either as a single transaction or as more than one transaction.

76.   An FHA early payment default is a mortgage loan that is 60 days past due within the first six months.

Exam

1. An FHA mortgage:
   A. Is 100% insured
   B. Is partially guaranteed
   C. Has a 5% late fee
   D. Is not assumable

2. FHA maximum loan amounts:
   A. Are set by the U.S. Department of State
   B. Do not include the Up Front Mortgage Insurance Premium
   C. Are set at $500,000
   D. Are set at $1,000,000

3. A VA mortgage has all the following features **EXCEPT**:
   A. It is partially guaranteed
   B. It has a mortgage insurance premium
   C. It has a 4% late fee
   D. No required down payment

4. A VA appraisal is known as a:
   A. Qualified appraisal
   B. Certificate of reasonable value
   C. Certificate of market value
   D. VA designated market appraisal

5. A USDA loan has:
   A. 100% financing
   B. No income limits
   C. A 5% late fee
   D. Has no geographical restrictions

6. A conventional mortgage does **NOT** have a:
   A. 3% minimum down payment
   B. 5% late fee
   C. Due-on-sale clause
   D. Borrower income limit

7. Interest rates are set by:
   A. FHA
   B. Lenders
   C. VA
   D. Fannie Mae

8.   A reverse mortgage is an example of:
      A.   Positive amortization
      B.   Negative amortization
      C.   Lender error
      D.   Bridge loan

9.   In an adjustable rate mortgage :
      A.   Index + fully indexed rate = margin
      B.   Fully indexed rate + margin = index
      C.   Index + margin = fully indexed rate
      D.   Index – margin = fully indexed rate

10.   Which of the following is expressed as basis points in an adjustable rate mortgage:
      A.   Index
      B.   Margin
      C.   Fully indexed rate
      D.   Term

11.   A 2/3/7 ARM has a:
      A.   Lifetime cap of 2%
      B.   Lifetime cap of 3%
      C.   Lifetime cap of 7%
      D.   Lifetime cap of 10%

12.   If a 15 year ARM has a starting interest rate of 5% and has an adjustment rate cap of 2% and a lifetime cap of 8%, what is the maximum interest rate that can be charged for the first adjustment period?
      A.   5 1/4 %
      B.   5 1/2 %
      C.   7 %
      D.   13 %

13.   A term mortgage is **NOT**:
      A.   Non-amortizing
      B.   Interest only
      C.   Satisfied by a final lump sum payment
      D.   Fully amortized

14.   A graduated payment mortgage:
      A.   Is for college graduates only
      B.   Has payments that start low and increase over time
      C.   Has payments that start high and decrease over time
      D.   Is only for borrowers with a minimum age of 62

15. Borrower's equity equals
    A. Appraised value – loan balance
    B. Appraised value – down payment
    C. Loan balance + down payment
    D. Loan balance – down payment

16. Escrow impounds are collected by the:
    A. Lender
    B. Attorney
    C. Police
    D. Seller

17. Private Mortgage Insurance is required for:
    A. FHA loans
    B. VA loans
    C. Jumbo loans
    D. Conventional loans when there is less than a 20% down payment

18. What type of mortgage has a fixed interest rate and increasing payments?
    A. Adjustable rate mortgage
    B. Package mortgage
    C. Growing equity mortgage
    D. Wraparound mortgage

19. The FHA is an agency within:
    A. Department of the Veteran's Affairs
    B. Department of HUD
    C. Department of Fannie Mae
    D. Private organization

20. PITI is an acronym for:
    A. Property, insurance, taxes and interest
    B. Property, interest, taxes and insurance
    C. Principal, insurance, taxes and interest
    D. Principal, interest, taxes and insurance

21. Which of the following is a common index used in ARMs:
    A. CD rate
    B. The London Inter-Bank Offered Rate
    C. The Chase Fluctuating Index
    D. The New York Times Index

22. A bi-weekly mortgage:
    A. Is paid every 2 weeks
    B. Is paid every 2 months
    C. Is not legal
    D. Has no mandatory payment schedule

23.   Which has the superior lien position?
    A.   Senior mortgage
    B.   Junior mortgage
    C.   Mortgages under $250,000
    D.   First signed mortgage

24.   80 basis points equals what percentage of the loan amount?
    A.   .08 %
    B.   .8%
    C.   8%
    D.   80%

25.   Which lien will most likely have the lowest lien position?
    A.   Property tax
    B.   Senior mortgage
    C.   Junior mortgage
    D.   IRS tax lien

26.   A gift letter does **NOT** include the:
    A.   Donor's name
    B.   Amount of the gift
    C.   Terms of repayment
    D.   Donor's address

27.   A partially amortized loan which consists of a lump sum payoff at the end of the term is:
    A.   Balloon mortgage
    B.   Package mortgage
    C.   Chattel mortgage
    D.   Buy-down mortgage

28.   A mortgage with payments due every two weeks is a:
    A.   Package mortgage
    B.   Bridge loan
    C.   Bi-weekly mortgage
    D.   Blanket mortgage

29.   A VA appraisal is known as a:
    A.   Certificate of Eligibility
    B.   Certificate of Occupancy
    C.   Certificate of Reasonable Value
    D.   Certificate of Domicile

30.   The fluctuating economic indicator used in an ARM is the:
    A.   Index
    B.   Margin
    C.   Collateral
    D.   Basis point

31.   A loan in which interest is subsidized for a stated period of time is a:
       A.   Buy-down mortgage
       B.   Term mortgage
       C.   Bridge loan
       D.   Collateral loan

32.   Which of the following CANNOT contribute money towards the borrower's down
       payment:
       A.   Employer
       B.   Real estate agent
       C.   Domestic partner
       D.   Borrower's relative

33.   The maximum FHA seller concession is:
       A.   3%
       B.   4%
       C.   6%
       D.   9%

34.   The maximum VA seller concession is:
       A.   3% + standard closing costs
       B.   4% + standard closing costs
       C.   6% + standard closing costs
       D.   9% + standard closing costs

35.   What is the minimum down payment usually required for non-owner occupied rental
       properties?
       A.   5%
       B.   10%
       C.   15%
       D.   20%

36.   Borrowers must be notified of an ARM rate change how many months before the initial
       reset?
       A.   1
       B.   3
       C.   6
       D.   9

Answer Key

1.	A	26.	C
2.	B	27.	A
3.	B	28.	C
4.	B	29.	C
5.	A	30.	A
6.	D	31.	A
7.	B	32.	B
8.	B	33.	C
9.	C	34.	B (answer may be simply 4% for national exam)
10.	B	35.	D
11.	C	36.	C
12.	C		
13.	D		
14.	B		
15.	A		
16.	A		
17.	D		
18.	C		
19.	B		
20.	D		
21.	B		
22.	A		
23.	A		
24.	B		
25.	D		

5

Basic Concepts of Mortgage Financing

To start this chapter on financing, we offer a quick review of percentages, decimals and fractions and how to convert from one form to another. Everyone should have a calculator to work the problems in this chapter.

I.   Using a Calculator

When working with the calculator, set the decimal place to 4 (if your calculator has this feature) and don't hit the equal sign until the problem is complete since this may cause incorrect answers due to rounding errors. Results round up on 5; .045 equals .05 when converting an answer to dollars and cents. **Clear the calculator before each problem.**

Fractions are reduced to their lowest form. You will never see an interest rate expressed as 4/8, it will be reduced to 1/2. To do this, find the largest number that can be evenly divided into the top number (numerator) and the bottom number (denominator). In the case of 4/8, that number would be 4. Divide the 4/8 numerator and denominator by 4 and the result is 1/2.

Before you take the exam, make sure that you completely understand the following chart because answers are in a multiple-choice format, and the correct answer could be expressed as a fraction, decimal or percent.

Fraction	Decimal	Percent
1/8	.125	12.5%
1/4	.25	25%
3/8	.375	37.5%
1/2	.50	50%
5/8	.625	62.5%
3/4	.75	75%
7/8	.875	87.5%
1	1.0	100%

To convert a decimal to a percent, multiply by 100 and add a percent sign. A shortcut is to move the decimal place 2 positions to the right. This is the same as multiplying by 100. Likewise, to convert a percent to a decimal, divide by 100 and drop the percent sign or move the decimal place 2 positions to the left.

Problem 1:

1. How is 5 1/8% expressed as a decimal?   _____

2. How is 8.625 expressed as a fraction?   _____

3. How is 11 6/8 expressed as a reduced fraction?   _____

II.   Discount and Origination Points

Discount points are paid to the lender for lowering the interest rate, and origination points are paid to the loan originator as a fee for his service.

When the loan originator is quoting interest rates to a borrower, he may be looking at a rate table for a particular lender that has a range of possible interest rates and fees or rebates. A par interest rate is the "break-even" rate for the lender. If a borrower wants a rate lower than par, the lender charges the borrower discount points. Discounts can be either temporary or fixed, and the cost of the points is a closing cost, which is typically paid by the buyer who also pays the origination points.

> One discount point   = 1% of the loan amount
>
> One origination point = 1% of the loan amount

For fixed discounts, the borrower gets a lower interest rate for the life of the loan, but has to pay an additional 1% of the loan amount at closing for each point. Is it worth it? It all depends on how long the property is held before it is sold or refinanced. How long does it take for the savings realized by the difference between the two mortgage payments to exceed the initial cost of the points?

There are also buy down points to temporarily lower the interest rate. For example, an FHA 2-1 buy down allows a purchaser to reduce the initial interest rate on the mortgage by 2% the first year, 1% the next year, and 0% every year thereafter.

Problem 2:

1. What is the cost of 3 discount points on a $100,000 loan? _____

2. What is the cost of 1 1/2 origination points and 1 discount point on a $150,000 loan? _____

III.   Mortgage Interest Calculations

When a loan closes, the first payment will not be due for at least a month. For example, if the loan closes on January 20, the first payment is due March 1. You might think that the lender will be missing the February payment but that is not entirely true because mortgage interest is paid in arrears. As you already know, the monthly payment consists of interest and loan reduction payments (P & I). The portion of the March payment that consists of interest is actually paying the interest for February, and the loan reduction is credited to March. In the first few years of a loan, the majority of the monthly payment consists of an interest payment, so the fact that the lender loses one month of the first loan reduction payment (February in this case) is negligible.

But, what about the interest during the remainder of the month in which the deal closes? In this example, the deal closes on January 20; therefore, the borrowers pay the lender for 12 days of per diem interest that corresponds to the 12 days in the month that they own the property. This is a closing cost to the borrowers. Per diem interest is calculated using a 365-day year.

Suppose there are 10 days left in the month including the closing date, and the loan amount was $100,000 at 7% interest. How much interest does the borrower owe the lender at closing?

Solution:

> Multiply the loan amount by the interest rate to give annual interest
>
> Divide that calculated annual interest by 365 days in a year to give the daily amount of interest
>
> Multiply the daily interest by the number of days remaining in the month
>
> (($100,000 loan x 7% interest)/365 days) x 10 days = $191.78

Problem 3:

1. The loan closes on May 2. When is the first mortgage payment due?   _____

2. There are 5 days left in the month including the closing date. The loan amount is $250,000 and the interest rate is 7 1/4%. How much interest does the borrower owe?   _____

When the seller is ready to pay off the loan balance, an estoppel letter is sent by the closing agent to the lender requesting the amount of the final payoff. When calculating the amount, the lender will need to take into account the fact that the interest has not been paid for the month of closing since it is paid in arrears.

IV.   Loan-to-Value Ratios

The loan-to-value ratio (LTV) is a value that expresses the percent of lender financing. To obtain this number divide the loan amount by the smaller of the purchase price or appraisal value. Lenders will generally not lend any more than the appraised value of the home. The LTV is usually expressed as a percent to one decimal place.

$$\frac{\text{Loan amount}}{\text{the lesser of the sale price or appraisal value}}$$

Likewise:

Loan amount + down payment = purchase price
and
Market value − loan balance = owner's equity

When there is more than one mortgage loan involved, we can calculate the combined loan-to-value (CLTV) ratio. This is also called the total loan-to-value (TLTV) ratio.

$$\frac{\text{Total loan amounts}}{\text{the lesser of the sale price or appraisal value}}$$

Problem 4:

1. The purchase price is $100,000 and the loan amount is $80,000.

    What is the LTV?   _____

    What is the down payment?   _____

    What is the amount of the owner's equity?   _____

2. The purchase price is $300,000, the loan amount is $250,000 and the appraisal value is $275,000

    What is the LTV?   _____

3. The purchase price is $400,000. There is an assumed mortgage of $200,000 and the maximum LTV cannot exceed 95%.

    How much is the new second mortgage?   _____

    What is the borrower's down payment?   _____

    What is the CLTV?   _____

V.   Late Charges and Monthly Payments

Monthly mortgage payments consist of principal and interest and perhaps one month of property tax, one month of mortgage insurance (PMI or MIP) and one month of hazard insurance (PITI).

Mortgage insurance is usually assessed if the LTV is greater than 80%, and hazard insurance and property taxes are usually escrowed. The lender may allow the escrows to be waived; in this case, the borrowers will have to pay the bills themselves when they become due.

Late fees are charged after the 15th of the month and are calculated as a percentage of the principal and interest payment (P&I) only. FHA and VA late fees are 4% and conventional loans are 5%.

Suppose that the payment is late on a conventional loan and that the monthly P&I is $1,000. What is the late charge?

$$\$1{,}000 \times 5\% = \$50$$

Problem 5:

1. The borrower's May mortgage payment has not yet been received on May 17. He has a $200,000 conventional loan, monthly P&I is $1,080, annual PMI is $2,000, annual hazard insurance is $3,000 and annual property taxes are $4,550. What is the late charge? _____

2. The borrower's June payment is late on an FHA loan. The monthly P&I is $1200. What is the late fee? _____

VI.   Debt Ratios

Lenders assess the risk of the borrowers. Part of this process is to look at the borrowers' gross monthly income (before any deductions) and the total amount of monthly debt including the projected monthly housing expenses. Lenders use two ratios that summarize this information.

Housing Expense Ratio

The first ratio is the Housing Expense Ratio and includes all the projected monthly housing costs divided by gross monthly income. Housing costs may include principal, interest, monthly property tax, monthly hazard insurance, monthly mortgage insurance, monthly condo maintenance fees and monthly Homeowner Association (HOA) fees.

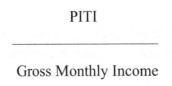

$$\frac{\text{PITI}}{\text{Gross Monthly Income}}$$

For standard qualification purposes, Fannie Mae requires a maximum ratio of 28%, FHA has a standard value of 31%, and the VA does not consider this ratio.

Total Debt to Income Ratio

The second ratio is the Total Debt to Income Ratio and includes credit card payments, lease payments, alimony and child support payments, and any monthly recurring debt. The next chapter in this book details the Fannie Mae standards for debt inclusion. For now, just memorize the formula.

$$\frac{PITI + other\ monthly\ debt}{Gross\ Monthly\ Income}$$

For standard qualification purposes, Fannie Mae requires a maximum Total Debt to Income Ratio of 36% for manually underwritten loans and 50% for Desktop Underwriter (DU) loans, FHA is 43% and VA is 41%. Qualified Mortgage maximum is 43%.

Problem 6:

1. Monthly PITI payments are estimated to be $1400 and the borrower's gross monthly income is $5,000. His other debt totals $200 a month.

What is the Housing Expense Ratio? _____

What is the Total Debt to Income Ratio? _____

Will the borrower qualify based on the ratios? _____

2. The monthly PITI is $900 and the other monthly debts are $250. According to Fannie Mae standard guidelines, what is the borrower's minimum gross monthly income to qualify?

_____

VII.   Gross Monthly Income

Fannie Mae provides a standard method for calculating gross monthly income if the borrower provides the loan originator with income from some other type of payment interval. In a nutshell, the loan originator needs to annualize the salary and divide by 12 to obtain a monthly income.

Annual Income divided by 12

Weekly income x 52 divided by 12

Hourly rate x weekly hours x 52 divided by 12

Problem 7:

1. The employee makes $1000 a week. What is his gross monthly income? _____

2. The employee works 37 hours a week at $15 per hour. What is his gross monthly income?

_____

VIII.   Total Monthly Payment

The total monthly payment consists of the principal and interest (P & I) payment for the loan, and any escrow impounds which the lender collects in order to pay the bill for certain items when they come due. These impounds can include property tax and all the possible types of home protection insurance policies that a homeowner may be carrying (hazard insurance, flood insurance, wind insurance and earthquake insurance).

To calculate the monthly payment, add the monthly P & I with one month of any hazard insurance premiums, one month of property tax and one month of mortgage insurance premiums.

Problem 8:

1. The loan amount is $250,000, monthly P & I is $600, annual hazard insurance is $1200, annual mortgage insurance premium is .5% of the loan amount and annual property taxes are $2000. What is the total monthly payment? _____

IX.   Closing Costs and Prepaid Items

Closing costs to the buyer on a new purchase can consist of the following charges: down payment, attorney fees, deed recording fees, property survey, funding fee or up front mortgage insurance premium, per diem mortgage interest, escrow impounds for insurance and property tax and any loan origination fees. Because the first mortgage payment isn't due until the second month after closing, the escrow amount at closing will include any money due that first subsequent month. Remember, if a borrower closes on February 15, the first mortgage payment is not due until April 1. You always skip a month between closing and the time the first payment is due, but the money still has to be collected that month for property taxes and insurance.

Closing costs to the seller include the unpaid loan balance plus pro-rated mortgage interest for the number of days in the month that the seller owns the property, not including the day of closing (per purchase contract).

Insurance

Typically, the lender requires the first year of the various types of homeowner's insurance (hazard, flood, wind) policies and first year's mortgage insurance premium to be paid outside of closing and effective on the settlement date or to be paid at closing.

Escrow Cushion

The Real Estate Settlement Procedures Act allows the lender to collect an additional 2 months of escrow payments to act as a cushion. This ensures that if the borrowers are late with their payments, the bills are still paid. Therefore, the charges at closing may include additional charges for this cushion.

Refinances

For refinances, the situation is a little different since insurance policies are already in effect, but the lenders still want a year paid in advance. To calculate the amount of an insurance escrow payment for a refinance, take the number of months the current annual policy has been in effect and add a two-month cushion to that. So, if the original policy went into effect in July, and the refinance is closing 5 years later in September, the escrow is for August, September + 2 months cushion. If the original policy went into effect in July, and they are closing the refinance in February, then there are 7 months (July - February) + 2 months cushion premium due.

(See the following escrow table.)

Hazard/Flood Months of Required Escrow
(Refinances Only)
Original Closing Month

New Closing Month	Jan	Feb	March	April	May	June	July	Aug	Sept	Oct	Nov	Dec
Jan	2	13	12	11	10	9	8	7	6	5	4	3
Feb	3	2	13	12	11	10	9	8	7	6	5	4
March	4	3	2	13	12	11	10	9	8	7	6	5
April	5	4	3	2	13	12	11	10	9	8	7	6
May	6	5	4	3	2	13	12	11	10	9	8	7
June	7	6	5	4	3	2	13	12	11	10	9	8
July	8	7	6	5	4	3	2	13	12	11	10	9
August	9	8	7	6	5	4	3	2	13	12	11	10
Sept	10	9	8	7	6	5	4	3	2	13	12	11
Oct	11	10	9	8	7	6	5	4	3	2	13	12
Nov	12	11	10	9	8	7	6	5	4	3	2	13
Dec	13	12	11	10	9	8	7	6	5	4	3	2

Answers to Sample Problems

1-1	5.125		
1-2	8 5/8		
1-3	11 3/4		
2-1	$3,000		
2-2	$3,750		
3-1	July 1		
3-2	$248.29		
4-1	80%	$20,000	$20,000 or 20%
4-2	90.9%		
4-3	$180,000	$20,000	95%
5-1	$54		
5-2	$48		
6-1	28%	32%	Yes
6-2	$3,194.44		
7-1	$4,333.33		
7-2	$2,405		
8-1	$970.84		

Important Points to Remember

1.   Each discount point and each origination point cost 1% of the loan amount.
2.   Discount points are a one-time closing cost usually paid by the borrower.
3.   Discount points are paid to the lender for lowering the interest rate, and origination points are paid to the loan originator as a fee for service.
4.   Mortgage interest is paid in arrears.
5.   Prorated mortgage interest, paid by the borrower at closing = ((loan amount x interest rate)/365 days) x number of days left in month including closing day.
6.   The first mortgage payment due date always skips one calendar month.
7.   The Loan-to-Value Ratio (LTV) = loan amount/appraisal value or purchase price, whichever is less.
8.   Late fees are due after the 15th of the month.
9.   FHA, USDA and VA late fees are 4% and conventional mortgages are 5% of P&I.
10.   The Housing Expense Ratio = PITI/Gross Monthly Income. Fannie Mae requires a maximum of 28% and FHA is 31 %. The VA does not consider it.
11.   The Total Debt to Income Ratio = PITI + other monthly debt/Gross Monthly Income.
12.   For standard qualification purposes, Fannie Mae requires a maximum Total Debt to Income Ratio of 36% for manually underwritten loans and 50% for DU loans, FHA is 43% and VA is 41%. Qualified Mortgage maximum is 43%.
13.   Gross Monthly Income = Annual Income/12.
14.   Gross Monthly Income = (Weekly Income x 52)/12.
15.   Gross Monthly Income = (Hourly rate x weekly hours x 52)/12.
16.   To calculate the amount of an insurance escrow payment for a refinance take the number of months the current annual policy has been in effect and add a two-month cushion to that.

Exam

1.   What is the cost of 2 3/4 discount points on a $450,000 loan?
   A. $1,237.50
   B. $3,375.00
   C. $12,375.00
   D. $13,750.00

2.   There are 10 days left in the month when the loan closes. The purchase price is $325,000 and the loan amount is $280,000 at 6.75% interest. How much interest does the borrower owe for the remainder of that month?
   A. $517.81
   B. $601.03
   C. $720.15
   D. $813.22

3.   The purchase price is $300,000; the appraisal value is $290,000, and the LTV is 80%. What is the loan amount?
   A. $220,000
   B. $232,000
   C. $240,000
   D. $248,000

4.   The monthly PITI is $1000, and the gross monthly income is $5000. According to standard Fannie Mae guidelines, what is the Housing Expense ratio?
   A.   5%
   B.   20%
   C.   36%
   D.   50%

5.   An employee works 40 hours a week at $12.50 per hour. What is his gross monthly income?
   A. $2,000.00
   B. $2,166.67
   C. $2,245.78
   D. $2,400.00

6.   The borrower's October mortgage payment has not yet been received on October 17. He has a $175,000 VA loan; monthly P&I is $1280; annual PMI is $1,800; annual hazard insurance is $2,400, and annual property taxes are $3,550. What is the late charge?
   A. $42.20
   B. $48.00
   C. $51.20
   D. $64.30

7.   A property originally closed in November, 2012. A refinance of that property is closing in March, 2013. How many months of hazard insurance will be collected at closing?

A.   3
B.   5
C.   6
D.   7

Answer Key

1. C
2. A
3. B
4. B
5. B
6. C
7. C

6

The Loan Application

Working with loan applicants isn't particularly difficult; however, the successful loan originator needs to know the right questions to ask and be comfortable asking them. This takes practice since most new loan originators have no prior experience discussing income and debt with a stranger. But, stick with it because it gets easier over time.

I.   Overview

An individual who is new to financing might be feeling overwhelmed at this point, and that is completely understandable. Earlier chapters in this text explained the difference between a note and a mortgage, FHA, VA and conventional mortgages, lots of different loan products (fixed rate, ARM, reverse mortgages, etc.), mortgage insurance, tax and hazard insurance escrow impounds, and the laws that regulate the industry.

In Chapter 1 of this book, there is an extensive discussion of disclosures which is relatively clear-cut if a borrower takes the time to fill out a loan application, and the loan is funded. But what happens if someone reaches you by phone and starts asking questions? Is this an application? Do you have to give them any disclosures? The answer is ... it depends on the way you answer them.

According to the Equal Credit Opportunity Act, an inquiry is a discussion about available loan products and financing terms. **A pre-qualification request is an inquiry and not an application** and doesn't result in a loan originator's approval or denial of a loan; therefore, no disclosures are needed. Pre-qualification letters are non-binding and usually state something to the effect that it appears the individual would qualify for a loan of X dollars based on a cursory review.

On the other hand, if a creditor analyzes a prospective borrower's **pre-approval request** and denies the loan due to a bankruptcy on the credit report, this has to be considered as an application and an adverse action notice must be delivered. However, if the lender chooses to write a pre-approval letter, stating the loan amount, interest rate, product type, term and expiration date, this is a legally binding commitment. If there is a property address, a Loan Estimate is definitely triggered. If there is no property address, company policy determines whether or not a Loan Estimate is delivered. To further complicate things, the RESPA Special Information booklet, mortgage servicing disclosure and a list of housing counseling agencies only need to be delivered after the creditor receives the application AND the additional qualifying financial documents.

An inquiry becomes a loan application (either verbally or in writing) when it includes all six of the following items:

- Consumer name.

- Consumer social security number.

- Consumer monthly income.

- Property address with zip code.

- Estimated value of the property.

- Estimated amount of mortgage loan sought.

For ECOA purposes, an inquiry also becomes an application that requires an adverse action notice if the lender denies the loan, regardless of how much information has been received.

Disclosures can be delivered in one of four ways:

- Face-to-face.

- Electronically.

- Standard mail.

- Overnight delivery.

The rest of this chapter covers some of the "mechanics" of the loan originator's daily routine. There's a lot to it; but, if you break it down into steps, it's not quite so daunting:

- Interview the applicant. Find out if he plans to live in the house or if it's an investment property; ask how long he plans to keep the property; determine if he is a veteran, and whether or not there are multiple borrowers. After that, you tell him what kind of documentation you need from him and advise him to have a home inspection.

- Complete the loan application.

- "Pull" the credit report. This helps loan originators decide what lender to use and what the best product is for their borrowers. If the credit is very bad, they may use a lender who specializes in these types of borrowers. If the credit is very good, there may be products available to them that aren't available to other borrowers.

- Calculate the debt-to-income ratios to see if the borrowers qualify. Maybe they need to pay off some credit cards to lower their amount of debt before the application is submitted to a lender.

- Gather all the documentation together, have them sign all necessary forms and distribute all required disclosures and booklets to them. Submit the package to the chosen lender's underwriter.

The remainder of the book makes frequent references to Fannie Mae. Fannie Mae was created as a government agency in 1938 and later become a public company listed on the New York Stock Exchange. Its purpose is to buy mortgages and notes from the primary lenders so that money remains in circulation; the lender loans the money to a consumer, and Fannie Mae buys the mortgage and note so that the lender now has more money to loan. (The secondary mortgage market will be discussed in more detail in the following chapter.) Fannie Mae is the largest institutional buyer of conventional mortgages in the secondary mortgage market, and therefore, it has a lot of clout. Fannie Mae establishes the standards for residential loans, and if the lenders want to sell their loans to Fannie Mae, they follow the standards. If the borrowers qualify for Fannie Mae approval, they get more favorable interest rates.

II.   Interview

Interviews can be done in person or over the telephone, and the purpose is to help consumers chose a product which is best for them. As a loan originator, you may realize by the end of the interview that you can't help them because they have unrealistic expectations, they tell you that they have a horrendous credit history or a variety of other factors. If that's the case, thank them for thinking of you and move on to your next applicant.

However, if you broker loans for a wide variety of lenders, some of whom specialize in "difficult" cases, you may be able to proceed and find a suitable product for your client. Talk to them and find out what type of loan it is (new purchase for a primary residence, second home or investment property or a refinance); how long they plan to keep the property; how much money they plan to put down, and the sales price of the property if it is a new purchase. Do they already know the type of mortgage they want (fixed rate or ARM)? If not, explain the loan types and help them decide.

This initial interview may indicate that they can't get approved under the current conditions but perhaps you can offer some suggestions, such as:

- Making a larger down payment.

- Using a co-borrower (with a good credit score) to increase qualifying income.

- Paying off some existing credit balances.

- Procuring a gift from an approved donor to finance the down payment.

- Working for another year. (Need a 2-year work history).

- Waiting longer after a bankruptcy, foreclosure or short sale.

- Establishing a credit history, if they always pay cash for everything.

- Saving enough money for the down payment, closing costs and for two months of mortgage payments after the closing.

- Contacting creditors to clear up any credit report discrepancies that are lowering the score.

In other cases, it looks like the borrower will be approved, but they feel that the mortgage payment is too high. You might want to:

- Lower the interest rate (which may reduce your commission).

- Suggest they purchase discount points to lower the rate.

- Recommend a larger down payment if they have the funds.

- Perhaps switch from an ARM to a fixed rate (or vice versa) and see if interest rates are lower.

- Suggest a 30-year loan if they are currently looking at 15 years.

- Possibly eliminate the property tax and insurance escrows if they qualify. In these cases, it is the borrower's responsibility to pay on time or risk foreclosure.

The following is a checklist of documents that you may need to collect from the applicant:

- **Contracts and Deeds**

  - Copy of the Sales and Purchase Contract (if new purchase).
  - Copy of the deed and note (if a refinance).

- **Employment Income**

  - 2 years of W-2s.
  - 30 days previous paystubs.
  - Self-employment income.
  - 2 years personal tax returns.
  - 2 years business tax returns.
  - Profit and Loss Statement (year-to-date report).
  - Balance Sheet (snapshot-in-time).

- **Retirement Income**

  - Social Security benefits statement.
  - Pension award letter from company.
  - Document other income with 1099s.

- **These must continue for 3 years past application date to be considered as income**

  - Alimony and child support income.
  - A copy of the divorce decree or separation agreement.
  - 12 months canceled checks of alimony or child support received.

- **Investment property income.**

  - A copy of the rental agreement.

- **Other Income**

  - 2 years documentation of commission, bonus or dividends income.
  - 2 years documentation of stocks and dividends paid.
  - 2 years of automobile income that was paid in excess of expenses.

- Disability benefits with a remaining term of at least 3 years.
- Unemployment benefits that are documented, have been received for the past 2 years and are likely to continue.

- **Assets**

  - 2 months bank/brokerage statements as check for "seasoned" funds. (Don't want an undisclosed "gift" deposited a week before closing to be used for closing costs.)

- **Identification**

  - Driver's license, passport or other government identification with a photograph as required by the USA Patriot Act.

- **Contact Information**

  - Name and phone number of real estate agent.
  - Name and phone number of hazard insurance company.
  - Name and phone number of title company.
  - Name and phone number for homeowners or condo associations.

- **Address and Employment History**

  - 2 years of residential addresses.
  - 2 years of employment history.

III.   Loan Application (1003)

The 1003 includes signature lines for the applicant to indicate whether the application is for joint or individual credit. This information is found at the top of the first page.

Once the loan originator enters some basic information such as the type of loan, name, social security number, address and employment history, he needs to enter monthly gross net income and projected monthly housing expenses. The loan originator must adhere to the following Fannie Mae standards.

Gross Monthly Income

If the applicant is an employee and gives the originator something other than gross monthly income (pay before any deductions), the following calculations must be used to derive a monthly wage:

Annual income divided by 12

Weekly income x 52 divided by 12

Hourly rate x weekly hours x 52 divided by 12

The guidelines for inclusion of income are as follows:

- Employment income must be verifiable for the past 2 tax years; 2 years of W-2s will suffice. Any source of income that isn't verifiable isn't acceptable to the lender.

- Commission, overtime, bonus, part-time, interest and dividend income must be averaged over 2 years.

- Automobile allowances must be documented over the past 2 years.

- Retirement and pension income must continue for 3 years beyond the application date in order to be included.

- Receipt of alimony or child support payments must continue for 3 years beyond the application date in order to be included.

- Disability benefits with a remaining term of at least 3 years.

- Unemployment benefits that are documented, received for the past 2 years and are likely to continue.

- 75 % of rental income from an investment property can be included; rent from boarders in the primary residence or second home may not be included.

The applicant will most likely be required to sign one or two IRS forms: an IRS 4506-T (Request for Transcript of Tax Return) and/or an IRS 8821 (Tax Information Authorization) so that the lender can verify their income.

Projected Monthly Housing Expenses

The projected monthly housing expense is the estimate of the combined monthly housing expenses for the new property. Insurance can include hazard, wind, flood and mortgage insurance (PMI or MIP).

Liabilities

When the borrower's credit report includes any revolving charge account with an outstanding balance that suggests that more than ten payments remain to be paid, the lender always must consider the payment on the account as part of the borrower's recurring monthly debt obligations. This applies even if the loan application indicates that the debt will be paid off at (or prior to) loan closing. Installment debt with ten or fewer monthly payments remaining also may be considered as a recurring debt obligation if it significantly affects the borrower's ability to meet his or her credit obligations. If the credit report doesn't show a required minimum payment amount, the lender should use an amount equal to five percent of the outstanding balance.

All installment debt that has more than 10 monthly payments remaining and is not secured by a financial asset (student loans, automobile loans, and home equity loans) should be included in the calculation of the borrower's monthly debt obligations. However, the loan originator should also include any installment debt with ten or fewer monthly payments remaining if it significantly affects the borrower's ability to meet his credit obligations.

Student loans with deferred payments must also be considered as a monthly debt. If no monthly payment is stated on the credit report, the loan originator should obtain a copy of the borrower's original payment agreement and use that amount to include in the calculation of the total monthly debt obligation.

Because the expiration of a lease agreement for rental housing or an automobile typically leads to either a new lease agreement, the buyout of the existing lease, or the purchase of a new vehicle or house, Fannie Mae requires that lease payments always be considered a recurring monthly debt obligation, regardless of the number of months remaining on the lease.

When the borrower owns mortgaged real estate (other than investment properties), the full mortgage payment (principal, interest, taxes, and insurance) that the borrower is obligated to pay is considered as part of the borrower's recurring monthly debt obligations.

Payments for alimony or child support must continue for 10 months beyond the application date in order to be included.

Reserves

Any bank or brokerage account that is to be used for qualifying purposes should be entered here with the name of the institution, the account number and the value of the account. At a minimum, the total of the accounts should equal closing costs and 2 months of mortgage PITI payments for conventional loans. The actual required amount of funds available for future PITI payments depends on the borrower's qualifications, type of loan, type of property and individual lender requirements. In general:

- **Conventional Loans**

  - Primary residence - 2 months (could be as high as 6 months).

  - Vacation homes - 3-4 months.

  - Investment property - 6 months.

- **VA Loans**

  - No reserves for 1-2 units.

  - 3-4 units - 6 months.

- **FHA Loans**

  - No reserves for 1-2 units.

  - 3-4 units - 3 months.

Acceptable source of funds include:

- Savings and Brokerage Accounts.

- Vested portion of retirement accounts.

- Vested portion of life insurance policy.

- Business accounts.

Unacceptable funds include:

- Undocumented funds.

- Non-vested portion of retirement accounts.

- Non-vested portion of life insurance policies.

MISCELLANEOUS	DEBT	INCOME
2 year home addresses	Alimony & child support payments that continue for more than 10 months	Bonuses, commissions, overtime and dividends averaged over 2 years
2 year employment history	Installment charge accounts with more than 10 payments left	Receipt of alimony and child support that is expected to continue for at least 3 years
2 months bank statements	5 % of credit card balance if there is no monthly minimum payment	Disability benefits with a remaining term of at least 3 years
2 months liquid reserves	Always count auto lease no matter how many months are left	Unemployment benefits that have been received for 2 years and are expected to continue
30 day pay stub	Always count deferred student loans	75 % of rental income
2 year W-2s		Retirement and pension income that is expected to continue for 3 or more years
Profit and Loss Statement if self-employed		
Balance Sheet if self-employed		
2 year business tax returns if self employed		

IV.   Refinancing

According to the Truth-in-Lending Act, the term refinance applies to the satisfaction of an existing obligation and its replacement by a new obligation. All the new-purchase disclosure requirements also apply to a refinance.

Motivations

Homeowners consider refinancing in a number of circumstances including falling interest rates; to shorten the loan term in order to build up equity faster; to lengthen the loan term and lower the monthly mortgage payment; to convert an adjustable-rate mortgage to a fixed rate and to take equity out of the home.

Cash-Out

A cash-out refinance occurs when a homeowner refinances for a larger mortgage than his current loan balance. The homeowner can receive part of the difference between the two amounts. For example, suppose a home has a $100,000 loan balance, and the property appraises for $200,000. If the lender allows an 80 percent cash-out, the borrower walks away with approximately $60,000 ($200,000 times .80 minus $100,000 minus closing costs) in tax-free money. The monthly mortgage payment is probably much larger now, but a smart and lucky investor can turn that $60,000 windfall into a fortune.

Qualifications

The borrower typically needs to qualify for a refinance in much the same way as for a purchase loan. Credit, debt and income are still important factors. If the property has depreciated in value and appraises for less than the current mortgage balance, the borrower may not be able to refinance.

FHA's Streamline Refinance Program

If the current mortgage is an FHA loan, and the borrower is current on the past three months of mortgage payments, an FHA Streamline Refinance is a likely choice. There is no verification of employment, income, debt or credit score with this program. The FHA believes that past payment history is sufficient proof of the borrower's ability and intent to pay the mortgage on time. In addition, an appraisal is not required, and funding is based on the original purchase price. This is a great option for borrowers who owe more on the mortgage than the current value of the home and are unable to obtain a conventional refinance. Cash-out refinances aren't allowed in this program.

Junior Mortgage Liens

The date and time of recording determine the position of the mortgage lien and indicate the order in which loans are paid off. The first loan recorded is less risky for the lender because it will get a least a partial payment during a foreclosure or short sale. However, the equity line of credit lender may not get anything since that is a junior lien, which is only paid after the senior lien.

When a borrower refinances the primary senior mortgage, the original lien is satisfied, removed from the property, and a new mortgage lien is recorded. Junior lien holders (equity lines of credit and second mortgages) need to agree to allow the new mortgage lien to assume the senior position (resubordination) because the junior lien has the legal right to move into the senior position. Alternatively, the junior liens are paid off. If neither of these circumstances occurs, the refinance is not likely to happen. The primary mortgage lender won't agree to assume the risk associated with a lower lien position.

Right of Rescission

Most refinancing loans are subject to the Right of Rescission rule that gives the borrower the right to cancel the loan within three business days after signing the closing documents. The loan isn't funded until this "cooling-off" period expires.

V.   Locking a Rate

A lock, which is also called a rate lock or rate commitment, is a lender's promise to hold a certain interest rate and a certain number of points for the borrower, usually for a specified period of time, while the loan application is processed. If the borrowers choose to allow the interest rate to float, they run the risk of being in a situation where interest rates are rising, and they end up no longer qualifying for the loan. In that case, they have to find a different product or put down a larger down payment. Each lock-in agreement must be in writing and must contain:

- Expiration date of the lock-in, if any.

- Interest rate locked in, if any.

- Discount points locked in, if any.

- Commitment fee locked in, if any.

- Lock-in fee, if any.

Lock-in agreements received by a mortgage lender by mail or through a broker must be signed by the mortgage lender in order to become effective. The borrower can cancel the agreement at any time prior to the lender sending the signed agreement back to the borrower or his mortgage company. If a borrower does elect to cancel the agreement, the lender must promptly refund any paid lock-in fee.

VI.   Credit Reports

The three national credit repositories are Equifax, Experian and TransUnion, and Fannie Mae requests that mortgage lenders obtain credit reports for all borrowers from at least two of the sites. Canceled checks for rent and utilities payments may be used in some cases for individuals who don't have a credit history.

Public Records

The report contains credit information as well as public record information such as bankruptcy, foreclosure and perhaps evictions for each locality in which the borrower has resided during the most recent two-year period. Bankruptcy is kept in the file for 10 years, but the other public data is removed after 7 years. Fannie Mae only requires a seven-year review.

Alterations

Don't ever try to alter a credit report using white-out or similar material. If you submit this to a lender, you may find yourself facing fraud charges. The credit report must include the full name, address, and telephone number of the reporting agency, as well as the names of the national repositories that the agency used to provide information for the report.

Content

The credit report must indicate the dates that accounts were last updated with the creditors. Each account with a balance must have been checked with the creditor within 90 days from the date of the credit report. All inquiries that were made in the previous 90 days must be shown on the report.

For each debt listed, the credit report must provide the creditor's name, the date the account was opened, the amount of the highest credit, the current status of the account, the required payment amount, the unpaid balance, and a payment history.

Timeframes

Credit documents must be no more than 120 days old on the date the note is signed. This includes new construction.

Credit Scores

The FICO credit score developed by Fair Isaac Corporation is the one most commonly used in the industry. Individuals are graded based on their credit payment history and their amount of total available credit. For example, it's better for your score to use 25 percent of a $20,000 credit line than to use 50 percent of that limit. Lenders generally want to see three lines of credit. If you interview someone who is thinking about buying a house and brags that he doesn't use credit cards, you should advise him to get three cards; use them and pay them off in full each month. FICO credit scores range from 300-850; higher scores are better than lower ones.

Representative Credit Score

Fannie Mae recommends that a lender obtain a minimum of two credit scores for every borrower. This enables the lender to select a single applicable score for underwriting each borrower; use the lower score when two credit scores are obtained or the middle score when three credit scores are obtained.

When there is only one borrower, the single applicable score used to underwrite that borrower is the "representative" credit score for the mortgage. If more than one individual is applying for the same mortgage, the lender should determine the single applicable credit score for each individual borrower and select the lowest applicable score from the group as the "representative" credit score for the mortgage. The "representative" credit score for the mortgage should be used to underwrite and evaluate the comprehensive risk for the mortgage application.

VII.   Fannie Mae Guidelines

If lenders want to sell their loans to Fannie Mae, they have to follow the guidelines. Lenders can have more stringent underwriting criteria, but not less.

First-Time Homebuyer

A first-time homebuyer is someone who is purchasing an owner-occupied primary residence and who has not had an ownership interest in a residential property for the past three years, unless he or she is a displaced homemaker or single parent that qualifies as an exception. If there is more than one applicant, only one of the applicants has to qualify as a first-time homebuyer. The lender may have special programs or down payment assistance available for these individuals.

Eligibility

Four years is generally the minimum time required by Fannie Mae between a bankruptcy discharge or short sale and filing a new mortgage loan application. (If the bankruptcy had documented extenuating circumstances, then only two years is required.) It is seven years following a foreclosure or three years with extenuating circumstances.

The borrower should be a natural person. A mortgage is not eligible for purchase by Fannie Mae if the borrower is a corporation, partnership, or real estate syndication. There is no maximum age limit for a borrower.

The property consists of 1-4 units, and the borrower must usually hold title in fee simple. Fannie Mae requires borrowers to have a social security number or Individual Taxpayer Identification Number.

Co-signers

A guarantor or co-signer doesn't have an ownership interest in the security property but signs the mortgage note. This individual has a joint liability for the note with the borrower who is the owner of the note.

Self-Employed

Twenty-five percent of ownership in a business is required for an individual to be considered self-employed. Verification of income requires two years of personal and business income tax returns. A year-to-date Profit and Loss Statement and a Balance Sheet may also be required. A Profit and Loss Statement summarizes the company's assets and liabilities over a range of time and a balance sheet depicts the company's book value at a single moment in time. It's a snapshot of value.

Escrows

First mortgages generally must provide for the deposit of escrow funds to pay as they come due – taxes, ground rents, premiums for hazard insurance and flood insurance. The lender may waive the escrow deposit account requirement of an individual first mortgage as long as the standard escrow provision remains in the mortgage documents. When the lender waives this requirement,

Fannie Mae retains the right to enforce the requirement if the borrower fails to act responsibly. In some states, escrow funds are called impound funds.

Verification

In addition to reviewing documents supplied by a borrower, a loan originator will have the borrower sign consent forms that allow the loan originator (or loan processor) to validate the information with a financial institution and employer. These forms include:

- Verification of Deposit (VOD) - Fannie Mae 1006

- Verification of Employment (VOE) - Fannie Mae 1005. They may follow this up with a phone call.

A borrower's payment history on previous mortgages or rent must be verified for 12 months. Fannie Mae will accept a standard mortgage verification or loan payment history from the mortgage servicer or the borrower's canceled checks for the last 12 months or the borrower's year-end mortgage account statement provided it includes a payment receipt history.

Credit Card Charges

Fannie Mae permits the cost for application "lock-in" fees to be charged to the borrower's credit card as long as the total amount of such charges does not exceed one percent of the mortgage amount. The actual cost of a credit report or an appraisal — up to $500 — may be charged to the credit card (and does not have to be considered in the one-percent limitation).

Financing Limitations

When the mortgage that is being delivered to Fannie Mae is secured by the borrower's principal residence, Fannie Mae doesn't impose any limitations on the number of mortgages that the borrower is currently financing. But, if the mortgage is secured by a second home or an investment property, the borrower may not own more than ten properties (including his principal residence) that are currently being financed. In this case, the investor can probably still get a loan, but the interest rate will likely be higher if it can't be sold to Fannie Mae.

Signatures

When a married applicant qualifies for a mortgage based on his own financial capacity (without any assets or income the spouse being taken into consideration), the spouse doesn't need to sign the note. However, Fannie Mae requires the spouse to sign the mortgage, and Fannie Mae must be guaranteed a lien position superior to the non-purchasing spouse.

A co-signer or co-borrower who doesn't take title to the property may still be required to sign the mortgage note. Fannie Mae will not accept a co-borrower's income for qualifying purposes, unless the co-borrower also signs the mortgage note.

A power of attorney authorization can be used to allow an alternate signer on any document except the loan application.

Late Fees

Fannie Mae requires that the note for a conventional first mortgage has a 5% late charge on any installment NOT received by the 15th day after it is due. The late charge is computed only on the P&I portion of the payment.

Maximum Term

The maximum term for a first mortgage is 30 years.

Balloon Mortgages

Most balloon mortgages are not purchased by Fannie Mae since they aren't Qualified Mortgages. Two exceptions are short-term bridge loans and originations by small lenders.

VIII.   Loan Processing

Loan processing may be done by the loan originator or a dedicated third party individual. Regardless of who does it, the loan processor validates the information in the application, collects all the verifying documents and packages everything together to send to the lender's underwriter.

Once all the necessary documents have been collected, the processor prepares the Fannie Mae 1008 Transmittal Summary, which is a form that summarizes the applicant's data, and places it as the first sheet of paper in the file. The entire package is then sent to the underwriter.

Important Points to Remember

1. Fannie Mae was created as a government agency in 1938 and later become a public company listed on the New York Stock Exchange.

2. The purpose of Fannie Mae is to buy mortgages and notes from the primary lenders so that money remains in circulation.

3. Fannie Mae is the largest institutional buyer of conventional mortgages in the secondary mortgage market.

4. Fannie Mae buys conventional, FHA and VA loans.

5. The interview process may uncover the fact that the applicant needs a co-borrower in order to qualify for the loan.

6. The loan originator collects all the information and sends the package to an underwriter.

7. Employment income must be verifiable for the past 2 tax years. Any source of income which is not verifiable is not acceptable to the lender.

8. Commission, Overtime, Bonus, Part-time, Interest and Dividend income must be averaged over 2 years.

9. Retirement and pension income must continue for 3 years beyond the application date in order to be included as income.

10. Receipt of alimony or child support payments must continue for 3 years beyond the application date in order to be included as income.

11. 75 % of rental income from an investment property can be included; rent from boarders in their primary residence or second home may not be included.

12. Generally, all installment debt that is not secured by a financial asset, including student loans, automobile loans, and home equity loans, should be considered as part of the borrower's recurring monthly debt obligations only if there are more than 10 monthly payments remaining to be paid on the account.

13. Any installment charge account with an outstanding balance that suggests that more than 10 payments remain to be paid must always be included.

14. If the credit report does not show a required minimum payment amount, the lender should use an amount equal to five percent of the outstanding balance.

15. Lease payments must always be considered a recurring monthly debt obligation, regardless of the number of months remaining on the lease.

16. Payment for alimony or child support must continue for 10 months beyond the application date in order to be included as debt.

17. Fannie Mae emphasizes the Total Obligations Ratio and is looking for a maximum value of 36% to qualify under the standards.

18. At a minimum, the borrower should have 2 months of mortgage payments after closing as reserves in a bank or brokerage account.

19. The applicant will most likely be required to sign one or two IRS forms: an IRS 4506-T (Request for Transcript of Tax Return) and/or an IRS 8821 (Tax Information Authorization) so that the lender can verify the income.

20. Applications can be taken face-to-face, over the phone, through the mail or over the Internet.

21. An applicant's interest rates can float or be locked-in.

22.   A rate lock is a lender promise to hold a certain interest rate and a certain number of points for the borrower, usually for a specified period of time, while the loan application is processed.

23.   Each lock-in agreement must be in writing and contain: expiration date of the lock, the interest rate, any discount points, any commitment fee and lock-in fee if these exist.

24.   The borrower may rescind any lock-in agreement until a written confirmation of the agreement has been signed by the lender and mailed to the borrower.

25.   Fannie Mae requires the lender to obtain a written credit report for each borrower on the loan application who has an individual credit record.

26.   The credit report must be based on data provided by the following national credit repositories—Equifax, Experian, or TransUnion.

27.   A traditional credit report must include both credit and public record information for each locality in which the borrower has resided during the most recent two-year period.

28.   Fannie Mae requires only a seven-year history to be reviewed for all credit and public record information.

29.   Bankruptcy information can be kept in the credit report for 10 years.

30.   Each account with a balance must have been checked with the creditor within 90 days of the date of the credit report. All inquiries that were made in the previous 90 days must be shown on the report.

31.   Credit documents must be no more than 120 days old on the date the note is signed. This includes new construction.

32.   FICO credit scores were developed by Fair Isaac Corporation.

33.   Fannie Mae recommends that a lender obtain a minimum of two credit scores for every borrower. If there are two scores, use the lower; if there are three scores, use the middle. This is the representative score for a single borrower.

34.   If more than one individual is applying for the same mortgage, the lender should determine the single applicable credit score for each individual borrower and then select the lowest applicable score from the group as the "representative" credit score for the mortgage.

35.   A first-time homebuyer is someone who is purchasing an owner-occupied primary residence and who has not had an ownership interest in an owner-occupied property for the past three years.

36.   Four years is generally the minimum time required by Fannie Mae between a bankruptcy discharge or short sale and filing a new mortgage loan application. This is seven years following a foreclosure.

37.   The borrower should be a natural person and not a corporation.

38.   There is no maximum age limit for a borrower.

39.   A guarantor or co-signer is a credit applicant who does not have an ownership interest in the security property, but who signs the mortgage note and thus has a joint liability for the note with the borrower who is the owner of the note.

40.   Fannie Mae requires a borrower to have a social security number or Individual Taxpayer Identification Number.

41.   25% of ownership in a business is required for an individual to be considered self-employed. Verification of income requires 2 years of personal and business income tax returns. A year-to-date Profit and Loss Statement and a Balance Sheet may also be required.

42. A Profit and Loss Statement summarizes the company's assets and liabilities over a range of time. A balance sheet depicts the company's book value at a single moment in time. It is a snapshot of value.

43. The maximum term for a Fannie Mae loan is 30 years.

44. Fannie Mae emphasizes the borrower's continuity of stable income vs. stability of employment.

45. A borrower's payment history on previous mortgages or rent must be verified for 12 months.

46. A borrower may charge $500 for an appraisal and up to 1% of the loan amount to his credit card to pay for lock-in fees.

47. When the mortgage that is being delivered to Fannie Mae is secured by the borrower's principal residence, Fannie Mae has no limitations on the number of mortgages that the borrower can currently be financing. But, if the mortgage is secured by a second home or an investment property, the borrower may not be financing more than ten properties.

48. When a married applicant qualifies for a mortgage based on his or her own financial capacity (without any assets or income of his or her spouse being taken into consideration), the spouse does not need to sign the note.

49. Fannie Mae requires the non-qualifying spouse to sign the mortgage or any other documentation required to evidence that the spouse is relinquishing all rights to the property.

50. Fannie Mae will not accept a co-borrower's income for qualifying purposes, unless the co-borrower also signs the mortgage note.

51. Fannie Mae requires that the note for a conventional first mortgage provides for the borrower to pay a 5% late charge on any installment not received by the 15th day after it is due. The late charge is computed only on the P&I portion of the payment.

52. Fannie Mae does not purchase most balloon mortgages (short-term bridge loan is one exception).

53. At the time of the loan application the lender normally requires the applicant to sign a form authorizing the lender to obtain verifications of bank balances (Fannie Mae 1006) and payroll information (Fannie Mae 1005).

54. The Fannie Mae 1008 Transmittal Summary is a form that summarizes the applicant's data and will usually be the top sheet in the loan package when it is sent to the underwriter.

55. An FHA Streamline Refinance doesn't require an appraisal, or income and credit verification.

56. A refinance is the satisfaction of an existing obligation and its replacement by a new obligation.

57. A power of attorney authorization can be used to allow an alternate signer on any document except the loan application.

58. Verbal or written receipt of the following 6 pieces of information constitutes a loan application which triggers disclosures: consumer name, consumer social security number, consumer monthly income, property address, estimated property value and estimated mortgage loan amount.

59. An inquiry also becomes an application that requires an adverse action notice if the lender denies the loan, regardless of how much information has been received.

60. Verification of Deposit (VOD) - Fannie Mae 1006.

61.   Verification of Employment (VOE) - Fannie Mae 1005

62.   Disclosure notices can be delivered face-to-face, electronically, mail or overnight delivery.

Exam

1.   How many years of home addresses are required on the typical loan application?
A.   1 year
B.   2 years
C.   3 years
D.   4 years

2.   How many years of employment history may be required on the loan application?
A.   1 year
B.   2 years
C.   3 years
D.   4 years

3.   Which of the following is **NOT** usually required by a loan applicant?
A.   Photo ID
B.   Personal references
C.   2 months of bank or brokerage statements
D.   30 days previous pay stub

4.   Commission, bonus or dividend income is usually averaged over:
A.   1 year
B.   2 years
C.   3 years
D.   4 years

5.   In order to be counted as income, retirement income must continue for how long after the loan application is signed?
A.   1 year
B.   2 years
C.   3 years
D.   4 years

6.   In order to be counted as income, alimony must continue for how long after the loan application is signed?
A.   1 year
B.   2 years
C.   3 years
D.   4 years

7.   If there is no minimum monthly credit card payment, what percent of the balance is used in the calculation of monthly debt?
A.   1%
B.   3%
C.   5%
D.   10%

8.   How many months must be left on a car lease payment in order to be included as a debt?
A.   More than 1 month
B.   More than 5 months
C.   More than 10 months
D.   Automobile lease payments are always included

9.   How many months must be left on an installment charge in order to be included as a debt?
A.   More than 1 month
B.   More than 3 months
C.   More than 5 months
D.   More than 10 months

10.   The Fannie Mae Total Obligations Ratio is:
A.   10%
B.   26%
C.   36%
D.   46%

11.   Payment for alimony must continue for how long after the application date in order to be included as a debt?
A.   1 month
B.   10 months
C.   2 years
D.   3 years

12.   A lock-in agreement does **NOT** include:
A.   Interest rate
B.   Expiration date
C.   Lock-in fee
D.   APR

13.   Which IRS form does a lender use to verify an applicant's income?
A.   2071
B.   321 - ML
C.   911 - R
D.   4506 - T

14.   Fannie Mae requires how many years of credit and public records review?
A.   1 year
B.   3 years
C.   5 years
D.   7 years

15. Bankruptcies can be kept on the credit report for a maximum of:
    A.   3 years
    B.   5 years
    C.   7 years
    D.   10 years

16. Credit reports for new construction cannot be older than:
    A.   30 days
    B.   90 days
    C.   120 days
    D.   180 days

17. FICO stands for:
    A.   Federal Interest Corporation
    B.   Fair Isaac Corporation
    C.   Freddie's Insurance Company
    D.   Fannie's International Credit organization

18. If two credit scores are obtained for a single borrower the representative score that is usually used is:
    A.   The higher score
    B.   The lower score
    C.   It doesn't matter
    D.   Whatever is the policy of the Mortgage Broker business

19. If three credit scores are obtained for a single borrower the representative score that is usually used is:
    A.   The higher score
    B.   The lower score
    C.   The middle score
    D.   Whatever is the policy of the Mortgage Broker business

20. The maximum age limit for a borrower is:
    A.   65
    B.   75
    C.   85
    D.   There is no maximum age limit

21. A guarantor or co-signer signs the:
    A.   Mortgage
    B.   Note
    C.   Deed
    D.   Mortgage and the note

22.   Which of the following is **NOT** a national credit repository?
          A.   Experian
          B.   Fannie Mae
          C.   TransUnion
          D.   Equifax

23.   What minimum percentage of ownership of a business is required for an individual to be considered self-employed?
          A.   10%
          B.   25%
          C.   50%
          D.   75%

24.   Which of the following is **NOT** an escrow impound?
          A.   Title insurance
          B.   Property insurance
          C.   Flood insurance
          D.   Hazard insurance

25.   Fannie Mae generally wants how many months of liquid financial reserves after closing?
          A.   1 month
          B.   2 months
          C.   3 months
          D.   4 months

26.   Fannie Mae requires a non-qualifying spouse whose income is not used in qualifying to sign the:
          A.   Mortgage
          B.   Note
          C.   Mortgage and the note
          D.   They are not required to sign anything

27.   A co-borrower whose income is used to qualify must sign the:
          A.   Mortgage
          B.   Note
          C.   Mortgage and the note
          D.   They are not required to sign anything

28.   If a mortgage is secured by the primary residence, Fannie Mae allows how many total properties to be financed?
          A.   No limit
          B.   3
          C.   5
          D.   10

29.   Which form is used to summarize the information in the loan package?
    A.   Fannie Mae 1006 – Verification of Deposit
    B.   Fannie Mae 1005 – Verification of Employment
    C.   Fannie Mae 1008 – Transmittal Summary
    D.   Fannie Mae 1003 – Loan Application

30.   Which form is used to verify employment information?
    A.   Fannie Mae 1006 – Verification of Deposit
    B.   Fannie Mae 1005 – Verification of Employment
    C.   Fannie Mae 1008 – Transmittal Summary
    D.   Fannie Mae 1003 – Loan Application

31.   Which form is used to verify bank accounts?
    A.   Fannie Mae 1006 – Verification of Deposit
    B.   Fannie Mae 1005 – Verification of Employment
    C.   Fannie Mae 1008 – Transmittal Summary
    D.   Fannie Mae 1003 – Loan Application

32.   Which piece of information is NOT required in order to have a legal loan application?
    A.   Consumer name
    B.   Consumer monthly income
    C.   Estimated property value
    D.   Consumer signature

Answer Key

1.	B	26.	A
2.	B	27.	C
3.	B	28.	A
4.	B	29.	C
5.	C	30.	B
6.	C	31.	A
7.	C	32.	D
8.	D		
9.	D		
10.	C		
11.	B		
12.	D		
13.	D		
14.	D		
15.	D		
16.	C		
17.	B		
18.	B		
19.	C		
20.	D		
21.	B		
22.	B		
23.	B		
24.	A		
25.	B		

7

Underwriting, Closing and the Secondary Market

Once the loan processor sends the completed loan application and supporting documents to the lender's underwriter, a number of activities are set in motion. The lender orders the appraisal that is reviewed by the underwriter, and the title company conducts a lien search on the property. If there are no issues with the appraisal or title, the title company orders a property survey, and the borrower is advised to contact an insurance company and arrange for coverage to start on the day of closing. After the closing, the lender normally assigns the mortgage and note to an investor who operates within the secondary mortgage market. Loan originators should make a point of staying in touch with past borrowers, since happy customers are an excellent source of referrals.

I.   Evaluating the Borrower

The underwriter is responsible for evaluating both the risk of the borrower and the property risk, and he must ensure that adequate hazard and flood insurance is available to protect the security of the lender. To assess a borrower, the underwriter analyzes the credit score and reviews the credit history, financial resources and continuity of stable income. The underwriter also evaluates the factors that affect the borrower's credit standing, i.e., slow payments, repossessions, liens, judgments, bankruptcy and charge-offs.

The underwriter reviews the debt-to-income ratios to determine if the math was done correctly during the qualifying process. For Fannie Mae standard qualification, he will be looking for a maximum total obligations ratio of 36%. It's 41% for VA and 43% for FHA loans.

Assessing an individual's risk may be done manually or by automatic underwriting systems. Fannie Mae's automated underwriting system is known as Desktop Underwriter (DU). Desktop Underwriter is a flexible, automated underwriting system that analyzes salaried, commission and self-employed borrowers for their credit worthiness and their ability to repay the debt. The system electronically evaluates each individual loan application along with the appropriate credit report information and provides the lender with a recommendation as to whether or not the loan meets the Fannie Mae criteria for loan approval. This system can be used for conventional, FHA or VA mortgage loans.

Desktop Underwriter can make a recommendation to approve/eligible. This means that based on the data presented the loan meets Fannie Mae's credit risk and eligibility requirements. Other standard responses are: approve a mortgage, refer it or refer it with caution to the lender's underwriter. After considering these responses, the lender always makes the final decision as to whether the loan application is approved.

Freddie Mac, a competitor of Fannie Mae, has an automated underwriting system called Loan Prospector (LP) that is available for approved lenders. This system provides one of three responses to the lender: Approve, Refer or Caution. This system can be used for conventional, FHA or VA mortgage loans.

An underwriter that has received the (DE) "Direct Endorsement Underwriter" designation from the FHA is enabled to approve FHA residential loans for a lender and proceed to closing without prior approval for mortgage insurance (MIP) from the FHA. This is an extremely competitive advantage for the lender.

II.   Property Appraisals

To assess if the property is adequate security for the loan, the underwriter will look at the property appraisal report. Fannie Mae holds the lender responsible for the quality of the appraisal. The appraiser is paid a flat fee for the report, and not a fee based on the value of the property. The FHA requires appraisers to perform a limited home inspection report with the appraisal, and VA-approved appraisers operate on a rotation system controlled by the VA.

The Dodd-Frank Act prohibits lenders from influencing any residential property appraiser. Lenders can't have any direct or indirect financial interest in the appraisal company. This replaces a similar 2009 Home Valuation Code of Contact (HVCC) that was implemented for Fannie Mae loans. The new regulation applies to all residential loans including the ones that lenders keep in their own portfolios and don't sell.

The appraiser performs a number of tasks: he goes to the property; observes the neighborhood; enters the structure and notes the general condition and materials used; sketches the structure; measures the outside square footage of the property and researches other recently sold similar properties. All of these are important steps in determining market value, which is the most probable price that a property should bring in a competitive and open market during an arm's-length transaction. An appraisal on a property with 2-4 units is called a Small Residential Income Property Appraisal.

The property must have been appraised within the 12 months that precede the date of the note and mortgage. When an appraisal report will be more than four months old on the date of the note and mortgage, the appraiser must inspect the exterior of the property and review current market data to determine whether the property declined in value since the date of the original appraisal.

Highest and Best Use

Many factors can affect market value, but the primary consideration is the highest and best use of the property. The use must be legally permissible (zoned for the use), physically possible (soil must be able to support any new foundation; property must have adequate drainage, etc.) and financially feasible (the income from the property must cover the cost of improvements). The appraiser will look at best use as if vacant and as improved (structure on land). If there is a structure on the property does it make sense to tear it down and replace it with a structure of another type? These are not issues that are normally of much concern in residential property appraisals, but they do play a major role in non-residential transactions.

Principle of Substitution

The Principle of Substitution states that a knowledgeable consumer will pay no more money for a property than the cost of acquiring an equally desirable alternative property; this applies to all three of the following appraisal methods.

Appraisal Methods

There are three basic approaches to estimating property value: Sales Comparison Approach (residential homes and vacant land), Cost Approach (new construction and special-use properties) and the Income Capitalization Approach (income producing properties).

Sales Comparison (Market Data) Approach

In the Sales Comparison Approach, the appraiser researches a minimum of three closed sales that are similar in characteristics to the subject property (the property being appraised). Since the chances are slim that these comparable sales (comps) are identical to the subject property, the appraiser will most likely have to make adjustments for the major differences and derive a new estimated closing cost for the comparable; i.e., what would the comps sell for if they were more like the subject? Adjustments to sale price are made upward if the comparable is not as good as the subject on a particular feature. Suppose the comp has a dirt front yard and the subject property is professionally landscaped. The appraiser may add $10,000 to the actual sale price of the comparable for the purposes of his report. Adjustments to sale price are made downward if the comparable is better than the subject on a particular feature.

Fannie Mae guidelines limit net adjustments to 15% of the gross sale price. Gross adjustments (the total dollar amount regardless of positive or negative) are limited to 25% of gross sales price.

$$\text{Sales Price of Comparable} \quad + \text{ or } - \text{ Adjustments} \quad = \quad \text{Adjusted Sales Price}$$

Once the appraiser calculates the adjusted sales price for each comparable, he must rank how close each one resembles the subject. To do this, he assigns a weight to each comparable; the weights must add up to 1.00.

For example, suppose the first comparable is next door to the subject and has a one-car garage instead of the subject's two. The second comparable is five streets away in the same subdivision and has a one-car garage, better landscaping and is 100 sq. ft. smaller than the subject. The third comparable is in a similar neighborhood, has a two car garage and a pool (like the subject).

Multiply the adjusted sales price by the assigned weight and add the resulting calculated values. The market value calculation might look something like this:

Comparable	Adjusted Sales Price	Weight	Calculated Value
1	$150,000	.40	$60,000
2	$148,000	.35	$51,800
3	$155,000	.25	$38,750

	Subject Market Value		$150,550

In this approach, the closed sales are the most important although the appraiser may include active listings to better determine if a market is declining or appreciating in value. As you can see, this calculation is subjective and is the reason why two appraisal values for the same property may differ by tens of thousands of dollars.

Cost Approach

In the Cost Approach, the appraiser estimates the cost to reproduce or replace the structures as if they were new; he subtracts a value for depreciation because the structure is not new, and adds in the value of the land and improvements such as landscaping or a driveway.

Reproduction or   -   Depreciation   +   Site Value   =   Value of Subject Property
Replacement Costs
of Improvements

Depreciation is the loss in value of the property. There are three categories of residential depreciation:

- **Physical Deterioration** - caused by aging or poor upkeep.

- **Functional Obsolescence** - caused by a change in buyer's tastes.

- **Economic Obsolescence** - caused by a deteriorating neighborhood.

Appreciation is the increase in value of a property due to improving neighborhood, property improvements or overall rise in an area's market value.

Income Capitalization Approach

The Income Capitalization Approach is based on the yearly net operating income, or investment return, that a buyer expects from a property. The IRV formula is frequently used where:

I = annual net operating income

R = capitalization rate

V = property value

Given two of the variables, the third can be calculated:

$I = R \times V$

$V = I/R$

$R = I/V$

For example, if the net annual operating income (I) = $40,000, and the capitalization rate in the area (R) is 8%, then an estimate of the value of the property (V) = $40,000 /.08 = $500,000, which is a figure that can be used to help determine the value of the property.

Another example: if the offer price for a property (V) is $1,000,000, and the annual operating income (I) is $100,000, then the capitalization rate (R) = $100,000 / $1,000,000 = 10%.

If the investor wants a higher return on their investment (R), he must either pay less for the property (V) or increase the cash flow (I).

Final Reconciliation

Most appraisal reports require the use of at least two of these three appraisal methods (Sales Comparison, Cost and Income) to determine market value, and in an ideal world, all three of the approaches would result in the same market value for the property. However, the appraiser most likely has to reconcile the three values to arrive at one conclusive appraisal value. The Uniform Residential Appraisal Report (URAR), which is required by Fannie Mae, has space for the appraiser to enter a value for the subject using each of the three methods. The appraiser then explains which approach (and value) is most applicable to this particular subject.

Gross Rent Multiplier (GRM)

The GRM is an additional way to quickly determine a ballpark figure for the value of a property based on the average sale price and rents of the area's comparable properties.

> Market Value / Monthly Rent = Neighborhood Gross Rent Multiplier (GRM)

> Neighborhood GRM x Subject Monthly Rent = Subject Market Value

The first step is to calculate the GRM for the neighborhood by finding the average comparable sales price and divide that by the average monthly rent for the area.

> Comparable property sells for $120,000 / $1,200 average monthly rent = GRM of 100

Now, if the *subject* property has a monthly rent of $1,300:

100 GRM x $1,300 = $130,000 as a rough estimate of the value of the property.

Gross Income Multiplier (GIM)

The GIM is very similar to the GRM except that it uses _annual_ gross income that includes the rent and any other generated income including money from vending machines, washers and dryers, and parking.

Market Value / Annual Gross Income = GIM

Neighborhood GIM x Annual Income of Subject = Market Value

Completion Escrow Account

If minor repairs or construction that doesn't affect occupancy won't be completed until after the loan is funded, the lender may proceed with the closing. However, all parties must agree that the improvements will be finished within 180 days after the date of the mortgage note. The appraisal report must show both the cost of completing the postponed items and the "as completed" value of the property after completion of the postponed improvements although no dollar-for-dollar adjustments should be made. The cost of completing any minor improvements must not represent more than two percent of the "as completed" appraised value of the property.

The lender establishes a "completion escrow" for the postponed improvements, by withholding from the purchase proceeds funds equal to at least 120 percent of the estimated cost for completing the improvements. However, if the contractor or builder offers a guaranteed "fixed price" contract for completion of the improvements, the funds in the "completion escrow" only need to equal the full amount of the contract price.

The lender and the borrower enter into an escrow agreement that determines how the lender will manage and disburse funds from the escrow account. Once a certificate of completion is obtained, the lender releases the final draw from the escrow account.

III.   Loan Commitment or Denial

On receipt of the appraisal, the underwriter evaluates the report and other physical aspects of the property to determine if any adverse conditions exist that might increase the risk for the lender; i.e., is the property in a flood zone. The underwriter reviews the appraisal to determine acceptability as to age of property, roof condition, location and road accessibility.

Once the underwriter reviews all the documents, the lender makes the decision to issue a loan commitment, a conditional loan commitment, to deny the loan, or to make a counter-offer that alters the borrower's original requested terms.

Commitment Letter

A commitment letter from the lender states the terms of the loan (amount, interest rate, term and expiration date for acceptance) and is a legally binding, written promise from the lender to the mortgagor. The disclosure of the APR is not required in a loan commitment. The borrower must accept the offer within the specified time limit and when this occurs, the contract is formed. A lender issues a standby commitment to a borrower only under certain conditions. The most common example would be a commitment to repay a construction lender in the event a permanent mortgage lender can't be found. A commitment fee is normally charged since the borrower retains the option of closing the loan or allowing the commitment to lapse.

Contingencies

Usually, however, there are outstanding contingencies that must be satisfied before the loan commitment can be issued, so the lender issues a conditional approval instead of a loan commitment. These contingencies may include: failure to receive credit approval from the PMI carrier; unpaid taxes appearing on the title search; evidence of payoff of certain debts of the borrower such as delinquent taxes, judgments, charge-offs and tax liens; receipt of proper hazard insurance or flood insurance; survey reveals a curable/incurable encroachment, and repairs to a property required prior to closing. Some lenders may request a wood destroying organism (WDO) inspection and may not close without a WDO clearance letter that states there is no current active infestation. Any treatment is completed prior to closing. The underwriter monitors the situation and when all the documents are received and everything else is in order, the underwriter recommends that the lender issues the commitment letter.

Counter-Offers

If the lender can't satisfy the borrower's original request, it may issue a counter-offer that changes one or more of the requested terms of the loan. The borrower has 90 days to accept a counter-offer unless it has been accompanied by an adverse action notice.

Adverse Action

Adverse action occurs when a lender denies an applicant's request for a loan, or when the borrower rejects a counter-offer. The lender is required to notify the applicant of the reasons why the loan was denied within 30 days after receipt of the completed application. Providing adverse action notices is mandated by the Equal Credit Opportunity Act (Regulation B), and the law requires that at a minimum, the borrower is provided with the following information:

- Name, address, and telephone number of the consumer reporting agency.

- A statement that the consumer reporting agency did not make the decision and cannot provide the specific reasons why the action was taken.

- Information about the consumer's right to obtain copies of their report and to dispute information in the report. The telephone number provided must be a toll-free number if the credit report used in the adverse action was from a national reporting agency.

The Consumer Financial Protection Bureau handles all complaints about mortgage loan rejections and related adverse action notices.

IV.   Pre-Closing Procedures

Many steps, which require good communication between all the parties, have to be accomplished prior to closing. A closing agent is responsible for overseeing this process and is usually a representative from a title company, lender or lawyer's office. These tasks must be done in a timely manner so that the closing isn't delayed. The lender provides instructions to the closing agent to ensure that all the lender's required documentation has been collected and that its policies have been followed.

Property Inspections

Property inspections are usually completed before the appraisal. A knowledgeable home inspector checks for plumbing leaks, electrical problems, foundation weakness and climbs up and inspects the condition of the roof. Many home inspectors do a preliminary test for termites by knocking on the eaves. They'll recommend an exterminator if they see evidence of infestation. These exterminators treat the cause and issue a Wood Destroying Organism (WDO) clearance letter.

Some lenders routinely require WDO clearance letters prior to closing. It's possible that the lender may require that any property repairs be completed prior to closing.

Title Insurance

The primary purpose of title insurance is to protect the owner and the mortgagee from financial loss caused by past defects of record in the title. What are defects? Things such as undiscovered liens, forged documents, fraud, undisclosed heirs and mistakes in recording legal documents are all factors that can appear after the closing and may affect the borrower's right to own the property free and clear. Title insurance will pay the liens as well as the court costs.

The American Land Title Association (ALTA), founded in 1907, is the national trade association and voice of the abstract and title insurance industry, and it standardized the forms used by the title companies.

Before the title insurance policy is issued, the title company will do a search of public records to try and uncover any impediments. For example, involuntary liens such as mechanic's liens or tax liens will have to be paid before title can be transferred. A voluntary lien, such as a mortgage, will be paid off at closing or assumed. The loan originator orders this preliminary title report once the appraisal has been completed.

A title insurance binder is a commitment that lists all the known defects. The insurance policy itself is issued after closing, and the title insurance premium is a one-time closing cost to either the seller or borrower. Who pays is a matter of convention and negotiation.

There are two types of title insurance policies:

- Mortgagor (homeowner).

- Mortgagee (lender).

The following chart summarizes the differences between the two.

	MORTGAGOR	MORTGAGEE
Coverage	Full Purchase Price	Loan Amount
Required	No	Yes, by lenders
Transferable	No	Yes

Either the seller or buyer (or both) will pay for the policies; the lender *requires* it, but does not *pay* for it. As a general rule of thumb, whoever pays for the title insurance picks the title company. Under RESPA, the seller may not require the purchaser, as a condition of the sale, to purchase title insurance from any particular title company.

The mortgagee's policy is required by the lenders while the mortgagor's policy is optional. Issuing the two policies at the same time is called simultaneous issue.

The homeowner's policy is not transferable. That means that when title transfers to a new owner, that new owner has the option of purchasing his own insurance, or doing without. The mortgagee policy, however, is transferable. A lender frequently assigns mortgages and notes to an investor in the secondary mortgage market. In this case, the title insurance is transferable, and the policy passes to the new assignee.

Survey

Lenders or title insurance companies often require a property survey. A survey is a drawing of the property showing the perimeter boundaries and marking the location of the house and other improvements.

All setback lines are indicated. Setbacks designate how close to the edges of the property a structure may be built. They are defined in building codes, deed restrictions, special covenants and zoning regulations. For example, there may be a 20-foot setback line from the front property line facing the street. This prevents houses from being built right at the street and makes for more attractive front yards. Surveys may indicate the elevation of the property above sea level and this can dramatically affect any flood insurance premiums.

An encumbrance is a claim or limitation on a property's use and includes setbacks, encroachments, easements and restrictive covenants.

The survey shows any encroachments on the property. For example, if the neighbor's fence or garage is on the seller's property, this is probably an unacceptable impediment that must be resolved before closing. Two of the most common unacceptable title impediments are unpaid real estate taxes and survey exceptions. Acceptable encroachments are removable hedges and fences, and public utility easements. Surveys are certified to lenders, title insurers and buyers.

An easement is a right of way that gives someone other than the property owner the right to be on the land for a specific purpose. Utility easements are common in residential areas; they allow the utility workers to access property on an as-needed basis.

A deed restriction or restrictive covenant limits the future use of property. A restrictive covenant affects the entire subdivision while a deed restriction affects one particular lot. For example, a restrictive covenant may state that all structures built on the property must have a minimum area of 2500 square feet. This prevents small houses from being built on large lots and should help maintain property values. Deed restrictions run with the land (can't be removed) and are usually put there by an owner. Restrictions have to stay on the deed but can't be enforced if they are discriminatory.

Legal Description

There are four methods of property description ranging from very primitive determination of boundary lines to more sophisticated methods. The crudest of these approaches is the Monument

Method in which property lines are delineated based on natural landmarks such as rivers, trees and boulders. It's obvious that these are subject to change over time.

The Government Land Survey Method was developed after the Revolutionary War and is based on a grid of intersecting lines that divide a state into townships, ranges and sections.

The Lot and Block Method is the most common and occurs after a subdivision is platted. A plat map is a recorded drawing showing all the blocks in a subdivision which have been subdivided into individual lots. The plat map may also indicate streets, green areas, utility lines, etc.

The Metes and Bounds Method is the most accurate and involves a surveyor measuring the distance (metes) and direction (bounds) between the metal plaques in the corners of the property. The direction of a boundary line is expressed using compass directions and is given in degrees, minutes and seconds. Distances are measured in feet. The surveyor must start and end his measurements at the same place (the Point of Beginning (POB)).

Hazard Insurance

Property insurance for home mortgages protects against loss or damage from fire and other hazards such as windstorm, hurricane and hail damage, and it is required by the lenders. If the mortgage is to be sold to Fannie Mae, the maximum allowable deductible for a first mortgage is 5 % of the face amount of the policy.

The hazard insurance premium is paid a year in advance and must be effective on the day of closing. The closing agent verifies that the policy meets the lender's requirements and has the correct owner's name and address, and the correct form of loss payable clause to protect the mortgagee. FHA's standard mortgage document requires that the mortgagee be named as a loss payee on the hazard insurance policy. This helps to ensure that the property owner will use the money for repairs and not simply pocket the cash.

Flood Insurance

The National Flood Insurance Program (NFIP) provides for low cost subsidized federal flood insurance for properties that are located in flood hazard areas. In these cases, the insurance is required, and lenders are responsible for determining whether the property is located in a hazard area. Personal belongings are not required to be insured. Prior to the passage of this law, flood insurance was mostly unavailable or too expensive for the general public.

The Federal Emergency Management Agency (FEMA) administers the NFIP and produces Flood Insurance Rate Maps that indicate all the flood hazard areas in a community. There are 10 different flood-zone ratings that are based on the level of risk in each zone. The maximum coverage available for flood insurance through NFIP on a 1-4 family residential property is $250,000 on the dwelling and $100,000 on the contents. Flood insurance is based on the standard that a designated flood elevation has a 1% chance of flooding every year.

Flood insurance coverage is either 100 percent of the replacement cost of the building or the maximum insurance available through the NFI program or the unpaid balance of the mortgage, whichever is lowest.

A Flood Certification Fee is charged to the borrower at closing to cover the costs of determining whether the property is located in a flood zone.

Wind Insurance

High-risk areas may need a separate policy for wind insurance if they are going to be covered for hurricane damage. The homeowner's hazard insurance company will inform the borrower if this additional coverage is recommended. When a hazard insurance policy provides for a separate wind-loss deductible (either in the policy itself or in a separate endorsement), that deductible may be the higher of $2,000 or two percent of the face amount of the policy.

Force-Placed Insurance

Lenders can require borrowers to obtain certain types of insurance coverage, but they can't force the borrower to purchase a policy from a particular company. However, if the borrower refuses to obtain coverage or allows a policy to lapse, the lender has the right to pick a company and obtain insurance. This is known as force-placed insurance, and the premiums may be higher on these policies than for a company that was selected by the borrower.

Payoff Letter

If the borrower is not assuming a loan and is obtaining his own financing, then the seller's loan is paid off at the closing. The closing agent sends an estoppel letter to the lender requesting the payoff amount. Because mortgage interest is paid in arrears, the seller has not yet paid that month's mortgage interest. Therefore, the lender will calculate the month's pro-rated mortgage interest and add that to the loan balance. The payoff letter (estoppel certificate) indicates the principal balance and the daily interest to be charged through the date of closing.

V.   Preparation and Explanation of Closing Documents

The closing agent must be knowledgeable about all aspects of the loan transaction and be confident and able to answer the questions that are raised. This can be a stressful time for both the buyer and the seller. People aren't paid unless the deal closes, so it's vital that the closer is a calm professional.

Settlement Statement

The HUD-1 Settlement Statement/Closing Disclosure is required to be used as the standard real estate settlement form in all transactions in the United States that involve federally-related mortgage loans and have closing costs for the borrower. The HUD-1/Closing Disclosure itemizes all cash coming in and all disbursements, including charges that have been paid outside of closing (POC), such as an advance one-year hazard insurance policy payment; it summarizes all the financial details for both the buyer and the seller. RESPA states the borrower should be given a copy of the HUD-1 at least one day prior to settlement; however, in actuality, changes can continue up until the last minute. The Closing Disclosure must be delivered three business days before closing. Everyone involved in the deal should review the form for accuracy. The closing agent prepares all the documents involved in the closing, which are reviewed by the underwriter.

Charges

The closing agent must be able to explain and calculate all the charges on the HUD-1/Closing Disclosure because questions can arise at the closing table. Typical charges include:

- Real estate transfer taxes.

- Appraisal.

- Pro-rated mortgage interest payments.

- Lender fees.

- Origination fees.

- Property survey.

- Title search.

- Title policy.

- Credit report charge.

Signatures

The agent must be sure which parties need to sign the note and the mortgage. This is because an individual's name may be on the deed and mortgage but not on the note (if his income was not used for qualifying purposes, there is no reason for him to sign the note). Likewise, his name may only be on the note and not on the deed or mortgage if he's a co-signer with no ownership interest in the property.

First Payment

The new owners will be told that their first mortgage payment will not be due until the second month following the closing, and they may be told that their mortgage interest is paid in arrears. So, for example, if the day of closing was January 15, the first mortgage payment is due March 1.

Adjustable-Rate Mortgage

If the financing involves an adjustable-rate mortgage, the closer should be able to explain the caps and adjustment periods to the borrower. He may go further and explain how the index can vary and is outside the control of the lender. The borrower should have already received the "Consumer Handbook on Adjustable-Rate Mortgages" or a similar guide.

Completion Escrow

If there are repairs that need to be done on the home after the closing, the agent will explain to the borrower that an escrow account will be established for at least 120% of the cost of the repairs. The lender monitors the work to ensure that the repairs are completed.

Closing Sequence

After the buyers and sellers sign the closing documents and the lender funds the loan, the real estate transfer taxes are paid, and the mortgage or deed of trust is recorded in the county where the property is located.

Right of Rescission

Normally, when a loan is not a refinance, funding and closing occur simultaneously in most states. However, under certain circumstances, funding is delayed for three business days after closing and the receipt by the borrower of the right of rescission notice. This three business day interval is a cooling-off period, which allows the borrower to cancel the transaction. It's called the rescission period and applies to refinance loans, home improvement loans and second mortgage loans for primary residences only. The right of rescission does not apply to a first mortgage purchase of a property.

Completed Mortgage Loan File

The loan originator must keep a record of all documents related to a transaction including:

- Loan application.

- Real estate contract.

- Loan Estimate.

- Federal Disclosures.

- Adverse action notice, if applicable.

- Rate-lock agreement.

- Signed Closing Disclosure.

VI.   Methods of Funding the Loan

There are usually two types of funds required during the financing of a property acquisition. The borrower needs money for the down payment and closing costs, and the lender needs a source of cash to fund the loan.

Borrower Funding

As a general rule, lenders want the borrower to have documented seasoned funds, and many title companies only accept wire transfers to pay for closing costs. After the closing documents are signed, the lender wires the borrower's loan funds to the closing agent's account.

Generally, "sweat" equity is not an acceptable source of funds for the down payment, closing costs or financial reserves because it is often difficult to accurately assess the contributory value of the work.

Typical sources of funds are checking and savings accounts, vested retirement funds, trust accounts, stocks, bonds, mutual funds and personal gifts (under certain circumstances).

The proceeds from the sale of a currently owned home are a common and acceptable source for the down payment and closing costs on a new house; however, the lender does require a copy of the closing statement. Cash-on-hand is generally not an acceptable source of funds for the down payment under Fannie Mae guidelines.

Lender Funding

Direct investor funding occurs when the lender deals directly with the borrower without any middlemen.

Table funding occurs when the lender uses borrowed money from an investor to fund the loan, and after closing, the mortgage and note are immediately assigned to that investor. Funds for closing are usually wired to the closing agent's escrow account.

Warehouse funding occurs when a lender obtains funds for closing from a line of credit extended by a commercial bank. The lender pledges the mortgage and note as collateral for the funds, and the bank will hold them for a short period of time until they are sold to a permanent investor.

VII.   Mortgage Servicing

Mortgage servicing provides a predictable and steady income stream, and the servicing rights are frequently sold. When this happens, the mortgage payment must be sent to a new mailing address. Loan originators should be aware that when they broker a loan, there is no limit on the number of times the loan servicer may actually change after the loan is closed.

Because borrowers may have already sent their payment out to the original servicer before they get their notice of change, lenders are prohibited from charging a late fee for the first 60 days after a change in service if the borrower sent the payment on-time to the wrong servicer. The terms of the loan do not change when servicers change.

The loan servicer oversees the escrow impounds, pays the appropriate bills and administers the late fee charges.

Mortgage payments are due on the 1st of each month and are late after the 15th. The payment usually consists of principal, interest and escrow funds for property tax and hazard insurance. The payment may also include the monthly private mortgage insurance, if applicable. Late fees are assessed as a percentage of the over-due principal & interest payment: 4% for VA and FHA loans and 5% for conventional first mortgages.

The loan servicing company performs an annual escrow analysis and informs the borrower of any shortfall or refunds any excess. The servicer uses the funds in the borrower's escrow deposit account to pay taxes and other related charges before any penalty date. Whenever funds are available, the servicer must pay these expenses early enough to take advantage of the maximum allowable discounts.

VIII.   Secondary Mortgage Market

The lender who loans the money to the borrower is participating in the primary mortgage market. That lender, however, will most likely sell that mortgage and note to an investor in the secondary mortgage market. A secondary market is said to exist whenever primary investors and lenders buy and sell existing mortgages. Lenders who provide loans directly to borrowers make mortgage loans in the primary market. The secondary mortgage market consists of non-institutional investors who are acting as individuals and large institutional investors such as commercial banks, savings associations, pension funds, life insurance companies and government agencies. They buy the note and mortgage to have a positive income stream that's generated by the monthly mortgage payments. In return, the lenders' supply of money is replenished from the proceeds of the sale, so they now have more money to make more loans.

Assignments

When a lender sells a mortgage loan to an investor, this is called an assignment of mortgage and is recorded to give constructive notice of the transfer of ownership of the mortgage and note. The assignor can keep the servicing rights (selling a loan with servicing retained), or it can sell the servicing rights along with the mortgage and note to the assignee (selling a loan with servicing released). The terms of the loan don't change when servicing rights are transferred. When a loan is sold under a buy-back arrangement, the note is endorsed with recourse by the seller. Whenever a mortgage is assigned from one lender to another, the promissory note is also endorsed in favor of the new investor.

Fannie Mae

In 1938, the United States federal government established the Federal National Mortgage Association (FNMA), now known as Fannie Mae, to buy FHA loans. Fannie Mae became a share-holder owned corporation in 1968 and is now the largest institutional investor in the secondary mortgage market. It purchases FHA, VA, and conventional mortgages.

Freddie Mac

In 1970, the Federal Home Loan Mortgage Corporation (Freddie Mac) was chartered by the federal government to buy mortgages originated by Savings Associations. It became a share-holder company in 1989. It's now a competitor of Fannie Mae and it purchases FHA, VA, and conventional mortgages.

Government Conservators

After the financial meltdown of 2007-2008, auditors uncovered irregularities in the practices of Fannie Mae and Freddie Mac. Consequently, Congress passed the Housing and Economic Recovery Act on July 30, 2008, which allowed the U.S. government to take control of the two institutions. On September 9, 2008, the newly-created Federal Housing Finance Agency (FHFA) was appointed Conservator of Fannie and Freddie to save them from spiraling further downward and destroying the U.S. housing market. This effort was successful, and both entities are once again profitable. Shareholders are upset because dividends are paid only on the preferred shares owned by the U.S. Treasury. Talks continue in Congress about the need to replace or merge the two corporations. Stay tuned.

Ginnie Mae

The Government National Mortgage Association (Ginnie Mae) was formed in 1968 and is a wholly owned government corporation within the United States Department of Housing and Urban Development (HUD). Ginnie Mae does not buy or sell loans. The primary function of Ginnie Mae is to issue, administer and guarantee Ginnie Mae mortgage-backed securities that are based on FHA, VA and USDA loans. These securities can be purchased on the open market by individual investors. They are identified as "Security Holders" in the Ginnie Mae transaction and Ginnie Mae guarantees the payment of the principal and interest each month to the security holders. Ginnie Maes are the most popular type of mortgage-backed securities because they are guaranteed by the U.S. government and usually provide higher returns than U.S. Treasury bills. Individual banks and mortgage companies are the issuers of mortgage-backed securities. The issuer is responsible for paying the security holder each month, whether the payment is collected or not.

Standards

Because Fannie Mae and Freddie Mac buy so many loans in the secondary market, they can set the standards for the loans they will purchase. That's why the loan processing documents are called the Fannie Mae 1006 or the Fannie Mae 1008. Even the loan application is known as the Fannie Mae 1003. Because there is standardization in the way the information is gathered and the debt ratios calculated, there is lower risk, which leads to lower interest rates for Fannie Mae and Freddie Mac loans. However, they don't purchase all loans, as demonstrated in the next section.

Fannie Mae Criteria

Fannie Mae will purchase mortgages secured by residential properties in urban, suburban or rural areas. Fannie Mae doesn't purchase mortgages on agricultural-type properties such as farms, orchards, ranches or on undeveloped land or land development-type properties.

Fannie Mae won't purchase a mortgage that has an unacceptable title impediment. Unacceptable title impediments are delinquent or unpaid real estate taxes and/or survey exceptions. Some minor survey exceptions are acceptable, such as: public utility easements and/or encroachments by hedges or removable fences.

Fannie Mae will purchase first mortgages that are secured by residential properties for use by 1 to 4 families. The occupancy may be that of a principal residence, a second home or investment property.

Fannie Mae will purchase a conventional mortgage on a manufactured home. The manufactured home must be a one-family dwelling that is legally classified as real property. The unit must be built on a permanent chassis and attached to a permanent foundation system. Any towing hitch, wheels or axles must be removed, and the dwelling must assume the characteristics of site-built housing. The land on which the manufactured home is situated must be owned by the borrower, unless the home is located in a cooperative or condominium project. Mortgages on manufactured homes located on leasehold estates are not eligible for purchase by Fannie Mae.

Fannie Mae generally requires Private Mortgage Insurance (PMI) on all conventional first mortgage loans with a loan-to-value ratio greater than 80%. PMI insures the mortgage amount in excess of 80% against the borrower's default. PMI is of value to the borrower because it enables the lender to make a loan to the borrower with a smaller down payment.

Important Points to Remember

1.   The underwriter is responsible for evaluating both the risk of the borrower and the property.
2.   Assessing an individual's risk may be done manually or by automatic underwriting systems.
3.   Fannie Mae's automated underwriting system is known as Desktop Underwriter (DU).
4.   Freddie Mac's automated underwriting system is known as Loan Prospector (LP).
5.   These systems can be used for conventional, FHA and VA loans.
6.   The lender always makes the final decision to fund a loan.
7.   An underwriter that has received the (DE) "Direct Endorsement Underwriter" designation from the FHA is enabled to approve FHA residential loans for a lender and proceed to closing without prior approval for mortgage insurance (MIP) from the FHA.
8.   Fannie Mae holds the lender responsible for the quality of the appraisal.
9.   The appraiser must be paid a flat fee, and not a fee based on the appraisal value.
10.   An appraisal is valid for 12 months. It must be re-certified if the appraisal will be 4 months old or more at closing.
11.   Market value is the most probable price a property will bring in a fair and open market.
12.   To determine the highest and best use of a property, the use must be legally permissible, physically possible and financially feasible.
13.   Three approaches to estimating property value are: Sales Comparison Approach (residential and vacant land), Cost Approach (new construction and special-use properties) and Income Capitalization Approach (income producing properties).
14.   The Principle of Substitution states that a knowledgeable consumer will pay no more for a property than the cost of acquiring an equally desirable alternative property.
15.   In the Sales Comparison Approach, the appraiser researches a minimum of three closed sales that are similar in characteristics to the subject property.
16.   Adjustments to sale price are made upward if the comparable is not as good as the subject on a particular feature. Adjustments to sale price are made downward if the comparable is better than the subject on a particular feature.
17.   Sales Price of Comparables +- Adjustments = Value of Subject Property
18.   Closed sales are the most important type of comparable in the Sales Comparison Approach.
19.   In the Cost Approach, the appraiser estimates the cost to reproduce or replace the structures as if they were new; subtracts a value for depreciation because the structure is not new and adds in the value of the land and any improvements.

Reproduction or   -   Depreciation   +   Site Value = Value of Subject Property
Replacement Costs
of Improvements

20.   Depreciation is the loss in property value.
21.   Appreciation is an increase in property value.
22.   Functional obsolescence is caused by a change in buyer's tastes.
23.   Economic obsolescence is caused by a deteriorating neighborhood.
24.   Physical deterioration is caused by aging or poor upkeep.

25. The appraiser reconciles the values arrived at by all three methods to derive one final estimate of value.

26. The IRV formula is a good starting point in valuing an income producing property. $I = R \times V$ where I is the annual net operating income, V = value of the property, and R is the capitalization rate. If you know two, you can solve for the third variable.

27. If the investor wants a higher return on their investment (cap rate R), he must either pay less for the property (value V) or increase the cash flow (annual net operating income I).

28. Gross Rent Multiplier (GRM) is another method used to value an income producing property based on its sale price and projected rental income as compared to other similar properties in the subject's neighborhood.

29. Market Value/Monthly Rent = Neighborhood Gross Rent Multiplier.

30. Neighborhood Gross Rent Multiplier x Subject Monthly Rent = Subject Market Value.

31. Gross Income Multiplier (GIM) is similar to the GRM except the calculation is based on annual rental income plus other additional income generated by the property. This additional income may come from vending machines, laundry facilities and parking.

32. The lender must establish a completion escrow for the postponed improvements, by withholding from the purchase proceeds funds equal to at least 120 percent of the estimated cost for completing the improvements.

33. A commitment letter from the lender states the terms of the loan (amount, interest rate and expiration date for acceptance) and is a legally binding, written promise from the lender to the mortgagor.

34. Adverse action occurs when a lender denies an applicant's request for a loan or when the borrower rejects a counter-offer.

35. The Consumer Financial Protection Bureau handles all complaints about mortgage loan rejections and related adverse action notices.

36. Title insurance protects the homeowner (mortgagor) and the lender (mortgagee) against defects that occurred in the past: undisclosed liens, heirs, fraudulent documents, etc.

37. The mortgagor title insurance policy is based on full purchase price, is not transferable and is optional.

38. The mortgagee title insurance policy is based on loan amount, is transferable and is required by the lender.

39. A title commitment binder is issued after a search of the public records.

40. Either the seller or buyer (or both) will pay for the title policies.

41. Issuing both the homeowner's and the lender's title policy at the same time is called simultaneous issue.

42. A property survey is required and is certified to lenders, title insurers and buyers.

43. An easement is a right of way that gives someone other than the property owner the right to be on the land for a specific purpose.

44. A deed restriction or restrictive covenant limits the future use of a property.

45. There are four types of legal descriptions for properties: the Monument Method, the Government Land Survey Method, Lot and Block Method, and the Metes and Bounds Method.

46. The Lot and Block Method is the most common.

47. The Metes and Bounds Method is the most accurate.

48. In the Metes and Bounds Method the surveyor must start and end his measurements at the Point of Beginning (POB).

49. The hazard insurance premium is paid a year in advance and must be effective on the day of closing.

50. A Flood Certification Fee is charged to the borrower at closing to cover the costs of determining whether or not the property is in a flood zone.

51. FEMA maintains the flood maps.

52. Closing agent sends an estoppel letter to the seller's lender requesting the payoff amount.

53. The HUD-1 or Closing Disclosure is required to be used as the standard real estate settlement form in all residential transactions in the United States which involve federally related mortgage loans.

54. RESPA states the borrower should be given a copy of the HUD-1 at least one day prior to settlement. The Closing Disclosure is given 3 business days prior to settlement.

55. Fannie Mae requires guaranteed funds such as a cashier's check from a bank or reputable financial institution to pay the closing costs; personal checks are not acceptable.

56. Sweat equity is not an acceptable source of funds.

57. The proceeds from the sale of a currently owned home are a common and acceptable source for the down payment and closing costs on a new house. A photocopy of the HUD-1/Closing Disclosure should be submitted to the lender.

58. Direct investor funding occurs when the lender deals directly with the borrower without any middlemen.

59. Table funding occurs when the lender uses borrowed money from an investor to fund the loan. After closing, the mortgage and note are immediately assigned to that investor.

60. Warehouse funding occurs when a lender obtains funds for closing from a line of credit extended by a commercial bank.

61. Mortgage payments are due on the 1st of each month and are late after the 15th.

62. The payment usually consists of principal, interest and escrow funds for property tax and hazard insurance. The payment may also include the monthly private mortgage insurance, if applicable.

63. Late fees are assessed as a percentage of the over-due Principal & Interest payment: 4% for VA and FHA loans and 5% for conventional first mortgages.

64. The servicer must analyze the escrow account each year and estimate the funds needed for the upcoming year.

65. The terms of the loan do not change when the servicer changes.

66. Lenders are prohibited from charging a late fee for the first 60 days after a change in service if the borrower sent the payment on-time to the wrong servicer.

67. The lender who loans the money to the borrower is participating in the primary mortgage market.

68. A mortgage and note may be sold to an investor in the secondary mortgage market.

69. When a lender sells a mortgage loan to another lender this is called an assignment of mortgage.

70. The assignor is the seller of the mortgage and note.

71. The assignee receives the mortgage and the note.

72. The assignor can keep the servicing rights (selling a loan with servicing retained).

73. The assignor can sell the servicing rights along with the mortgage and note to the assignee (selling a loan with servicing released).

74. The Federal National Mortgage Association (FNMA) is now known as Fannie Mae.

75. Fannie Mae is the largest institutional investor in the secondary mortgage market. It purchases FHA, VA and conventional loans from commercial banks.

76.   The Federal Home Loan Mortgage Corporation (Freddie Mac) was chartered by the federal government to buy mortgages originated by Savings Associations.

77.   The Government National Mortgage Association (Ginnie Mae) is a wholly owned government corporation within the United States Department of Housing and Urban Development (HUD).

78.   Ginnie Mae does not buy or sell loans or issue mortgage-backed securities (MBS).

79.   Ginnie Mae guarantees investors the timely payment of principal and interest on MBS backed by federally insured or guaranteed loans — mainly loans insured by the Federal Housing Administration (FHA) or guaranteed by the Department of Veteran Affairs (VA).

80.   Fannie Mae will purchase mortgages secured by residential properties in urban, suburban or rural areas.

81.   Fannie Mae does NOT purchase mortgages on agricultural-type properties such as farms, orchards, ranches or on undeveloped land or land development-type properties.

82.   Fannie Mae will NOT purchase a mortgage that has an unacceptable title impediment.

83.   Fannie Mae will purchase first mortgages that are secured by residential properties for use by 1 to 4 families. The occupancy may be that of a principal residence, a second home or investment property.

84.   Fannie Mae will purchase a conventional mortgage on a manufactured home. The manufactured home must be a one-family dwelling that is legally classified as real property.

85.   Fannie Mae guidelines for appraisals using the Sales Comparison Method, limit net adjustments to 15% of the gross sale price. Gross adjustments (the total dollar amount regardless of positive or negative) are limited to 25% of gross sales price.

86.   The Uniform Residential Appraisal Report (URAR) is the Fannie Mae appraisal form.

87.   The Housing and Economic Recovery Act allowed the Federal Housing Finance Agency to take control of Fannie Mae and Freddie Mac in 2008.

88.   An encumbrance is a claim or limitation on a property's use and includes setbacks, encroachments, easements and restrictive covenants.

89.   An appraisal on a property with 2-4 units is called a Small Residential Income Property Appraisal.

90.   The maximum coverage available for flood insurance through NFIP on a 1-4 family residential property is $250,000 on the dwelling and $100,000 on the contents. Flood insurance is based on the standard that a designated flood elevation has a 1% chance of flooding every year.

Exam

1. Fannie Mae's automated underwriting system is known as:
    A.   Loan Prospector (LP)
    B.   Desktop Underwriter (DU)
    C.   Daniel's Underwriting System (DUS)
    D.   Limited Portfolio (LP)

2. Freddie Mac's automated underwriting system is known as:
    A.   Loan Prospector (LP)
    B.   Desktop Underwriter (DU)
    C.   Daniel's Underwriting System (DUS)
    D.   Limited Portfolio (LP)

3. Who makes the final decision as to whether a loan will be funded?
    A.   The automated underwriting system
    B.   The lender
    C.   The real estate agent
    D.   The closing agent

4. The automated underwriting systems can **NOT** be used for what types of loans?
    A.   FHA
    B.   VA
    C.   Conventional
    D.   Jumbo

5. Who does Fannie Mae hold responsible for the quality of the appraisal?
    A.   Appraiser
    B.   Real estate agent
    C.   Lender
    D.   Title company

6. An appraisal must be re-certified if it is older than:
    A.   1 month
    B.   4 months
    C.   6 months
    D.   12 months

7. The most probable price which a property should bring in an open market is:
    A.   Median price
    B.   Market value
    C.   Going rate
    D.   Insurance value

8.   The highest and best use of the property is **NOT**:
      A.   Legally permissible
      B.   Physically possible
      C.   Financially feasible
      D.   Based on possible future zoning changes

9.   The appraisal approach that best applies to residential property is:
      A.   Sales Comparison Approach
      B.   Cost Approach
      C.   Residential Approach
      D.   Income Capitalization Approach

10.   The appraisal approach that best applies to vacant land is:
      A.   Sales Comparison Approach
      B.   Cost Approach
      C.   Residential Approach
      D.   Income Capitalization Approach

11.   The appraisal approach that best applies to a school is:
      A.   Sales Comparison Approach
      B.   Cost Approach
      C.   Residential Approach
      D.   Income Capitalization Approach

12.   What is the minimum number of closed sales comparables that can be used in the Sales Comparison Approach?
      A.   1
      B.   3
      C.   6
      D.   8

13.   What is the most important type of comparable used in the Sales Comparison Approach?
      A.   Active
      B.   Pending
      C.   Closed
      D.   Expired

14.   An office building has an annual net operating income of $50,000 and a capitalization rate of 9%. What is its value?
      A. $200,000
      B. $435,890
      C. $555,555
      D. $672,154

15. The method used to value income producing properties based on the rental incomes and sales prices of similar properties is called the:
    A.   GRM
    B.   BBQ
    C.   CDR
    D.   TRA

16. In a completion escrow account, what is the minimum estimated repair cost held in trust by the lender?
    A.   50 %
    B.   90 %
    C.   120 %
    D.   200 %

17. A legally binding letter from the lender to the mortgagor stating the terms of the loan is:
    A.   A commitment letter
    B.   A letter of intent
    C.   A discover notice
    D.   A conditional letter

18. Who handles complaints regarding mortgage loan rejections?
    A.   FCC
    B.   FHA
    C.   VA
    D.   CFPB

19. All of the following apply to a mortgagor's title insurance policy **EXCEPT**:
    A.   It is for the amount of the purchase price
    B.   It is based on loan amount
    C.   It is optional
    D.   It is not transferable

20. Surveys are **NOT** certified to:
    A.   Lenders
    B.   Title insurers
    C.   Buyers
    D.   Real estate broker

21. What gives someone other than the owner the right to be on the property for a specific purpose?
    A.   Mechanic's lien
    B.   Easement
    C.   Encumbrance
    D.   Declaration of intention

22.   What is a clause in the deed that limits the future use of a property?
    A.   Deed restriction
    B.   Encumbrance
    C.   Title lien
    D.   Owner's privilege

23.   The most common type of legal description for residential subdivisions is:
    A.   The monument method
    B.   Lot and block
    C.   Metes and bounds
    D.   Government land survey method

24.   The most accurate type of legal description for residential subdivisions is:
    A.   The monument method
    B.   Lot and block
    C.   Metes and bounds
    D.   Government land survey method

25.   A fee charged to the borrower for determining whether or not a property was in a flood zone is a:
    A.   Mapper fee
    B.   Flood certification fee
    C.   FEMA fee
    D.   Reviewer fee

26.   Which form is used as the standard settlement form?
    A.   HUD-1/Closing Disclosure
    B.   FHA Closing Statement
    C.   U.S.A. Settlement Statement
    D.   National Closing Statement

27.   The day of closing is May 15. When is the first loan payment due?
    A.   June 1
    B.   July 1
    C.   August 1
    D.   June 16

28.   Which of the following is an acceptable source of funds at closing?
    A.   Sweat equity
    B.   Cash on hand
    C.   Personal check
    D.   Wire transfer

29.   What type of funding occurs when a lender obtains funds from a line of credit at a commercial bank?
    A.   Credit lending
    B.   Table funding
    C.   Warehouse funding
    D.   Temporary funding

30.   The late fee for FHA and VA loans is:
    A.   3 % of principal and interest
    B.   4 % of principal and interest
    C.   5 % of principal and interest
    D.   10 % of principal and interest

31.   When a lender sells a mortgage loan to another lender this is called:
    A.   Assignment of mortgage
    B.   Note transfer
    C.   Vendor selling
    D.   Linking a mortgage

32.   When an assignor keeps the servicing rights this is known as:
    A.   Selling a loan with escrow impounds
    B.   Selling a loan with servicing released
    C.   Selling a loan with servicing retained
    D.   Selling a loan pro norma

33.   Ginnie Mae does:
    A.   Buy loans
    B.   Sell Loans
    C.   Fund loans
    D.   Guarantee loans

34.   Fannie Mae was established in:
    A.   1914
    B.   1938
    C.   1962
    D.   1980

35.   Fannie Mae will not purchase a mortgage secured by a:
    A.   Urban area residential property
    B.   Orchard
    C.   Rural area residential property
    D.   Suburban area residential property

36.   Which title insurance policy is transferable?
        A.   Mortgagor
        B.   Mortgagee
        C.   Restricted use
        D.   Conforming

37.   The title company considers unpaid property taxes to be an:
        A.   Encroachment
        B.   Encumbrance
        C.   Easement
        D.   Engress

38.   The principle of value that focuses on the most profitable, legal use to which a property can be put is:
        A.   Principle of Satisfaction
        B.   Principle of Substitution
        C.   Principle of Highest and Best Use
        D.   Principle of Conformity

39.   A Point of Beginning is used in what type of survey?
        A.   Government Land Survey
        B.   Plat Map
        C.   Metes and Bounds
        D.   Circle Grid

40.   A neighbor's fence that crosses over on to another's property is an example of an:
        A.   Encroachment
        B.   Encumbrance
        C.   Exculpation
        D.   Egress

41.   An outstanding claim on a property that limits the ability to sell the property is a:
        A.   Title defect
        B.   Subordination
        C.   Penalty
        D.   Fault fee

42.   The national trade association and voice of the abstract and title insurance industry is:
        A.   TICOA
        B.   ATC
        C.   ALTA
        D.   TITLE NOW

Answer Key

1.	B	26.	A
2.	A	27.	B
3.	B	28.	D
4.	D	29.	C
5.	C	30.	B
6.	B	31.	A
7.	B	32.	C
8.	D	33.	D
9.	A	34.	B
10.	A	35.	B
11.	B	36.	B
12.	B	37.	B
13.	C	38.	C
14.	C	39.	C
15.	A	40.	A
16.	C	41.	A
17.	A	42.	C
18.	D		
19.	B		
20.	D		
21.	B		
22.	A		
23.	B		
24.	C		
25.	B		

8

Ethics and Fraud

Webster's defines ethics as "a set of moral principles and the principles of conduct governing an individual or a group." Violations of sound ethical practices are not always illegal, but they can be. If an individual belongs to a professional organization that enforces a strict code of conduct, ethical violations may lead to fines and expulsion, but not jail time. For the national loan originator examination, you might be presented with a variety of situational problems and asked to choose if any ethical or legal constraints have been violated. Take your time and read the question as many times as you need. Put yourself in the subject's place and ask, "Would I want to be treated that way?" If the answer is no, then your commonsense moral compass is probably leading you to the right answer.

The rest of this chapter contains links to websites containing Frequently Asked Questions (FAQ). You are strongly advised to read this material although some of it may not reflect changes implemented by the Consumer Financial Protection Board (CFPB). You should also review Chapter 1 that discusses federal consumer protection laws.

In particular, the HUD FAQs haven't been updated since its enforcement power for RESPA, Gramm-Leach-Bliley Act, TILA and ECOA transferred to CFPB in 2011. Although some regulatory details may have changed, the underlying ethical issues presented in the questions remain the same. The federal laws discussed in this text generally apply only to residential, financed loans and not to cash or commercial transactions.

I.   Real Estate Settlement Procedures Act (RESPA)

Many of the RESPA issues concern violations of unearned referral fees. Recently, there has been an increase of Affiliated Business Arrangements in which one parent company offers multiple settlement services under its umbrella. Unfortunately, there has also been a subsequent increase in related federal lawsuits. If a mortgage company has an affiliated real estate company, the mortgage side of the business can't pay for cruises to the top producing real estate agents that refer them the most business. Ethical quandaries arise when you have knowledge of violations and don't report them, or you fail to do anything to try and change the practice.

Another prominent example is title companies that bring in real estate companies as partners and pay them a share of the profits. The government considers many of these arrangements to be merely kickbacks because the closings are not held in the real estate offices, and the only added benefit they are bringing to the table is the referral of business. Some of the main issues that RESPA addresses include:

- **Kickbacks and Referrals**

  Nothing of value can be given in exchange for the referral of business among settlement providers with the exception of one real estate brokerage firm paying a referral fee to another real estate company.

- **Estimate of Closing Costs**

- **Closing Statement**

Frequently Asked Questions and Answers

Website: http://portal.hud.gov/hudportal/HUD?src=/program_offices/housing/ramh/res/resconsu

Website: http://www.fdic.gov/regulations/laws/rules/6500-2900.html

II.   Gramm-Leach-Bliley Act

The Gramm-Leach-Bliley Act applies to financial institutions that give loans or financial advice. This includes mortgage brokers, lenders, tax preparers and debt collectors. The law distinguishes between a consumer and a customer. A consumer is an individual who obtains assistance from a financial institution for personal, family or household reasons (check cashing). A customer is a consumer with a continuing relationship with a financial institution (mortgage loan). The key points of this law include:

- **Financial Privacy Rule**

  Individuals must receive a Privacy Notice that provides them with the opportunity to opt-out of different types of information sharing. A privacy notice is automatically sent to *customers* once a year. *Consumers* only receive a Privacy Notice and the right to opt-out if the information is shared with a nonaffiliated company. Notices must be mailed or delivered in person.

- **Pre-Texting**

  Financial institutions aren't allowed to obtain confidential information under false pretenses.

- **Safeguards Rules**

  Financial institutions and any institution with whom they share information, must implement procedures to safeguard individuals' private information.

Frequently Asked Questions and Answers

Website: http://www.ftc.gov/privacy/glbact/glb-faq.htm

Website: http://www.maine.gov/pfr/insurance/consumer/faq_rights.htm

III.   Truth-in-Lending Act (TILA)

TILA focuses on the fact that various disclosures must be given in a timely fashion. Forensic mortgage auditors who are defending homeowners against lender foreclosures are having a field day with this law. When the country was experiencing a time of loose credit, many of the compliance issues were overlooked, and the buyer never received the disclosures.

TILA also regulates "truth in advertising" for lenders and loan officers. Don't imply in your marketing that borrowers have unqualified access to credit. If you mention a particular loan program with favorable terms it must be available to a significant number of borrowers; you can't "bait and switch."

Disclosures

The following disclosures are required in particular circumstances:

- **Truth-in-Lending Disclosure Statement**

  The APR disclosure statement must be sent to the loan applicant within three business days of receiving the signed application. If the APR is quoted incorrectly by more than 1/8 % for a fixed-rate loan and 1/4 % for an ARM, it must be re-disclosed before settlement, and the APR must be finalized at least three days before closing. This disclosure is only used for the following loans: reverse mortgage, home equity line of credit, mobile homes and dwellings not attached to land.

- **Consumer Handbook on Adjustable-Rate Mortgages**

  If the individual applies for an adjustable-rate mortgage, creditors must give applicants either the "Consumer Handbook on Adjustable-Rate Mortgages" pamphlet or something similar within three business days of receiving a signed loan application.

- **Right to Rescind**

  The Right to Rescind notice provides a three business day cooling-off period for a consumer who uses their primary residence as security for a refinance, home improvement or second mortgage loan.

- **APR and Trigger Terms**

  If any triggering term (interest rate, down payment, payment amount, number of payments, term of repayment or amount of any finance charge, etc.) is specified in an advertisement for credit, then the APR and the amount and terms of repayment must also be disclosed.

High-Cost Home Loans

Predatory lending, which forces borrowers to pay exorbitant fees or higher interest rates, typically affects senior citizens, lower income individuals, and borrowers with poor credit histories. These applicants are more likely to be financially naive or unable to qualify for a conforming loan. In order to protect these people, the federal government has issued rules that must be followed when the buyer is forced to pay closing costs that exceed five percent of the loan amount.

A high-cost home loan is legal and is defined as one in which the total fees and points payable by the consumer at or before closing exceed five percent of the loan amount. These types of loans may be difficult to sell in the secondary mortgage market, and many lenders avoid them. The Home Ownership and Equity Protection Act (HOEPA) regulates these loans and requires the following disclosures and practices:

- HOEPA disclosure form delivered to applicant.

- Prepay penalties prohibited for high-cost home loans.

- Balloon mortgages prohibited.

- Borrowers must have a documented ability to repay the loan prior to funding.

- Borrowers must receive homeownership counseling from a HUD-approved counselor prior to funding.

- No negative amortization.

- No pressure tactics.

- No escalation clause.

Frequently Asked Questions and Answers

Website: http://www.consumerfinance.gov/askcfpb/search?selected_facets=tag_exact%3ATruth-in-Lending+disclosure

Website: http://www.consumerfinance.gov/askcfpb/search?selected_facets=tag_exact%3Aclosing

IV.   Equal Credit Opportunity Act (ECOA)

ECOA sets up protected classes of individuals. The loan originator should not ask applicants questions about their religion or how many children they plan to have. Casual conversation might be a good way to put the borrower at ease, but talk about the weather. The ECOA key points include:

- **Protected Classes**

  ECOA prohibits a lender from discouraging someone from applying for a mortgage or rejecting the application because of race, color, religion, national origin, sex, marital status, age or receipt of public assistance.

- **Appraisals**

  The lender must send the borrower copies of all valuation reports at least three business days before closing.

- **Adverse Action Notice**

    A lender has 30 days after receipt of an application to notify the applicant of its action on the application. If the application is denied, the applicant can request a statement of reasons within 60 days of receiving an adverse action notice, and the lender has 30 days after the applicant's request to provide him with the information.

Frequently Asked Questions and Answers

Website: http://www.consumerfinance.gov/askcfpb/search?q=Equal+Credit+Opportunity+Act+

V.   Appraisal

An appraisal is a licensed individual's opinion of value for a particular property. It's not rocket science and there can legitimately be a significant variance in the derived values among different appraisers. The problem comes when an appraiser inflates the value of a home for unscrupulous purposes. Many mortgage fraud schemes involve illegal activities on the part of the appraisers who are frequently part of a ring of criminal settlement service providers; criminal loan originators and title companies have all played a role in some of our country's financial woes.

One measure that was taken to control for fraudulent appraisals was the adoption of the Home Valuation Code of Conduct (HVCC or Code), which became effective in 2009 for single-family mortgage loans (except government-insured loans) delivered to Fannie Mae. Once this went into effect, mortgage brokers were no longer allowed to choose the appraiser. The 2010 Dodd-Frank Act extended these provisions to include all mortgage loans, including ones that aren't sold to Fannie Mae.

State licensing laws require appraisers to adhere to the Uniform Standards of Professional Appraisal Practice (USPAP). One component of USPAP is the Ethics Rule that contains the following four sections:

- **Conduct**

    An appraiser must be impartial and nondiscriminatory. The report can't be fraudulent, and the appraiser can't be grossly negligent. The appraiser must disclose if he has already evaluated this property within the past three years unless the prior client specifically instructed him not to disclose. In this case, the appraiser can't value the property again for three years.

- **Management**

  Appraisers must disclose the fact that they were paid for the assignment, but they aren't required to disclose the amount of payment. The appraiser can't accept assignments that are contingent on arriving at a predetermined opinion of value. Appraisers can't engage in false advertising or affix the signature of another appraiser without permission.

- **Confidentiality**

  An appraiser must keep client information and appraisal results confidential. Results can only be reported to the client, client-authorized individuals, state regulatory agencies and peer review committees.

- **Record Keeping**

  An appraiser must complete a workfile prior to submitting an appraisal report. The file must contain the name of the client, identity of authorized users, copy of all client reports, transcripts of oral reports and supporting documents used in the valuation. The appraiser must keep a copy of the workfile for a minimum of five years and two years after any judicial action in which the appraiser testified in court.

Frequently Asked Questions and Answers

Website: http://www.freddiemac.com/singlefamily/appraiser_independence_faq.html

VI.   Mortgage Fraud

Mortgage fraud is the intentional misrepresentation or omission of material facts that harmed the lenders or underwriters who relied on the information to fund a loan. The FBI defines two types of mortgage fraud:

- Fraud for housing in which borrowers make false statements on the loan application.

- Fraud for profit, which is perpetrated by appraisers, closing agents, real estate agents, loan originators, loan processors, underwriters, loan servicers, buyers and sellers. Unfortunately, many of the professionals often work together to commit the crime.

Common Mechanisms for Mortgage Fraud

Loan documents are subjected to much scrutiny and verification; however, adept criminals still manage to get loans approved. Some common ways of initiating the fraud include:

- **Asset Rental** - someone deposits temporary funds or assets in a borrower's bank account so that he will qualify for a loan. The loan applicant usually pays the depositor a rental fee for the use of the money.

- **Fake Down Payment** - someone falsifies the borrower's down payment verification through fake or altered documentation.

- **Fraudulent Appraisal** - appraiser deliberately creates an inflated appraisal report to mislead the lender.

- **Fraudulent Documentation** - forged or altered information on documents submitted to the lender for loan approval.

- **Fraudulent Shell Company** - illegal use of a shell company to hide financial information.

- **Identity Theft** - use of someone's stolen social security number or credit card information to obtain a loan approval.

- **Silent Second** - buyer obtains seller financing for the down payment and doesn't disclose this fact to the lender. The lien may go unrecorded.

- **Straw/Nominee Borrower** - individual with a good credit history is paid to represent himself as the borrower.

Red Flags for Mortgage Fraud

The Fair and Accurate Credit Transaction Act identified five categories of warning signs (red flags) that indicated the possible occurrence of identity theft. Consequently, the Red Flags Rule requires certain types of creditors with transactional accounts to create a written program to train employees in the recognition of these red flags and instruct them in the appropriate response to the threat. While identity theft plays a role in fictitious loans, there are many other mechanisms in mortgage fraud. Some of these warning signs for these other methods include the following:

- Property seller isn't the owner of record.

- Recent quitclaim deed transferred ownership.

- Early payment default.

- Incomplete or illegible appraisal.

- Unexplained large deposits in borrower's bank account.

- One individual has many outstanding loans.

- Credit history doesn't indicate a financial hardship in a short sale or loan modification.

- Incomplete leases.

- Numerous changes in wiring instructions.

- No real estate agent used in the transaction.

- No employment or income verification.

- No on-site audits of loan servicers.

Common Mortgage Fraud Schemes

Determined individuals will always be able to cheat the system by either dreaming up brand new schemes or by putting a new twist on an old one. The FBI website is an interesting place to visit and learn about the latest methods criminals are using to commit fraud. Some of the more common schemes are presented here:

- **Air Loan**

    This might be the most extreme form of mortgage fraud because neither the borrower nor the property exists. This type of scheme involves a group of individuals working together to defraud the lender.

- **Builder Bailout**

    This type of fraud is most likely to happen when a developer needs money and is under pressure to sell the remaining units in a subdivision or housing complex. In this situation, he might raise the sales price of the property, but offer undisclosed down payment assistance or excessive concessions. If the property appraises for the increased sales price, the lender is acquiring a loan that is worth more than the unit. Builders may bribe appraisers to inflate the value on the report, and they might use straw buyers to accelerate the liquidation of the remaining inventory.

- **Buy and Bail**

  A buy and bail happens when a homeowner is underwater on the mortgage (loan balance is higher than the market value), or circumstances are about to change that will have an adverse effect on the homeowner's finances (looming lay-off or interest rate adjustment coming due). The individual proceeds to buy a cheaper "investment" property (not owner-occupied) while he still has good credit, and walks away from his primary residence immediately after closing. In this case, the buyer may collaborate with or invent existing tenants and create a fictitious lease that shows an adequate cash flow to pay the housing expenses for the investment property.

- **Chunking**

  This scheme involves an innocent buyer and a devious seller. The seller poses as an agent, approaches the buyer and encourages him to buy one or more of his investment properties. Unbeknownst to the borrower, the "agent" submits the loan application to multiple lenders, arranges multiple closings for the same property within a very short timeframe, has power-of-attorney to sign for the borrower, pockets the loan proceeds and leaves the buyer facing the need to pay multiple lenders. The property forecloses, and the lenders suffer losses. This scheme usually involves the cooperation of a title company or real estate broker since the down payment funds need to be falsified for each sale. The same strategy can be accomplished with a straw buyer who has sufficient assets and good credit. In another version, the "agent" obtains one signed loan application, changes the property address and submits the altered loan application to a number of different lenders for the purchase of multiple properties.

- **Double Selling**

  Double selling is a scheme undertaken by a criminal loan originator who may be cooperating with a homeowner. One scenario involves the submission of an equity line of credit application to multiple lenders. The borrower's asset information may be altered in order for him to qualify. The loans are approved; multiple closings are completed before there is time to record any of the liens, and the borrower and loan originator split the money. Another situation proceeds without the homeowner's knowledge. The loan originator uses a warehouse lender to provide short-term financing for the loan and then sells the loan to multiple investors. He pays off the warehouse lender and pockets the rest of the money.

- **Equity Skimming**

  Many of the equity-skimming schemes involve the use of an inflated appraisal and a dishonest buyer or homeowner. In one case, an appraiser overvalues the property; the sale price is increased to match the appraisal value, and the buyer receives the difference in cash after the closing. In another case, inflated appraisals allow a homeowner to participate in cash-out refinances.

- **Fictitious Loan**

A fictitious loan is one in which the applicant has no attention of making a mortgage payment. Typically, the borrower's identity has been stolen or fabricated, and the loan funds are received by the perpetrator.

- **Loan Modification and Refinance Fraud**

Borrowers approved for a loan modification are generally facing financial difficulties. Falsifying a lower income in order to qualify for the modification, is the most common fraudulent method used in these schemes. Refinance fraud, on the other hand, typically involves the use of an inflated appraisal value.

- **Mortgage Servicing Fraud**

Mortgage servicing usually involves a company collecting the monthly mortgage payments; maintaining the borrower's escrow account; paying for property and hazard insurance from this account and forwarding proceeds to the loan owner if it sells a loan it services. There are many opportunities for servicing fraud including cases where the servicer sold the loan and kept the proceeds; the servicer continued to make the monthly payments so that the owner of the loan was unaware of the fraud.

- **Phantom Sale**

A phantom sale occurs when an individual finds an abandoned home, records a false quitclaim deed and proceeds to take out a loan on the property or sell it.

- **Property Flip Fraud**

Property flips typically involve properties that are bought and sold within a short period of time. Other flips happen when the property isn't selling, and the homeowner is highly motivated to sell it. Many flips are legal, but some are not. An inflated appraisal is often the mechanism of choice for the fraudulent flipper. For example, a buyer approaches the seller of a property that's been on the market for a long time and is desperate to sell. The investor offers an amount of money that's much higher than the list price and that's supported by an inflated appraisal. At closing, the seller receives the proceeds of the loan and disburses the difference between the sale price and original list price to the investors.

- **Reverse Mortgage Fraud**

The amount of eligible funds in a reverse mortgage depends primarily on the appraisal value of the home and on the age of the youngest applicant. Consequently, inflated appraisals and altered birth dates are likely sources of fraud.

- **Short Sale Fraud**

    A short sale occurs when a homeowner owes more on the mortgage balance than the current market value of the home, and the lender agrees to sell at or below market value and "forgive" the difference; the lender releases the mortgage lien for less than the balance of the loan amount. These properties typically sell below market value. This is an alternative to foreclosure, and the lender usually requires that the homeowner has a financial hardship and is unable to continue making the mortgage payments. The buyers have to attest that it's an arm's-length transaction. Fraud occurs when the buyer is related or affiliated with the seller, or financial records are altered to show a financial hardship. Short sale fraud also occurs when the perpetrator uses a straw buyer to purchase and ultimately default on a home loan. This creates a short sale situation that the perpetrator can take advantage of to purchase the home at a discount.

Website: http://www.ffiec.gov/exam/Mtg_Fraud_wp_Feb2010.pdf

Website: http://www.fbi.gov/stats-services/publications/financial-crimes-report-2010-2011/financial-crimes-report-2010-2011#Mortgage

VII.   Ethical Behavior

There are opportunities for fraud and unethical behavior along every step of a lending transaction and by every participant involved in the settlement. Pay attention to the warning signs and report any suspicious behavior or documents to your manager. If you conduct yourself professionally and treat your applicants with respect, you'll earn a reputation as a straight shooter, and referrals will pour in.

Consumers

"Buyers are liars." This is a famous real estate saying that has a variety of endings such as "and sellers are too." or "and sellers are story tellers." or "and sellers are worse." Take your pick. Being in this business can be frustrating. Unethical behavior on the part of buyers includes falsifying documents and acting as straw buyers. On the other hand, unethical sellers might not be the lawful owners of the offered property or may be relatives of the short-sale buyer.

Underwriters

Underwriters have the obligation not to arbitrarily deny or limit financial services to specific neighborhoods. This is usually done because of the race or ethnicity of the residents. This type of selective lending is called redlining, and it's illegal. Underwriters also need to consider both the property and the borrower. Suspicious appraisals and documents should be scrupulously reviewed.

Investors

Investors can't state on the loan application that a property is owner-occupied if it's actually a rental. Leases can't be altered or forged to show increased cash flow or to prove the existence of fictitious tenants. Investors can't work with fraudulent appraisers to inflate the value of flipped properties.

Real Estate Licensees

Loan originators and title companies can't pay real estate agents a referral fee. Real estate sales associates must comply with the Fair Housing Act that prohibits housing discrimination on the basis of race, color, religion, sex, disability, familial status, and national origin. They can't "steer" buyers into or away from particular neighborhoods based on their ethnic or racial demographics. Blockbusting occurs when a real estate agent spreads the rumor that a specific ethnic group is planning to move into the neighborhood and advises residents to sell before the property values drop.

Closing Agents

Closing agents must follow the lender's closing instructions and accurately account for all escrowed funds. The HUD-1/Closing Disclosure should be checked for errors prior to closing, and no arrangements can be made for the disbursements of funds that don't appear on the closing statement.

Employers

Lenders and mortgage brokers can't pressure their employees to steer applicants to higher priced mortgage loans that aren't in the borrower's best interest.

Mortgage Loan Originators

Loan originators shouldn't falsify documents, create fictitious borrowers or encourage rate-locks when interest rates are going down. An ethical loan originator explains the details of the chosen loan product to the borrower and carefully reviews the loan application for accuracy. Originators need to include disclosed monthly debts that don't appear in the credit report in the calculation of the total obligation ratio.

Important Points to Remember

1. RESPA applies to transactions involving residential financed home loans and does not cover cash sales, seller financing or property rentals.
2. Nothing of value can be given in exchange for the referral of business with the exception of real estate brokerage firms that are allowed to exchange referrals between themselves.
3. The Good Faith Estimate is not required if there is no property address (pre-approval).
4. Escrow accounts must refund the borrower any annual surplus that exceeds $50.
5. The Gramm-Leach-Bliley Act applies to financial institutions that give loans or financial advice. This includes mortgage brokers, lenders, tax preparers and debt collectors.
6. A consumer is an individual who obtains or has obtained a financial product or service from a financial institution for personal, family or household reasons. A customer is a consumer with a continuing relationship with a financial institution.
7. A privacy notice must be given to a customer by mail or in-person.
8. Consumers and customers have the right to opt-out of having their information shared with certain third parties.
9. Pre-texting is the illegal practice of obtaining consumer information from financial institutions under false pretenses.
10. HOEPA applies when the total fees and points payable by the consumer at or before closing exceed 5% of the loan amount.
11. A finance charge is the cost of credit expressed in dollars.
12. The TILA and Regulation Z require that the initial disclosure package (Good Faith Estimate, Truth-in-Lending, and state-specific disclosures) must be sent to the applicant within 3 business days of the day the application is taken or received and that from the day of mailing, the settlement or closing can't occur for at least 7 business days. These disclosures are only used for the following loans: reverse mortgage, home equity line of credit, mobile homes and dwellings not attached to land.
13. A business day includes Saturdays, but does not include Sundays and recognized Federal Holidays.
14. If there are changes to a borrower's loan program, loan terms, and/or APR, the initial disclosure package must be re-disclosed to the borrower prior to closing.
15. If the borrower's APR increases or decreases by more than .125% for a fixed-rate loan, or by more than .25% for an adjustable-rate mortgage (ARM), the initial package must be re-disclosed.
16. ECOA prohibits a lender from discouraging individuals from applying for a mortgage or reject their application because of their race, color, religion, national origin, sex, marital status, age, or because they receive public assistance.
17. The Home Valuation Code of Conduct (HVCC) prevents a mortgage broker from choosing the appraiser for loans that are sold to Fannie Mae. The Dodd-Frank Act extended the law to include all mortgages.
18. The lender must provide a copy of the appraisal report to the borrower within three business days prior to closing.
19. The FBI investigates mortgage fraud in two distinct areas: fraud for profit and fraud for housing.
20. Illegal property flipping is best described as purchasing properties and artificially inflating their value through false appraisals.

21.   Predatory lending typically affects senior citizens, lower income borrowers and applicants with low credit scores. Predatory lending forces borrowers to pay exorbitant loan origination/settlement fees, subprime or higher interest rates, and in some cases, unreasonable service fees.

22.   A builder-bailout scheme can occur when a builder or developer experiences difficulty selling his inventory and resorts to using fraudulent means to unload properties.

23.   Short sale fraud schemes occur when the perpetrator uses a straw buyer to purchase and ultimately default on a home loan, creating a short sale situation so that the perpetrator can take advantage and purchase the home at a discount.

24.   Property appraisers must be licensed and adhere to the Uniform Standards of Professional Appraisal Practice (USPAP).

25.   Redlining is the illegal practice by lenders of arbitrarily denying or limiting financial services to specific neighborhoods.

26.   The Fair Housing Act prohibits housing discrimination on the basis of race, color, religion, sex, disability, familial status, and national origin.

27.   Steering is the illegal practice by real estate agents of directing buyers into or out of certain neighborhoods based on their ethnicity or race.

28.   Blockbusting occurs when a real estate agent spreads the rumor that a specific ethnic group is planning to move into the neighborhood and advises residents to sell before the property values drop.

Exam

1. Under the federal fair housing law, the seven protected classes include:
    A. Race, color, source of income, handicap, national origin, marital status, religion
    B. Race, color, religion, sex, handicap, familial status, national origin
    C. Race, sexual orientation, sex, familial status, handicap, age, national origin
    D. Race, color, age, religion, sex, handicap, familial status

2. Under RESPA, a real estate professional may give in return for the referral of real estate settlement service business a:
    A. Caribbean cruise
    B. $50 bill
    C. Thank you
    D. Kickback

3. A real estate broker may pay a referral fee to:
    A. A closing agent
    B. A past customer
    C. A mortgage broker
    D. Another real estate brokerage firm

4. Who can provide closed sales comparables to an appraiser?
    A. Real estate agent
    B. Underwriter
    C. Mortgage broker
    D. Lender

5. Which of the following is NOT a common type of mortgage fraud?
    A. Rehabilitation
    B. Equity skimming
    C. Inflated appraisals
    D. Property flipping

6. What type of mortgage fraud scam occurs when a buyer borrows the down payment from the seller without the lender's knowledge?
    A. Equity skimming
    B. Air loan
    C. Silent second
    D. Property flipping

7. What is the mortgage fraud scam called when a broker invents borrowers and properties?
    A. Equity skimming
    B. Air loan
    C. Silent second
    D. Property flipping

8.   What are the two distinct areas of mortgage fraud that the FBI investigates?
      A.   Fraud for profit and fraud for housing
      B.   East coast and west coast
      C.   Domestic and international
      D.   Appraisers and mortgage brokers

9.   Which of the following is NOT a mortgage fraud indicator?
      A.   Inflated appraisal
      B.   Higher than normal commissions
      C.   High credit score
      D.   Request to sign blank forms

10.   A lender's refusal to lend in a particular neighborhood is known as:
      A.   Referential lending
      B.   Redemption
      C.   Railroading
      D.   Redlining

Answer Key

1. B
2. C
3. D
4. A
5. A
6. C
7. B
8. A
9. C
10. D

9

Mortgage Terminology

2-1 Buydown - A type of mortgage with a set of two initial temporary interest rates. In a 2-1 the interest for the first year is 2 percent lower than the permanent interest rate, and 1 percent lower the second year. The initial interest rate reductions are either paid for by the borrower in order to help them qualify for a mortgage (their debt-to-income ratios would be based on the first year's reduced interest rate), or might be paid for by a builder as incentive to purchase a home.

Accrued Interest - Interest earned since last settlement date but not yet due or payable.

Actual Notice - Notice which is not recorded in public records.

Adverse Action (as defined in ECOA) - A refusal to grant credit in the amount or on the terms requested in an application.

Amortization - Liquidation of a debt by regular, usually monthly, installments of principal and interest.

Annual Percentage Rate (APR) - The actual interest rate, taking into account points and other finance charges, for the projected life of a mortgage.

Appraiser - The individual performing an appraisal. When the property is connected to a mortgage loan, the lender chooses the appraiser and borrower typically pays the fees.

Appraisal - An estimate of a property's value as of a given date, determined by a qualified professional appraiser. The value may be based on replacement cost, the sales of comparable properties or the property's income-producing ability.

Assigned Loan - Transfer of ownership of a mortgage from one person to another.

Assumable Loan - A mortgage loan that can be taken over (assumed) by the buyer when a home is sold. An assumption of a mortgage is a transaction in which the buyer of real property takes over the seller's existing mortgage; the seller remains liable unless released by the lender from the obligation (assumption with novation.) If the mortgage contains a due-on-sale clause, the loan may not be assumed without the lender's consent.

Average Prime Offer Rate (APOR) - Annual percentage rate that is derived from average interest rates, points, and other loan pricing terms currently offered to consumers by a representative sample of creditors for mortgage transactions that have low-risk pricing characteristics.

Business Day (as defined in TILA) - A day on which the creditor's offices are open to the public for carrying on substantially all of its business functions.

Business Day (for delivery of a closing disclosure) - Same as above.

Business Day in a Mortgage Rescission (as defined in TILA) - All calendar days except Sundays and the legal public holidays.

Capacity of a Borrower - Borrower's ability to make their mortgage payments on time. This depends on income and income stability (job history and security), assets and savings, and the amount of your income each month that is left over after housing costs, debts and other obligations.

Cash Out Refinance - A mortgage refinancing transaction in which the new mortgage amount is greater than the existing mortgage amount, plus loan settlement costs. The purpose of a cash-out refinance is to extract equity from the borrower's home.

Chattel Mortgage - A mortgage on personal property.

Consumer Credit - Consumer credit is a debt that a person incurs when purchasing a good or service. Consumer credit includes purchases obtained with credit cards, lines of credit and some loans.

Conveyance - Conveyance is the act of transferring an ownership interest in real property from one party to another. Conveyance also refers to the written instrument, such as a deed or lease that transfers legal title of a property from the seller to the buyer.

Creditor (as defined in FACTA) - Any person or business who arranges for the extension, renewal, or continuation of credit.

Construction Loan - A short-term loan for financing improvements to real estate, such as the building of a new home. The lender advances funds to the borrower as needed while construction progresses. Upon completion of the construction the borrower must obtain permanent financing or repay the construction loan in full.

Constructive Notice - Notice which is recorded in public records.

Daily Simple Interest - A simple interest mortgage calculates interest on a daily basis, as opposed to a traditional mortgage where interest is calculated on a monthly basis. On a simple-interest mortgage, the daily interest charge is calculated by dividing the interest rate by 365 days, and then multiplying that number by the outstanding mortgage balance. If you multiply the daily interest charge by the number of days in the month, you will get the monthly interest charge. Because the total number of days counted in a simple-interest mortgage calculation is greater than a traditional mortgage calculation, the total interest paid on a simple interest mortgage will be slightly larger than a traditional mortgage.

Debt-to-Income Ratio Assessment - The ratio between a borrower's monthly payment obligations divided by gross monthly income.

Delinquent Loan - The situation that arises when a mortgage payment is late.

Discount Points - A percentage of the loan amount paid to the lender to buy down the interest rate. Each point costs one percent of the loan amount.

Disintermediation - Withdrawal of funds out of savings accounts and into stocks, bonds and real estate.

Dwelling - A residential structure that contains one to four units, whether or not that structure is attached to real property. The term includes an individual condominium unit, cooperative unit, mobile home, and trailer, if it is used as a residence.

Early Payment Default - Occurs when a mortgage payment is more than 90 days late or defaults during its first year. Strong indicator of mortgage fraud.

Easement - A right to the use of, or access to, land owned by another.

Elderly (as defined in ECOA) - Age 62 or older.

Eminent Domain - Condemnation of private property for public good.

Entitlement - The amount of money the VA promises to pay back the lender in case of borrower default.. Lenders usually loan 4 times that amount.

Escrow Accounts - An account that a mortgage servicer establishes on behalf of a borrower to pay taxes, insurance premiums, or other charges when they are due. Sometimes referred to as an "impound" or "reserve" account.

Examples of Origination Services - Inputting application into the computer, verifying credit, employment and income, selecting a loan product and interest rate, locking interest rate, sending out required disclosure forms, requesting an appraisal, underwriting and funding the loan.

Federal Mortgage Loans - Mortgage loans that provide full (FHA, USDA) or partial (VA) government reimbursement to approved lenders in the case of borrower default.

FHA Mortgage - A mortgage that is insured by the FHA. The FHA-approved lender is insured against suffering any loss on the loan.

FHA - Federal Housing Administration, an agency within the US Department of Housing and Urban Development (HUD).

Finance Charge - The total amount of interest and loan charges a borrower would pay over the entire life of the mortgage loan. Loan charges include origination charges, discount points, mortgage insurance, and lender fees.

Fraud Alert (as defined in FACTA) - A statement in the file of a consumer that notifies all prospective users of a consumer report relating to the consumer that the consumer may be a victim of fraud, including identity theft.

Fully Indexed Rate - The interest rate calculated using the index value and margin at the time of an adjustable-rate mortgage consummation.

High Cost Loans - Mortgage loans in which the APR exceeds the Average Prime Offer Rate by 6.5 percent for a first-lien mortgage or 8.5 points for a subordinate lien loan; total lender and broker fees exceed 5 percent of loan amount, and the loan has a prepayment penalty in effect for more than 3 years or the prepay penalty exceeds 2 percent of the amount prepaid. Origination of a high cost loan triggers HOEPA disclosures.

High Interest Rates - Interest rates that exceed a specified threshold require HOEPA disclosures.

High Priced Mortgage (as defined in TILA) - A high-priced mortgage loan is one with an APR 1.5 percent higher than the Average Prime Offer Rate for a first-lien mortgage or 3.5 percent higher for a subordinate mortgage.

Interest - A fee charged for the use of money.

Intermediation - Withdrawal of funds out of real estate, stocks and bonds and into savings accounts.

Junior Liens - A loan that is subordinate to the primary loan (first-lien mortgage loan) such as a second or third mortgage.

Legal Title Granted via a Mortgage - Full and legal ownership of real property with the borrowers receiving the deed at closing. Lenders in states with legal title must file a foreclosure lawsuit in order to foreclose. In states with equitable title, property owners don't receive full legal title until the loan is paid off and they receive a deed of reconveyance. Foreclosures in equitable title states can occur outside the court system.

Lender Credits - The lender may offer to give the borrower a credit to help with closing costs. Typically, the lender will either increase the loan amount to cover these costs, or charge a higher interest rate in exchange for the credit.

Leverage - Use of borrowed funds to increase yield.

Loan Consumption - This occurs when the closing documents are signed and the loan is funded.

Loan Payment Collection - Mortgage payments are due the first of the month and late after the 15th. Payments are frequently sent to loan servicers who manage borrowers accounts.

Loan-to-Value Ratio - The relationship between the loan amount and the value of the property (the lower of appraised value or sales price), expressed as a percentage of the property's value.

Mortgage Broker - A person (other than an employee of a lender) that renders origination services and serves as an intermediary between a borrower and a lender in a transaction involving a federally related mortgage loan, including a person that closes the loan in its own name in a table-funded transaction.

Mortgage Investor - Individual or company that purchase mortgages after the closing.

Mortgage Lender - The lender providing funds for a mortgage. Lenders also manage the credit and financial information review, the property and the loan application process through closing.

Net Worth - Assets minus liabilities.

Non-Conforming Loan - A loan that does not conform to Federal National Mortgage Association (FNMA) or Federal Home Loan Mortgage Corporation (FHLMC) guidelines. Jumbo loans are nonconforming.

Non-Traditional Mortgages - Residential mortgage loan products that allow borrowers to defer repayment of principal and, sometimes, interest. They include such products as "interest-only" mortgages where a borrower pays no loan principal for the first few years of the loan, and "payment option" adjustable-rate mortgages (ARMs) where a borrower has flexible payment options with the potential for negative amortization.

Note Endorsed With Recourse - Mortgage note that does not limit recovery solely from a property.

Payment Shock - The surprise borrowers receive when an adjustable-rate mortgage's interest rate increases more than expected.

Premium Pricing - A credit from a lender for the interest rate chosen. Premium pricing may be used to pay a borrower's actual closing costs and/or prepaid items.

Prepaids - Prepaid expenses at closing may include property taxes, homeowner's insurance, and mortgage interest that will accrue before the first mortgage payment is due.

Primary Mortgage Market - The entities involved in originating a mortgage loan including mortgage brokers and lenders are operating in the primary mortgage market.

Qualified Mortgage - Category of loans that have certain, more stable features that help make it more likely that a borrower will be able to afford a mortgage loan. Interest-only loans, negative amortizing loans, balloon loans and terms longer than 30 years aren't allowed.

Rate Lock Agreement - An agreement in which an interest rate is "locked in" or guaranteed for a specified period of time prior to closing.

Referral (as defined in RESPA) - A referral includes any oral or written action directed to a person in order to influence the selection of a settlement provider paid for by that consumer.

Residential Mortgage Loan (as defined in TILA) - A mortgage on the consumer's principal dwelling to finance the acquisition or initial construction of that dwelling.

Residual Income Qualification Test - The amount of money left each month after all major expenses are paid. The VA publishes a chart of desired minimum amounts, and lenders are encouraged to weight this factor more heavily than debt-to-income ratios. Residual income is also one factor considered in a Qualified Mortgage.

Secondary Market -The market in which mortgage loan and mortgage-backed securities are bought and sold.

Servicing Transfers - Servicing of a loan can be sold, assigned or transferred to another entity. This process requires a borrower disclosure containing the contact information of the new servicer.

Settlement - The process of completing a loan transaction at which time the mortgage documents are signed and then recorded, funds are disbursed, and the property is transferred to the buyer (if applicable). Also called closing or escrow in different jurisdictions.

Steering - A loan originator may not direct a consumer to a particular mortgage product that increases the loan originator's compensation unless that transaction is in the consumer's interest.

Subordinate Loans - Any mortgage with a lower priority than the first mortgage. This includes a second mortgage at the time of purchase or an equity line of credit.

Subordination - The act of lowering the priority of a mortgage lien.

Subprime - A subprime mortgage is generally a loan that is meant to be offered to prospective borrowers with impaired credit records. A higher interest rate is intended to compensate the lender for accepting the greater risk in lending to such borrowers.

Table Funding - An option which allows mortgage brokers or title companies approved for Wholesale Traditional Lending to originate, process and close loans in their own name. At settlement time, the loan is transferred to the lender who advances funds for the loan.

Third Party Providers - Settlement providers other than the lender including title company, hazard insurance company, credit report providers, appraisers, surveyors and pest inspectors.

Tolerances - The degree to which stated closing costs can vary between the Loan Estimate and the Closing Disclosure. There are three categories of closing costs. Some closing costs the lender can increase by any amount, some the lender can increase by up to 10 percent, and some the lender can't increase at all.

Types of Mortgages a Lender Cannot be Forced to Repurchase - A non-recourse loan.

Underwriting - The process used to determine loan approval. It involves evaluating the property and the borrower's credit and ability to pay the mortgage.

Yield Spread Premiums - Compensation paid by the lender to a mortgage broker when the selected interest rate is above par (the average rate).

Exam

1. A fee charged for the use of money is:
    A. Interest
    B. Usury
    C. Rent
    D. Lease

2. A mortgage on personal property is a(n):
    A. Chattel mortgage
    B. Reverse mortgage
    C. Ad valorem mortgage
    D. Participation Mortgage

3. One discount point equals one percent of the
    A. Purchase price
    B. Annual percentage rate
    C. Loan amount
    D. Appraisal value

4. Net worth is defined as:
    A. Cash plus real property
    B. Cash plus stocks and bonds
    C. Assets minus liabilities
    D. Liquid assets plus real property

5. The liquidation of a debt by regular, usually monthly, installments of principal and interest is:
    A. Amortization
    B. Hypothecation
    C. Assignment
    D. Novation

6. The withdrawal of funds out of savings accounts and into stocks and bonds is known as:
    A. Intermediation
    B. Disintermediation
    C. Acceleration
    D. Exculpation

7. The condemnation of private property for public good is:
    A. Eminent Domain
    B. Escheat
    C. Disintermediation
    D. Intestate

8.   Notice which is NOT recorded is known as:
    A.   Constructive notice
    B.   Actual notice
    C.   Selective notice
    D.   Lis pendens notice

9.   Notice which is recorded is known as:
    A.   Constructive notice
    B.   Actual notice
    C.   Selective notice
    D.   Lis pendens notice

10.   The use of borrowed funds to increase yield is:
    A.   Leverage
    B.   Acceleration
    C.   Defeasance
    D.   Forbearance

11.   A mortgage note that does **NOT** limit recovery solely from the property is called a:
    A.   Note Endorsed With Recourse
    B.   Hybrid Loan
    C.   Multi-level Loan
    D.   Non-recourse Note

12.   APOR stands for:
    A.   Average Price of Ratios
    B.   Annual Percentage of Refinancing
    C.   Average Prime Offer Rate
    D.   Annual Percentage of Reimbursement

13.   A discount point costs:
    A. $100
    B. $1,000
    C.   1 percent of loan amount
    D.   10 percent of loan amount

14.   ECOA defines elderly as:
    A.   55 years old
    B.   62 years old
    C.   65 years old
    D.   70 years old

15.   The right to use land owned by another is an:
    A.   Easement
    B.   Acquisition
    C.   Exposition
    D.   Alienation

16.   The act of lowering the priority of a mortgage lien is:
    A.   Reduction
    B.   Subordination
    C.   Degradation
    D.   Subtraction

17.   A loan offered to a consumer with poor credit is known as:
    A.   Subjugation
    B.   Alternative
    C.   Preliminary
    D.   Subprime

Answer Key

1.   A
2.   A
3.   C
4.   C
5.   A
6.   B
7.   A
8.   B
9.   A
10. A
11. A
12. C
13. C
14. B
15. A
16. B
17. D

Practice Final Exam #1

1. A discount point is BEST described as a charge the borrower pays to:
   A. A lender to decrease the interest rate on the mortgage loan
   B. A mortgage broker at the time of application to obtain a favorable rate
   C. The seller as part of the closing costs of a loan
   D . A lender to ensure against foreclosure

2. A buyer has made an earnest money payment of $5,000. The buyer pays an additional $2,000 in option money to be credited at closing on a property with a sale price of $160,000. If the required down payment is 20%, how much additional money will the buyer need to provide toward the down payment at closing?
   A. $32,000
   B. $27,000
   C. $30,000
   D. $25,000

3. If an applicant works 40 hours every week and is paid $13.52 per hour, what is the applicant's monthly income?
   A. $2,163.20
   B. $2,343.47
   C. $2,379.52
   D. $2,487.68

4. The requirement for private mortgage insurance is generally discontinued when the loan-to-value ratio falls below:
   A. 20 %
   B. 50 %
   C. 80 %
   D. 90 %

5. Which of the following documents itemizes all settlement costs including lender charges?
   A. Agreement of sale
   B. HUD-1/Closing Disclosure
   C. Form 1003
   D. Forbearance agreement

6. According to the Truth-in-Lending Act (TILA), the term "refinance" applies to:
   A. A change in a payment schedule
   B. A reduction in annual percentage rate
   C. The renewal of a single payment obligation with no change in the original terms
   D. The satisfaction of an existing obligation and its replacement by a new obligation

7.   What does a loan originator use to determine the estimated value of a property based on an analytical comparison of similar property sales?
      A.   An appraisal
      B.   A market survey
      C.   An area survey
      D.   A cost-benefit analysis

8.   Which of the following methods of disclosure does NOT meet the requirements of the Equal Credit Opportunity Act (ECOA)?
      A.   E-mail
      B.   Mailed letter
      C.   Telephone
      D.   Faxed letter

9.   The term "20 basis points" expressed as a percentage is:
      A.   0.02%
      B.   0.20%
      C.   2.00%
      D.   20.00%

10.   According to the Truth-in-Lending Act (TILA), which of the following fees is **EXCLUDED** from the calculation of the annual percentage rate?
      A.   Hazard insurance
      B.   Wire transfer
      C.   Prepaid interest
      D.   Mortgage insurance premiums

11.   FHA loans are:
      A.   Partially guaranteed
      B.   100% insured
      C.   Exempt
      D.   Entitled

12.   The late fee for a conventional loan is:
      A.   3 % of principal and interest
      B.   4 % of principal and interest
      C.   5 % of principal and interest
      D.   10 % of principal and interest

13.   A funding fee is required for a:
      A.   FHA loan
      B.   VA loan
      C.   Jumbo loan
      D.   Conventional loan

14. A Mortgage Insurance Premium is required on:
     A.   FHA loans
     B.   VA loans
     C.   Jumbo loans
     D.   Conventional loans

15. The mortgagee is the:
     A.   Borrower
     B.   Lender
     C.   Closing agent
     D.   Mortgage broker

16. The borrower does **NOT** sign which document:
     A.   Deed
     B.   HUD-1/Loan Disclosure
     C.   Mortgage
     D.   Note

17. Which document is usually **NOT** recorded?
     A.   Assignment of mortgage
     B.   Note
     C.   Deed
     D.   Mortgage

18. A mortgagee title insurance policy is **NOT**:
     A.   Based on loan amount
     B.   Transferable
     C.   Optional
     D.   Required by the lender

19. Which parties sign the deed?
     A.   Grantor, grantee and two witnesses
     B.   Grantor and two witnesses
     C.   Grantee and two witnesses
     D.   Grantee only

20. When the mortgagor and mortgagee title insurance policies are issued at the same time, this is known as:
     A.   Simultaneous issue
     B.   Concurrent issue
     C.   Subsequent issue
     D.   Dual issue

21.   A shrubbery hedge is one example of an:
   A.   Encumbrance
   B.   Easement
   C.   Entitlement
   D.   Acceptable title impediment

22.   A loan on personal property only is known as:
   A.   Package mortgage
   B.   Chattel mortgage
   C.   Furnishings mortgage
   D.   Exotic mortgage

23.   Which of the following is **NOT** a characteristic of a Tenants in Common form of ownership:
   A.   Equal shares
   B.   Buy at different times
   C.   Right of survivorship
   D.   Ability to will share

24.   PITI payments do **NOT** include which of the following:
   A.   Principal
   B.   Funding Fee
   C.   Hazard Insurance
   D.   Interest

25.   Who does Fannie Mae hold responsible for the quality of an appraisal?
   A.   Appraiser
   B.   Borrower
   C.   Mortgage broker
   D.   Lender

26.   Which law is known as Regulation B?
   A.   Truth-in-Lending
   B.   Real Estate Settlement Procedures Act
   C.   Equal Credit Opportunity Act
   D.   Patriot Act

27.   Which law prohibits discrimination by lenders?
   A.   Truth-in-Lending
   B.   Real Estate Settlement Procedures Act
   C.   Equal Credit Opportunity Act
   D.   Patriot Act

28. A property sold for $200,000 and was appraised at $180,000. The borrower received a loan for $150,000. What is the loan-to-value?
   A.   75 %
   B.   83.3 %
   C.   90 %
   D.   92.4 %

29. How many days does a lender have to send an adverse action notice?
   A.   5
   B.   10
   C.   30
   D.   60

30. The GFE/Loan Estimate must be mailed or given to the borrower within how many days after receiving the signed application?
   A.   3 business days
   B.   7 business days
   C.   10 business days
   D.   30 business days

31. The enforcement of a lien is known as a:
   A.   Closing
   B.   Foreclosure
   C.   Warranty inspection
   D.   Police action

32. What minimum percentage of ownership in a related service requires a conflict of interest disclosure?
   A.   5 %
   B.   10 %
   C.   25 %
   D.   50 %

33 What minimum percentage of ownership qualifies an individual as self-employed?
   A.   5 %
   B.   10 %
   C.   25 %
   D.   50 %

34. A salaried employee may have to produce which of the following documents to obtain a loan?
   A.   90 day pay stubs
   B.   2 years W2s
   C.   Profit and Loss statement
   D.   Balance sheet

35.   How many months must be left on an automobile lease to include it as a debt?
        A.   2 months
        B.   5 months
        C.   10 months
        D.   It is always included

36   Which law defines the right of rescission?
        A.   Truth-in-Lending
        B.   Real Estate Settlement Procedures Act
        C.   Equal Credit Opportunity Act
        D.   Patriot Act

37.   How long after the application date must social security payments continue to be received in order to count as income?
        A.   3 months
        B.   10 months
        C.   2 years
        D.   3 years

38.   Credit reports on new construction are good for how many days?
        A.   90 days
        B.   120 days
        C.   180 days
        D.   225 days

39.   Which clause in a mortgage allows a lender to increase the interest rate?
        A.   Defeasance
        B.   Escalation
        C.   Acceleration
        D.   Exculpatory

40.   Which clause in a mortgage prevents the lender from foreclosing unless the borrower is in default?
        A.   Defeasance
        B.   Escalation
        C.   Acceleration
        D.   Exculpatory

41.   The lender has how many days to send the Satisfaction of Mortgage letter to the borrower once the loan balance is paid?
        A.   30 days
        B.   60 days
        C.   90 days
        D.   120 days

42.   Which of the following increases cap rate?
       A.   Lower purchase price
       B.   Increase purchase price
       C.   Decrease cash flow
       D.   Increase interest rate

43.   Who should applicants contact if they have questions about their credit score or credit information?
       A.   Credit reporting agency
       B.   Lender
       C.   Mortgage broker
       D.   Attorney

44.   Who is responsible for maintaining the national flood maps?
       A.   HUD
       B.   FEMA
       C.   FHA
       D.   VA

45.   A VA appraisal is known as a:
       A.   CRV
       B.   Veteran's appraisal report
       C.   Fannie Mae 1025
       D.   AVA

46.   Fannie Mae's automated underwriting system is known as:
       A.   Fannie Mannie
       B.   Software helper
       C.   Desktop Underwriter
       D.   Loan Prospector

47.   There are 10 days left in the month. The purchase price is $150,000, the loan amount is $100,000 and the interest rate is 6%. How much mortgage interest must the borrower pay at closing?
       A. $164.38
       B. $250.00
       C. $440.20
       D. $2,739.73

48.   Private Mortgage Insurance is automatically canceled when the loan-to-value reaches what level?
       A.   55 %
       B.   70 %
       C.   78 %
       D.   80 %

49.   Which types of loans are meant for rural areas?
      A.   VA
      B.   FHA
      C.   USDA
      D.   RAL

50.   The purchase price of a home is $200,000 and the loan amount is $180,000. The
      borrower pays 6% interest with 1 discount point and 1 origination point. What is the cost
      of the points?
      A. $1,800
      B. $2,000
      C. $3,600
      D. $4,000

51.   If the Gross Rent Multiplier (GRM) decreases, the property value:
      A.   Increases
      B.   Decreases
      C.   Does not change
      D.   Can increase or decrease

52.   What is the maximum allowable amount of VA seller concessions?
      A.   2 %
      B.   3 %
      C.   4 %
      D.   5 %

53.   When a property increases in value for any reason this is known as:
      A.   Acceleration
      B.   Appreciation
      C.   Accumulation
      D.   Acclimation

54.   Which appraisal approach is most suitable for an office building?
      A.   Sales comparison approach
      B.   Cost approach
      C.   Income capitalization approach
      D.   Tenant collection approach

55.   Which of the following is incorrect regarding an adjustable-rate mortgage?
      A.   The index is fixed
      B.   The margin is fixed
      C.   There are rate caps on both the adjustment period and life of the loan
      D.   LIBOR is a typical index used

56.   Which of the following is **NOT** a fully amortized loan?
       A.   Term mortgage
       B.   Fixed-rate mortgage
       C.   Adjustable-rate mortgage
       D.   Bi-weekly mortgage

57.   Which of the following is a negatively amortizing loan?
       A.   Reverse mortgage
       B.   Balloon mortgage
       C.   Term mortgage
       D.   Wrap mortgage

58.   Fannie Mae does **NOT** require:
       A.   6 months of bank statements
       B.   Verifiable funds
       C.   2 years of addresses
       D.   Stable 2 year work history

59.   A note is the:
       A.   Document that conveys title
       B.   Pledge of the property as collateral for the loan
       C.   Borrower's IOU
       D.   Document that transfers contractual rights to another investor

60.   A mortgage is the:
       A.   Document that conveys title
       B.   Pledge of the property as collateral for the loan
       C.   Borrower's IOU
       D.   Document that transfers contractual rights to another investor

61.   An adjustable-rate mortgage can adjust after 2 years with an adjustment cap of 3 % per period and a lifetime cap of 7 %. The starting interest rate is 4%. What is the maximum interest that can be charged at the time of the first adjustment?
       A.   5 %
       B.   7 %
       C.   10 %
       D.   11 %

62.   What is the FHA minimum down payment?
       A. $0
       B.   3.5 %
       C.   5 %
       D.   10 %

63.   Which law is known as Regulation C?
      A.   Real Estate Settlement Procedures Act
      B.   Truth-in-Lending
      C.   Equal Credit Opportunity Act
      D.   Home Mortgage Disclosure Act

64.   What is the minimum down payment for a USDA loan?
      A. $0
      B.   3.5 %
      C.   5 %
      D.   10 %

65.   How many hours of continuing education are minimally required?
      A.   8 hours every year
      B.   14 hours every year
      C.   14 hours every 2 years
      D.   20 hours every 2 years

66.   Who is responsible for completing the HUD-1/Loan Disclosure?
      A.   The borrower
      B.   The closing agent
      C.   The loan originator
      D.   The grantor

67.   A mortgagor's title insurance policy is:
      A.   Transferable
      B.   Required
      C.   Based on purchase price
      D.   Never used

68.   The assignee of a mortgage and note is participating in the:
      A.   Primary lending market
      B.   Capital market
      C.   Secondary mortgage market
      D.   Options market

69.   VA loans are:
      A.   Partially guaranteed
      B.   Insured
      C.   Exempt
      D.   Entitled

70.   The late fee for a VA loan is:
      A.   3 % of principal and interest
      B.   4 % of principal and interest
      C.   5 % of principal and interest
      D.   10 % of principal and interest

71.   The purchase price of a home is $325,000 and the appraisal price is $350,000. If the first mortgage is in the amount of $200,000 and the second mortgage is $60,000. What is the combined loan-to-value ratio?
    A.   78.3 %
    B.   80.0 %
    C.   86.7 %
    D.   92.3 %

72.   The purchase price of a home is $375,000 and the buyer will assume a $175,000 first mortgage. The loan-to-value cannot exceed 85 %. What is the maximum amount of the new second mortgage?
    A. $130,000
    B. $143,750
    C. $162,030
    D. $171,260

73.   What clause in a mortgage allows the lender to call the entire loan balance due?
    A.   Defeasance
    B.   Escalation
    C.   Acceleration
    D.   Exculpatory

74.   What clause in a mortgage prevents the lender from recovering additional assets from the mortgagor if there is a shortfall in the foreclosure proceeds?
    A.   Forbearance
    B.   Escalation
    C.   Acceleration
    D.   Exculpatory

75.   What term describes the intentional delay of action on the part of the lender upon a borrower's default?
    A.   Forbearance
    B.   Escalation
    C.   Acceleration
    D.   Exculpatory

76   Which of the following does NOT appear in a lock-in agreement?
    A.   Expiration date
    B.   APR
    C.   Lock-in fee
    D.   Interest rate

77.   Freddie Mac was originally known as:
    A   Federal Home Loan Mortgage Corporation
    B.   Federal National Mortgage Association
    C.   Fair Discount Interest Rates
    D.   Free Certificate of Deposits

78.   Fannie Mae allows what amount of fees to be charged to a credit card?
    A.   1 % of the loan amount plus $500 for the appraisal and credit report
    B.   2 % of the loan amount plus $500 for the appraisal and credit report
    C.   3 % of the loan amount plus $500 for the appraisal and credit report
    D.   4 % of the loan amount plus $500 for the appraisal and credit report

79.   Loan Prospector can **NOT** be used for which type of loans?
    A.   Conventional
    B.   VA
    C.   FHA
    D.   Commercial

80.   A five bedroom, one bathroom house is an example of:
    A.   Appreciation
    B.   Functional obsolescence
    C.   Economic obsolescence
    D.   Residential allowance

81.   Which of the following is **NOT** a benefit of an FHA loan?
    A.   Favorable interest rates
    B.   Low down payment
    C.   No monthly mortgage insurance
    D.   Assumable

82.   A loan closes on May 14. When is the first mortgage payment due?
    A.   May 15
    B.   June 1
    C.   June 15
    D.   July 1

83.   Alimony payments must continue to be received for how long after the application date if they are to be included as income?
    A.   10 months
    B.   2 years
    C.   3 years
    D.   4 years

84.   Credit reports are good for how many days after they are pulled for qualifying purposes?
    A.   60
    B.   90
    C.   120
    D.   180

85. When title is transferred and the buyer assumes no liability for the note, this type of transference is known as:
    A.   Free and clear
    B.   Subject to the mortgage
    C.   Assumption
    D.   Novation

86. Which of the following is correct for an adjustable-rate mortgage?
    A.   Index – margin = fully indexed rate
    B.   Margin-index = fully indexed rate
    C.   Index + margin = fully indexed rate
    D.   Index – margin = fully indexed rate

87. The maximum term for a FHA loan is:
    A.   15 years
    B.   30 years
    C.   40 years
    D.   50 years

88. Which of the following is **NOT** an involuntary lien?
    A.   IRS lien
    B.   Judgment lien
    C.   Mortgage lien
    D.   Mechanic's lien

89. The most comprehensive form of ownership is:
    A.   Real Estate Investment Trust
    B.   Fee simple absolute
    C.   Tenants in common
    D.   Joint tenancy

90. Which is **NOT** a component of a valid contract?
    A.   Agreement
    B.   Consideration
    C.   Two witnesses
    D.   Competent parties

91. Which type of co-ownership permits the property to pass to an heir?
    A.   Collaboration
    B.   Tenants in common
    C.   Joint tenancy
    D.   Subordination

92.   The economic concept which states that a knowledgeable buyer will pay no more for one property than they would pay for an equally desirable comparable property is:
       A.   Principle of Substitution
       B.   Principle of Highest and Best Use
       C.   Principle of Market Value
       D.   Principle of Intelligent Purchases

93.   Which law allows consumers a free copy of their credit report every year?
       A.   Homeowner's Protection Act
       B.   The Fair and Accurate Credit Transaction Act
       C.   Truth-in-Lending
       D.   The Equal Credit Opportunity Act

94.   Which law requires the interviewer to complete the Government Monitoring section on the 1003?
       A.   Homeowner's Protection Act
       B.   The Fair and Accurate Credit Transaction Act
       C.   Truth-in-Lending
       D.   The Equal Credit Opportunity Act

95.   Which law entitles an applicant to a copy of his property appraisal report?
       A.   Homeowner's Protection Act
       B.   The Fair and Accurate Credit Transaction Act
       C.   Truth-in-Lending
       D.   The Equal Credit Opportunity Act

96.   Which law is also known as Regulation X?
       A.   Truth in Lending
       B.   Real Estate Settlement Procedures Act
       C.   Homeowner's Protection Act
       D.   The Equal Credit Opportunity Act

97.   Which law protects an individual's confidential information?
       A.   Truth-in-Lending
       B.   Real Estate Settlement Procedures Act
       C.   Homeowner's Protection Act
       D.   Gramm-Leach-Bliley Act

98.   Who enforces RESPA violations?
       A.   FTC
       B.   CFPB
       C.   FHA
       D.   FCC

99.   Which law requires that the Special Information booklet be given to borrowers?
    A.   Truth-in-Lending
    B.   Real Estate Settlement Procedures Act
    C.   Homeowner's Protection Act
    D.   The Equal Credit Opportunity Act

100.   What is the fine for violating the Federal Do Not Call rules?
    A. $5,000
    B. $11,000
    C. $43,792
    D. $60,000

Practice Final Exam #1 Answer Key

1.	A	26.	C	51.	B	76.	B
2.	D	27.	C	52.	C	77.	A
3.	B	28.	B	53.	B	78.	A
4.	C	29.	C	54.	C	79.	D
5.	B	30.	A	55.	A	80.	B
6.	D	31.	B	56.	A	81.	C
7.	A	32.	B	57.	A	82.	D
8.	C	33.	C	58.	A	83.	C
9.	B	34.	B	59.	C	84.	C
10.	A	35.	D	60.	B	85.	B
11.	B	36.	A	61.	B	86.	C
12.	C	37.	D	62.	B	87.	B
13.	B	38.	B	63.	D	88.	C
14.	A	39.	B	64.	A	89.	B
15.	B	40.	A	65.	A	90.	C
16.	A	41.	B	66.	B	91.	B
17.	B	42.	A	67.	C	92.	A
18.	C	43.	A	68.	C	93.	B
19.	B	44.	B	69.	A	94.	D
20.	A	45.	A	70.	B	95.	D
21.	D	46.	C	71.	B	96.	B
22.	B	47.	A	72.	B	97.	D
23.	C	48.	C	73.	C	98.	B
24.	B	49.	C	74.	D	99.	B
25.	D	50.	C	75.	A	100.	C

Practice Final Exam #2

1. Which of the following is NOT a loan origination activity?
    A. Assisting in a refinance
    B. Assisting in a purchase loan
    C. Assisting in a loan modification
    D. Changing the name of debtors on an existing loan

2. A unilateral contract is binding on:
    A. One party
    B. Two parties
    C. The negotiator
    D. No one

3. Loan originator organizations must keep compensation records for how many years?
    A. One
    B. Two
    C. Three
    D. Four

4. Mortgage companies must submit a residential loan origination activity report to the NMLSR every:
    A. Month
    B. Three months
    C. Six months
    D. Year

5. How many years must loan originator applicants wait after a felony fraud conviction, in order to qualify for a license?
    A. One year
    B. Two years
    C. Five years
    D. They aren't eligible for licensing

6. How many years must loan originator applicants wait after having a loan origination license revoked in another state, in order to qualify for a license?
    A. One year
    B. Two years
    C. They aren't eligible for licensing
    D. They can qualify immediately

7.   Who chooses force-placed hazard insurance companies?
       A.   Lender
       B.   Homeowner
       C.   Attorney
       D.   Loan originator

8.   Which of the following is required for an FHA Streamline refinance loan?
       A.   Credit verification
       B.   New appraisal
       C.   Current on mortgage payments for the last three months
       D.   Income and debt verification

9.   What law addresses loan originators' compensation issues?
       A.   Truth-in-Lending Act
       B.   Loan Origination Rule
       C.   Equal Credit Opportunity Act
       D.   Mortgage Compensation Act

10.   Commercial telemarketers are restricted to calling:
       A.   Only on weekends
       B.   Between 10 AM and 10 PM
       C.   Between 8 AM and 9 PM
       D.   There are no restrictions

11.   Commercial telemarketers must search the Do-Not-Call registry:
       A.   Every 7 days
       B.   Every 31 days
       C.   Every 180 days
       D.   Once a year

12.   In order to send a fax, advertisers must:
       A.   Have an established business relationship with recipient
       B.   Only fax to toll-free numbers
       C.   Include a personal cell phone number on the cover sheet
       D.   Not send faxes across state lines

13.   The first page of an advertiser's fax must include:
       A.   Company's mailing address
       B.   Company's email address
       C.   Company's phone number
       D.   Opt-out instructions

14.   What type of real estate co-ownership is only for married couples?
       A.   Tenants in common
       B.   Joint tenancy
       C.   Tenancy by the entirety
       D.   Spousal tenancy

15. Increasing neighborhood crime exemplifies what type of depreciation?
     A.   Economic obsolescence
     B.   Functional obsolescence
     C.   Physical deterioration
     D.   Unstable deterioration

16. What agency was established to respond to consumer financial complaints?
     A.   Federal Deposit Insurance Company
     B.   Federal Insurance Office
     C.   Financial Stability Oversight Council
     D.   Consumer Financial Protection Bureau

17. What law protects homeowners from foreclosure-prevention scams?
     A.   Foreclosure Mediation Rule
     B.   Mortgage Assistance Relief Services Rule
     C.   Truth-in-Lending Act
     D.   Homeowner's Protection Act

18. Individuals must file a report when they transport how much cash out of the country?
     A. $5,000 or more
     B. $10,000 or more
     C. $50,000 or more
     D. $100,000 or more

19. What type of federal report is filed when financial institutions detect suspicious activity?
     A.   Suspicious Activity Report
     B.   Treasury Alert Report
     C.   Unaccounted Funds Report
     D.   Unexplained Behavior Report

20. What agency becomes the receiver for some failing financial institutions?
     A.   Federal Deposit Insurance Company
     B.   Federal Insurance Office
     C.   Financial Stability Oversight Council
     D.   Consumer Financial Protection Bureau

21. The ability-to-repay regulation applies to:
     A.   Equity lines of credit
     B.   Reverse mortgages
     C.   Investment home purchases
     D.   Construction loans

22. Which of the following is NOT a feature of a qualified mortgage?
     A.   Positive amortization
     B.   30 year maximum loan term
     C.   Maximum debt-to-income ratio of 50 percent
     D.   No interest-only periods

23.   Individuals submit an annual Report of Foreign Bank and Financial Accounts to:
       A.   IRS
       B.   Mortgage lender
       C.   Federal Trade Commission
       D.   Fannie Mae

24.   Which of the following is part of the Mortgage Assistance Relief Services Rule?
       A.   Negotiators may be paid an up-front fee
       B.   Borrowers must pay a fee if they cancel their contract with the negotiator
       C.   Negotiators can't interfere with communication between borrowers and lenders
       D.   Negotiators only have to present reasonable lender offers to the borrower

25.   Loan originators aren't allowed to receive compensation:
       A.   Based on loan terms
       B.   From a consumer
       C.   From a lender
       D.   Based on the performance of the loan

26.   High-cost home loans require a borrower to:
       A.   Receive quotes from multiple lenders
       B.   Receive homeownership counseling
       C.   Receive free flood insurance
       D.   Receive 3% seller concessions

27.   The Truth-in-Lending Disclosure does NOT include:
       A.   APR
       B.   Finance charge
       C.   Total amount of payments
       D.   Borrower's credit score

28.   Which of the following is NOT true of high-cost home loans?
       A.   Borrower must have documented ability to pay the loan
       B.   Borrower must have a minimum credit score of 650
       C.   Prepay penalties are prohibited
       D.   Most balloon payments are prohibited

29.   Which of the following does NOT have zero variance between the GFE and HUD-1?
       A.   Title insurance
       B.   Real estate transfer taxes
       C.   Loan origination fees
       D.   Interest rate

30. Which of the following can have an unlimited variance between the GFE and HUD-1?
    A.   Hazard insurance
    B.   Recording fees
    C.   Appraisal
    D.   Credit report fee

31. What happens if the acceptable variance between the GFE and the HUD-1 is exceeded?
    A.   Loan originator faces criminal penalties
    B.   The loan can't be funded
    C.   The excess is refunded to the borrower within 30 days
    D.   The excess is refunded to the borrower within 60 days

32. Which law requires businesses to print only the last five card numbers on a credit card receipt?
    A.   Homeowner's Protection Act
    B.   Fact Act
    C.   Gramm-Leach-Bliley
    D.   Dodd-Frank

33. What happens if the acceptable variance between the Loan Estimate and the Closing Disclosure is exceeded?
    A.   Loan originator faces criminal penalties
    B.   The loan can't be funded
    C.   The excess is refunded to the borrower within 30 days
    D.   The excess is refunded to the borrower within 60 days

34. A higher-priced home loan is one that has:
    A.   More than 5 points in fees and points
    B.   More than 8 points in fees and points
    C.   APR exceeds the average prime rate by at least 1.5% for first-lien loans
    D.   Interest rate is higher than 10%

35. What is the shortest time in which a mortgage purchase loan can close?
    A.   3 business days
    B.   7 business days
    C.   14 days
    D.   30 days

36. What type of loan gives a borrower money each month?
    A.   Graduated payment mortgage
    B.   Reverse mortgage
    C.   Package mortgage
    D.   Wholesale mortgage

37. What type of mortgage is a non-recourse loan?
    A. Graduated payment mortgage
    B. Reverse mortgage
    C. Package mortgage
    D. Wholesale mortgage

38. A lender won't lose money funding what type of loan?
    A. FHA
    B. VA
    C. Conventional
    D. Construction

39. A lender that offers mortgage loans directly to the public is a:
    A. Participating lender
    B. Private lender
    C. Wholesale lender
    D. Retail lender

40. Which disclosure can be initially sent to the borrower within 45 days after closing?
    A. Affiliated Business Arrangement
    B. Good Faith Estimate
    C. Truth-in-Lending
    D. Initial Escrow Statement

41. What type of loan is short-term with money advanced in stages?
    A. Package
    B. Construction
    C. Wraparound
    D. Balloon

42. A loan originator who accepts an upfront fee for negotiating a loan modification is violating which law?
    A. RESPA
    B. TILA
    C. HMDA
    D. MARS

43. A lender that works with licensed loan originators is a:
    A. Participating lender
    B. Private lender
    C. Wholesale lender
    D. Retail lender

44. What type of mortgage is not guaranteed or insured by the government?
    A.   FHA
    B.   VA
    C.   USDA
    D.   Conventional

45. What agency became the conservator of Fannie Mae and Freddie Mac?
    A.   Federal Housing Finance Agency
    B.   Consumer Financial Protection Bureau
    C.   U.S. Department of Housing and Urban Development
    D.   Internal Revenue Service

46. HMDA requires lenders to submit their loan application registers to the:
    A.   Library of Congress
    B.   Federal Financial Institutions Examination Council
    C.   Federal Department of Books and Records
    D.   Nationwide Mortgage Licensing System and Registry

47. MIP is associated with what type of loan?
    A.   FHA
    B.   VA
    C.   Interest-Only
    D.   Conventional

48. UFMIP is associated with what type of loan?
    A.   FHA
    B.   VA
    C.   Interest-Only
    D.   Conventional

49. What law requires ARM borrowers to receive the Consumer Handbook on Adjustable-Rate Mortgages?
    A.   RESPA
    B.   ECOA
    C.   Gramm-Leach-Bliley
    D.   TILA

50. What law allowed the government to assume control over Fannie Mae and Freddie Mac?
    A.   Homeowner's Protection Act
    B.   Housing and Economic Recovery Act
    C.   Home Mortgage Disclosures Act
    D.   Truth-in-Lending Act

51. What law was passed in 2010 in response to the financial meltdown and recession?
     A.   Truth-in-Lending Act
     B.   Gramm-Leach-Bliley
     C.   Dodd-Frank Wall Street Reform and Consumer Act
     D.   Home Mortgage Disclosures Act

52. Lenders must maintain an escrow account for higher-priced mortgages for a minimum:
     A.   1 year
     B.   3 years
     C.   5 years
     D.   No escrow account is required

53. How much of a down payment does a borrower need if he doesn't want to pay PMI?
     A.   5 %
     B.   10 %
     C.   15 %
     D.   20 %

54. Borrowers with a high-cost loan can rescind the loan within how many business days?
     A.   3
     B.   7
     C.   15
     D.   There is no rescission period

55. Acceptable income for loan qualification includes:
     A.   1 year of sales commissions
     B.   Disability benefits with 2 years remaining
     C.   1 year of unemployment benefits
     D.   2 years of bonuses

56. Who determines the underwriting guidelines for conforming loans?
     A.   Federal Housing Finance Agency
     B.   Federal Trade Commission
     C.   U.S. Department of Housing and Urban Development
     D.   Fannie Mae

57. Which appraisal method subtracts a value for depreciation?
     A.   Sales Comparison
     B.   Cost
     C.   Income Capitalization
     D.   Gross Income Multiplier

58. What is the Fannie Mae appraisal report form?
     A.   USPAP
     B.   HVCC
     C.   USAPP
     D.   URAR

59. What lien has the highest priority and is paid off first when a property is sold?
    A. Property tax
    B. Senior mortgage lien
    C. Mechanic's lien
    D. Judgment lien

60. What document is assigned along with the mortgage?
    A. Deed
    B. GFE/Loan Estimate
    C. HUD-1/Closing Disclosure
    D. Promissory note

61. When does the borrower pay the first year of the hazard insurance premium?
    A. Each month for 12 months
    B. Before or at closing
    C. 6 months premium paid at closing; 6 months premium due 30 days after closing
    D. Every 2 months for a total of 6 payments during the first year after closing.

62. How many times may a loan originator receive credit for the same continuing education course?
    A. 1
    B. 2
    C. 3
    D. No limit

63. What type of valuation takes into account annual rent as well as other generated income?
    A. Sales Comparison
    B. Cost
    C. GRM
    D. GIM

64. What term describes the process of a senior mortgage lien-holder voluntarily changing into a junior mortgage lien-holder?
    A. Demotion
    B. Assignment
    C. Alienation
    D. Subordination

65.   Which of the following is an appropriate adjustment in a market data appraisal?
  A.   The comp has a two-car garage and the subject has a one-car garage. Subtract $5,000 from the comp's sale price.
  B.   The subject has a pool and the comp doesn't. Subtract $15,000 from the subject's estimated value.
  C.   The comp has a fireplace and the subject doesn't. Add $1,200 to the comp's sale price.
  D.   The subject has a dirt yard, and the comp is professionally landscaped. Add $8,000 to the subject's estimated value.

66.   Which of the following is NOT a valid component of a contract?
  A.   Competent parties
  B.   Mutual agreement
  C.   Down payment
  D.   Legal object

67.   Which of the following is NOT a valid requirement for a deed?
  A.   Names of the seller and the buyer
  B.   Must be signed in blue ink
  C.   Legal description of the property
  D.   Signed by grantor and two witnesses

68.   Which of the following is NOT required for self-employed qualification?
  A.   2-year business tax returns
  B.   60-day paystubs
  C.   Company balance sheet
  D.   Company profit-and-loss statement

69.   Ginnie Mae:
  A.   Buys and sells loans
  B.   Regulates loan originators
  C.   Guarantees Ginnie-Mae mortgage-backed securities
  D.   Sets guidelines for government loans

70.   Which law requires lenders to train employees to recognize the Red Flags of identity theft?
  A.   Homeowner's Protection Act
  B.   Fact Act
  C.   Gramm-Leach-Bliley
  D.   Dodd-Frank

71.   A California residential loan originator referred a borrower to a Florida residential loan originator. The California loan originator can receive a referral fee:
  A.   Only if he is also licensed in Florida
  B.   Only if the Florida loan originator is also licensed in California
  C.   Only with written permission from the lender
  D.   Never

72. Which law requires loan originators to shred credit reports?
    A.   Homeowner's Protection Act
    B.   Fact Act
    C.   Gramm-Leach-Bliley
    D.   No such law

73. Higher-priced loans for a flipped home require a second appraisal that is:
    A.   Performed by a different appraiser at no charge to the borrower
    B.   Performed by a different appraiser and paid for by the borrower
    C.   Performed by the same appraiser using different comparables at no charge to
          the borrower
    D.   Performed by the same appraiser using different comparables and paid for by
          the borrower

74. If a consumer makes an inquiry to a company, the company can call for:
    A.   6 weeks
    B.   3 months
    C.   6 months
    D.   18 months

75. Which of the following is NOT a loss mitigation option?
    A.   Loan modification
    B.   Refinance
    C.   Deed-in-lieu
    D.   Foreclosure

76. Which of the following is NOT part of the primary mortgage market?
    A.   Commercial bank
    B.   Seller financier
    C.   Insurance company
    D.   Credit union

77. Which is NOT a possible indication of a short sale fraud?
    A.   Buyer is a business partner of the seller
    B.   Seller has a poor credit history
    C.   Seller has an excellent credit history
    D.   The property appraises significantly below neighboring properties

78. An individual with a good credit history who is paid to represent himself as a buyer is a:
    A.   Straw buyer
    B.   Particular buyer
    C.   Promotion buyer
    D.   Demotion buyer

79.   A deficiency judgment occurs when a:
    A.   Borrower needs additional down payment funds
    B.   Seller wins a breach of contract lawsuit against the buyer
    C.   Lender sues for borrower's personal assets to pay balance of the note
    D.   Borrower needs additional private mortgage insurance

80.   What type of fraud occurs when a loan originator submits and closes one loan application with multiple lenders?
    A.   Chunking
    B.   Equity skimming
    C.   Buy and bail
    D.   Phantom sale

81.   What type of fraud occurs when a loan originator changes a borrower's birthdate to make him appear older?
    A.   Reverse mortgage
    B.   Equity skimming
    C.   Buy and bail
    D.   Phantom sale

82.   What type of funding occurs when a lender borrows money from an investor and assigns the mortgage and note to the investor immediately after closing?
    A.   Warehouse
    B.   Table
    C.   Direct investor
    D.   Temporary

83.   What is the practice called when a real estate agent only shows Hispanic buyers properties in Hispanic neighborhoods?
    A.   Redlining
    B.   Steering
    C.   Blockbusting
    D.   Conversion

84.   What is the practice called when a real estate agent spreads the rumor that a specific ethnic group is planning to move into the neighborhood and advises residents to sell before the property values drop?
    A.   Redlining
    B.   Steering
    C.   Blockbusting
    D.   Conversion

85. What is the term used when a lender allows a tenant's improvements to be applied toward down payment funds when the tenant purchases the home?
    A.   Home improvement funds
    B.   Restoration funds
    C.   Sweat equity
    D.   Good faith money

86. Anything that affects title to a property such as liens, easements or restrictions is a(n):
    A.   Encumbrance
    B.   Barrier
    C.   Covenant
    D.   Egress

87. What is the general term for the security pledged for the payment of a loan?
    A.   Repository
    B.   Collateral
    C.   Transaction account
    D.   Good faith

88. Purchase issues that must be resolved before closing are called:
    A.   Dynamics
    B.   Resolutions
    C.   Contingencies
    D.   Operations

89. Local laws that control the use of the land are called:
    A.   Contingencies
    B.   Operations
    C.   Habituations
    D.   Zoning

90. Which of the following is NOT characteristic of a warranty deed:
    A.   Guarantees the seller is true owner of the property
    B.   Guarantees the seller has the legal right to sell
    C.   Guarantees that there are no undisclosed liens on the property
    D.   Guarantees that the sale price is fair and reasonable

91. Monthly income before taxes and other deductions is known as:
    A.   Gross income
    B.   Net income
    C.   Assured income
    D.   Household income

92.   What protects lenders against losses when a borrower defaults on a loan?
    A.   Transactional account
    B.   Mortgage insurance
    C.   Deed restrictions
    D.   Title insurance

93.   Which federal agency guarantees mortgage backed securities that are based on FHA and VA loans?
    A.   FHA
    B.   VA
    C.   Ginnie Mae
    D.   Fannie Mae

94.   The lowest possible interest rate for an ARM loan is known as the:
    A.   Floor
    B.   Basin
    C.   Basement
    D.   Ground

95.   An FHA reverse mortgage loan is a:
    A.   FHARM
    B.   HECM
    C.   RMFHA
    D.   UFFHA

96.   What type of deed transfers ownership without making any guarantee of clear title?
    A.   General warranty deed
    B.   Special warranty deed
    C.   Power of attorney deed
    D.   Quitclaim deed

97.   What is the difference between the purchase price and the mortgage amount?
    A.   Good faith money
    B.   Escrow funds
    C.   Down payment
    D.   Discount points

98.   What is a claim against a property for the payment of a debt?
    A.   Lien
    B.   Title
    C.   Egress
    D.   Arbitration

99.   What is the interest rate commercial banks charge their most creditworthy customers?
       A.   Partial rate
       B.   Prime rate
       C.   Premium rate
       D.   Preferred rate

100.   What is the current name for the Federal Home Loan Mortgage Corporation?
       A.   Fannie Mae
       B.   Freddie Mac
       C.   FHA
       D.   Fed

Practice Final Exam #2 Answer Key

1.	C	26.	B	51.	C	76.	C
2.	A	27.	D	52.	C	77.	B
3.	C	28.	B	53.	D	78.	A
4.	B	29.	A	54.	A	79.	C
5.	D	30.	A	55.	D	80.	A
6.	C	31.	C	56.	D	81.	A
7.	A	32.	B	57.	B	82.	B
8.	C	33.	D	58.	D	83.	B
9.	B	34.	C	59.	A	84.	C
10.	C	35.	B	60.	D	85.	C
11.	B	36.	B	61.	B	86.	A
12.	A	37.	B	62.	A	87.	B
13.	D	38.	A	63.	D	88.	C
14.	C	39.	D	64.	D	89.	D
15.	A	40.	D	65.	A	90.	D
16.	D	41.	B	66.	C	91.	A
17.	B	42.	D	67.	B	92.	B
18.	B	43.	C	68.	B	93.	C
19.	A	44.	D	69.	C	94.	A
20.	A	45.	A	70.	B	95.	B
21.	C	46.	B	71.	D	96.	D
22.	C	47.	A	72.	D	97.	C
23.	A	48.	A	73.	A	98.	A
24.	C	49.	D	74.	B	99.	B
25.	A	50.	B	75.	D	100.	B

Made in the USA
Monee, IL
29 August 2024

64705904R00162